AF765105

# THE ROTH CONVERSIONS WINDOW

## HOW TO CONVERT AT 12-22% RATES IN THE OBBBA ERA BEFORE RMDS FORCE YOU INTO 24-32% BRACKETS AND TRIGGER UP TO $15,000/YEAR IN IRMAA SURCHARGES

BY

SCOTT BENNET

## Disclaimer

This book is designed to provide information about Roth IRA conversions, tax planning, and retirement strategies. It is sold with the understanding that the publisher and author are not engaged in rendering legal, accounting, tax, financial planning, or other professional services.

If professional advice or other expert assistance is required, the services of a competent professional should be sought.

## Tax and Financial Information

The information presented in this book is based on federal tax law, IRS regulations, Medicare rules, and CMS guidelines current as of January 2026. Tax laws, regulations, and individual circumstances vary and change frequently.

All examples, projections, and calculations in this book are for illustrative purposes only. Your actual results will vary based on:

## IRS and CMS Data

Tax brackets, RMD tables, IRMAA thresholds, and Medicare premium amounts referenced in this book are based on:

- IRS Publication 590-B (2024 and continuing)
- IRS Revenue Procedures (current through 2026)
- CMS Medicare Part B and Part D premium schedules (2026)
- Internal Revenue Code provisions current as of publication date

These figures are subject to annual adjustment for inflation and may change due to legislative action. Always verify current numbers with official IRS and CMS sources before making financial decisions.

## No Guarantee of Results

Past performance and hypothetical projections do not guarantee future results. Examples in this book showing tax savings, IRMAA avoidance, or other benefits are:

- Based on assumptions that may not apply to your situation
- Subject to changes in tax law
- Dependent on market performance
- Illustrative, not predictive

Actual outcomes will vary. Tax savings illustrated in this book may be higher or lower depending on individual circumstances.

## Errors and Omissions

While every effort has been made to ensure accuracy of information in this book, the publisher and author assume no responsibility for errors, omissions, or contrary interpretation of the subject matter.

The publisher and author shall have neither liability nor responsibility to any person or entity with respect to any loss or damage caused, or alleged to have been caused, directly or indirectly, by the information contained in this book.

## Third-Party References

This book references various financial institutions, software providers, government agencies, and other third parties for informational purposes only. These references do not constitute endorsements.

The author and publisher have no financial relationship with any entities mentioned in this book unless specifically disclosed.

## Data Sources and Attribution

Information in this book is derived from publicly available sources including:

- Internal Revenue Service (IRS) publications and regulations
- Centers for Medicare & Medicaid Services (CMS) premium schedules
- U.S. Congress legislative text and history
- Peer-reviewed financial planning research
- Publicly available tax planning resources

All data has been verified to the best of the author's ability as of the publication date.

## Updates and Corrections

For updates, corrections, or supplemental information related to this book:

**Email:** info@scottbennet.com

Significant changes to tax law, IRMAA thresholds, or RMD rules will be posted on the book's website as they occur.

## Limitation of Liability

To the maximum extent permitted by law, the author and publisher disclaim all liability for any loss, damage, or injury caused or alleged to be caused directly or indirectly by information in this book, including but not limited to:

- Financial losses from implementing strategies described

- Tax liabilities resulting from conversion decisions
- Penalties, interest, or fees from IRS or other agencies
- Investment losses
- Opportunity costs from deferred action
- Any consequential, incidental, or punitive damages

**Your use of this book constitutes acceptance of these terms.**
**Consult a tax professional familiar with your state's tax law before implementing conversion strategies.**

## Trademark Notices

- **Roth IRA®** is a registered trademark of the Internal Revenue Service
- **Medicare®** is a registered service mark of the U.S. Department of Health and Human Services
- All other trademarks, service marks, and trade names referenced in this book are the property of their respective owners

The G.A.P.S. System™ and related methodology described in this book are proprietary frameworks developed by the author.

Contents

# PREFACE

We need to tell you something that most financial professionals won't.

You have a window. It's open right now. And it's closing at age 73 whether you're ready or not.

This book exists because we've watched too many retirees discover this window after it slammed shut. They did everything right — saved diligently, retired comfortably, trusted their advisors. Then Required Minimum Distributions began at 73, and the tax bills arrived. Big ones. Year after year. Compounding.

Then IRMAA penalties hit. Medicare premiums doubled because IRA distributions pushed income over thresholds nobody warned them about. The couple managing just fine suddenly faced $2,600 in annual surcharges that lasted fifteen years.

Then one spouse died. The survivor's tax bracket jumped overnight. The same income that cost $24,000 in taxes as a couple now cost $35,000 as a widow. For the next twelve years.

These aren't hypothetical scenarios. This is what happens when people arrive at 73 unprepared.

We wrote this book because the financial industry has a gap years problem. Most advisors don't bring up Roth conversions until it's too late. Some don't bring them up at all. The reasons vary — compensation structures that don't reward tax planning, lack of expertise in conversion strategy, simple inertia. The result is the same: people who could have protected themselves didn't know they needed to.

You're different. You picked up this book. That means you're asking the right questions.

If you're between 60 and 72, you're in your gap years right now. This is the period when your income is temporarily low — you've stopped working, but you haven't started Social Security yet and RMDs haven't kicked in. You have control. You can decide how much to convert from traditional IRA to Roth, when to convert it, and at what tax rate.

Once you hit 73, the IRS decides for you. RMDs become mandatory. Your income spikes. Your tax rate climbs. IRMAA penalties trigger. The widow penalty compounds everything if one spouse dies. And you can't go back.

This book gives you the framework to act while the window is open. The G.A.P.S. System — Gap Years Identification, Arbitrage Calculation, Pre-RMD Positioning, Stack Protection. It's a methodology we've refined through years of implementation with real retirees facing real constraints.

We're not here to sell you anything beyond this book. No upselling. No consulting funnels. No expensive seminars. Just actionable information you can implement yourself or coordinate with your existing advisor.

You'll find practical guidance: which conversion profile matches your timeline, how to calculate safe amounts without triggering IRMAA, what to do if you only have three gap years left, how to coordinate conversions with Social Security timing.

Most importantly, you'll understand the cost of waiting. Every year you defer is one fewer gap year available. The problem doesn't pause while you "think about it." It compounds.

Your gap years are finite. This book shows you how to use them.

Turn the page. The window is waiting.

INTRODUCTION

# THE MOST DANGEROUS TWO WORDS IN RETIREMENT PLANNING: "I HAVE TIME"

Tom and Linda sat across from us in March 2024, nine months before Tom would turn 73.

They'd done everything right. Saved diligently. Maxed out 401(k) contributions for thirty years. Built an IRA worth $850,000. Retired at 65 with a plan. Followed financial news religiously.

Their advisor had been telling them since 2023: "We need to watch the 2025 deadline. TCJA brackets sunset December 31, 2025. After that, rates jump back to 2017 levels. We should think about conversions."

Tom and Linda were ready to act. They understood the urgency. They had the cash to pay conversion taxes.

Then July 4, 2025 arrived. President Trump signed the One Big Beautiful Bill Act. TCJA brackets became permanent.

Their advisor called the next week.

"Good news — the sunset is cancelled. Brackets are permanent now. No more deadline pressure. Let's wait and see how your situation develops before we commit to anything major."

Tom and Linda waited.

They watched 2025 end. The brackets stayed low, exactly as promised. No tax increase materialized. Their advisor's caution seemed prudent.

Tom turned 73 in December 2025.

His first Required Minimum Distribution hit in January 2026: $32,000. Added to their pension and Social Security, their Modified Adjusted Gross Income jumped from $195,000 to $227,000.

They crossed the IRMAA threshold at $218,000.

Result: $1,950 per year in Medicare surcharges. Every year. For both of them. Not because they spent irresponsibly or invested poorly — because the IRS forced Tom to take $32,000 he didn't need.

We ran the numbers. If Tom and Linda had converted $300,000 from traditional IRA to Roth between ages 65 and 70 — when their income was temporarily low, when they had full control — they would have paid roughly $66,000 in conversion taxes spread across five years.

Instead, over the next twenty years (ages 73-92), they'll pay approximately $145,000 in combined income taxes and IRMAA penalties.

The difference? $79,000 in lifetime costs they cannot recover.

Tom looked at the spreadsheet. "Our advisor said we had time now."

They did have time — legislative time. The brackets are permanent now.

What they didn't have was personal time. Their gap years — that narrow window between retirement and age 73 when income is low but control remains — closed silently while they waited for certainty that never mattered.

## The Problem Everyone Is Missing

OBBBA solved Congress's problem. It gave tax planners legislative stability. It eliminated the December 31, 2025 sunset cliff that had created years of uncertainty.

But it created a different problem: complacency.

Before OBBBA, there was external urgency. "Act before December 31, 2025 or lose the low brackets forever." That deadline drove decisions. People converted. They acted.

After OBBBA, that urgency vanished. Advisors said "wait and see." Retirees thought: "Now that brackets are permanent, I can take my time."

What everyone missed: your personal opportunity window has nothing to do with Congressional timelines.

Your gap years — typically ages 60 to 73, the period when you've stopped full-time work but haven't started Social Security or Required Minimum Distributions yet — exist regardless of what tax law does. These years are when your income is artificially low. When conversion taxes are minimized. When you still control your distribution timing.

At 73, that control ends. The IRS mandates withdrawals. Your income rises whether you want it to or not. IRMAA thresholds get crossed. Tax rates increase. The widow penalty looms.

OBBBA gave you infinite legislative time but couldn't extend your biological countdown.

The brackets aren't expiring. Your gap years are.

## What This Book Is (And What It Isn't)

This book compresses what we typically charge $5,000 to explain in comprehensive planning sessions into 200 pages you can read in an afternoon.

**What it IS:**

- A quantified analysis of what waiting costs ($50,000 to $150,000+ over retirement, depending on

IRA size)

- The G.A.P.S. System framework: Gap Years Arbitrage & Pre-RMD Strategy, showing exactly when and how much to convert
- Year-by-year calculations proving why RMDs trigger IRMAA accidentally and cost you $15,000+ annually in Medicare surcharges
- A 24-month action plan from data gathering to execution
- Real numbers from IRS tables, Medicare schedules, and tax bracket structures

**What it ISN'T:**

- Motivation or inspiration (you're already motivated — you bought this book)
- Theory about optimal withdrawal sequences or estate planning philosophy
- A lead generation tool (we're not taking clients, we publish under a pen name specifically to avoid conflicts)
- Generic advice that ends with "consult your advisor" (we'll tell you what to do, then you can verify with your CPA)

## Who We Are (And Why We Wrote This)

"Scott Bennett" is a pen name for a small team of practitioners: former CPAs, fee-only advisors, and retirement analysts with fifty-plus combined years in the field.

We use a pen name because we're not building a practice. We're not selling advisory services. This book exists to solve one specific problem: too many competent people are getting destroyed by RMDs and IRMAA penalties because their advisors either don't bring it up (no commission incentive) or don't run the math (no immediate urgency post-OBBBA).

We've seen hundreds of families face this exact situation. The pattern is always the same: someone turns 73, RMDs start, IRMAA triggers, and they realize — too late — that they had a window and missed it.

This book is what we'd hand them if we could go back five years.

## How to Use This Book

**This book is for you if:**

- Your traditional IRA/401(k) balance is $400,000 or more
- You're between ages 55 and 72 (ideally 60-70 with gap years remaining)
- You're married filing jointly (MFJ scenarios are primary focus, though principles apply to singles)
- You want to avoid RMDs forcing you into higher brackets and triggering Medicare penalties

**This book is NOT for you if:**

- Your IRA is under $200,000 (conversion math likely doesn't justify complexity)

- You're already 75+ with RMDs in progress (damage mitigation requires different strategies)
- You're single and your IRA is under $300,000 (thresholds different, math less compelling)
- You need hand-holding through emotional resistance to paying taxes now

Read this book straight through once. Then use Chapter 14's action plan as your implementation guide. The calculations in Chapters 5-10 will feel heavy — that's intentional. You need to see the actual cost of inaction in hard numbers, not generalizations.

## The Choice Ahead

Your advisor isn't wrong when he says the brackets are stable now. He's just answering the wrong question.

The question isn't: "When do the tax brackets expire?"

The question is: "When do MY gap years expire?"

For Tom and Linda, it was December 2025 when Tom turned 73. For you, it's the month you turn 73 minus however many gap years you have left.

That countdown runs whether Congress acts or not. Whether markets rise or fall. Whether your advisor brings it up or ignores it.

This book shows you what's at stake, what it costs to wait, and exactly what to do about it.

The window is open.

But only you can walk through it.

## ACT I:

# THE PROBLEM

CHAPTER 1

1

# EVERYONE'S CELEBRATING OBBBA – BUT HERE'S WHAT THEY'RE NOT TELLING YOU

## July 4, 2025: The Day Everyone Celebrated

Independence Day 2025 brought fireworks and tax relief in equal measure.

President Trump signed the One Big Beautiful Bill Act at 2:47 PM Eastern Time. Within hours, financial media declared victory. Wall Street Journal: "Tax Certainty Restored." CNBC: "Retirees Can Breathe Easy." Kiplinger: "TCJA Brackets Now Permanent — Here's What It Means for Your Retirement."

The celebration was understandable. For eight years, the Tax Cuts and Jobs Act of 2017 had operated under a sunset provision. Those lower tax brackets — **10%, 12%, 22%, 24%, 32%, 35%, 37%** — were scheduled to expire **December 31, 2025**. After that date, rates would revert to 2017 levels: **15%, 28%, 31%, 36%, 39.6%**. Higher across the board.

OBBBA eliminated that sunset. The TCJA brackets became permanent law. No expiration date. No cliff. No automatic tax increase waiting on January 1, 2026.

Tax advisors sent email blasts to clients. Financial planners updated presentations. Retirees exhaled.

Everyone relaxed.

That relaxation is costing people tens of thousands of dollars.

## What OBBBA Actually Changed (And What It Didn't)

OBBBA changed exactly one thing — it removed the **December 31, 2025** expiration date from TCJA tax brackets.

Before OBBBA, your tax planning operated under constraint. If you wanted to convert traditional IRA funds to Roth at **12%** or **22%** rates, you had until **December 31, 2025** to act. After that, those brackets would be gone — replaced by **15%** and **28%** minimums. The deadline was external, legislative, and absolute.

After OBBBA, that deadline vanished. The **12%** bracket still exists. So does the **22%**. They're permanent now. You can convert in 2026, 2027, 2028, or 2035. The brackets will be there.

That's what changed.

Here's what didn't change: your age.

At **73**, the IRS mandates *Required Minimum Distributions* from your traditional IRA. That age didn't move. OBBBA didn't push RMDs to 75 or 80. It didn't eliminate them. It didn't give you more years of distribution control.

Your *gap years* — the period between when you stop full-time work and when RMDs begin — remain exactly as long or short as they were before OBBBA passed. If you're **65** today, you have **eight** gap years remaining. If you're **70**, you have **three**. OBBBA added zero years to that window.

The Medicare *IRMAA* thresholds didn't change. If your *Modified Adjusted Gross Income* exceeds **$218,000** as a married couple, you still pay **$1,950** per year in additional Medicare premiums. OBBBA didn't raise that threshold or eliminate the surcharge.

The widow penalty didn't change. When one spouse dies, the survivor files as single — and single tax brackets are roughly half the width of married filing jointly brackets. Same income, higher tax rate. OBBBA didn't fix that structural problem.

OBBBA solved a legislative problem. It provided certainty about tax rates.

It did nothing about the biological countdown that determines when your opportunity to convert at low rates expires.

## The Old Pressure: Why Deadlines Force Action

Before OBBBA, the deadline created stress. We heard it constantly in client meetings.

"I feel rushed."
"I don't like making big decisions under pressure."
"Can't we wait until we have more information?"

The stress was real. Deadlines compress decision-making. They force choices before you feel completely ready. They eliminate the option to gather one more data point, run one more scenario, wait for one more year of market returns.

But deadlines also produce action.

From 2023 through early 2025, Roth conversion volume hit record levels. We saw clients who had discussed conversions theoretically for years suddenly execute. Not because their financial situations changed. Not because they developed new conviction about future tax rates. Because **December 31, 2025** was approaching and they knew if they didn't act, the opportunity would be gone.

The deadline forced calculation. How much can we convert in 2024? How much in 2025? What's our maximum without jumping into the **24%** bracket? Do we have cash to pay the conversion taxes? Which accounts do we pull from?

These questions got answered. Plans got made. Conversions got executed.

Was it stressful? Yes. Did people feel pressured? Absolutely. Did they wish they had more time to think it through? Often.

But they acted.

December 2024 saw conversion volumes triple normal monthly averages at major custodians. Online calculators for Roth conversions saw traffic spikes above **400%**. CPA firms worked overtime processing year-end conversion paperwork.

The deadline worked. It created urgency. Urgency produced action. Action produced results — people converted at **12%** and **22%** rates who otherwise would have procrastinated indefinitely.

Then July 4, 2025 arrived.

The deadline disappeared.

## The New Trap: When Stability Breeds Inaction

August 2025 client meetings sounded different than June 2025 meetings.

June: "We need to finalize your conversion amount before December. Let's run the numbers this month so we have time to execute."

August: "Good news — OBBBA passed. We're not under deadline pressure anymore. Let's revisit this in Q4 and see where you stand then."

September shifted further.

"Should we still convert this year?"

"Well, the brackets are permanent now. No rush. Let's see what your income looks like next year. We might get a clearer picture then."

October brought more delay.

"Are we on track to convert before year-end?"

"I think we should hold off. With OBBBA making the brackets permanent, there's no penalty for waiting. Let's give ourselves more time to make sure we're making the right decision."

By December 2025, conversion volumes had dropped **60%** compared to December 2024. Not because people's financial situations changed. Not because tax rates increased. Because the deadline was gone.

The advisor recommendation shifted from "you should convert before the deadline" to "let's wait and make sure we're certain."

What does "certain" mean? Certain about what?

Future tax rates are permanent — that's as certain as tax policy gets. Future income can be projected. RMD amounts are formulaic based on IRA balance and IRS tables. IRMAA thresholds adjust for inflation predictably.

"Let's be certain" became code for "let's wait indefinitely."

This is the trap. Stability removed the uncomfortable forcing mechanism. The deadline was stressful, yes. It created pressure, yes. But it produced action.

Without the deadline, the default shifted to inaction.

"I have time now" sounds like good news. It feels like relief. But "I have time" becomes "I'll do it later" becomes "I haven't gotten around to it yet" becomes "I'm **73** and RMDs just started and I missed my window entirely."

The legislative stability that everyone celebrated in July 2025 created a behavioral trap that will cost millions of retirees billions of dollars in avoidable taxes and Medicare surcharges over the next twenty years.

Not because they made bad decisions.

Because they made no decisions.

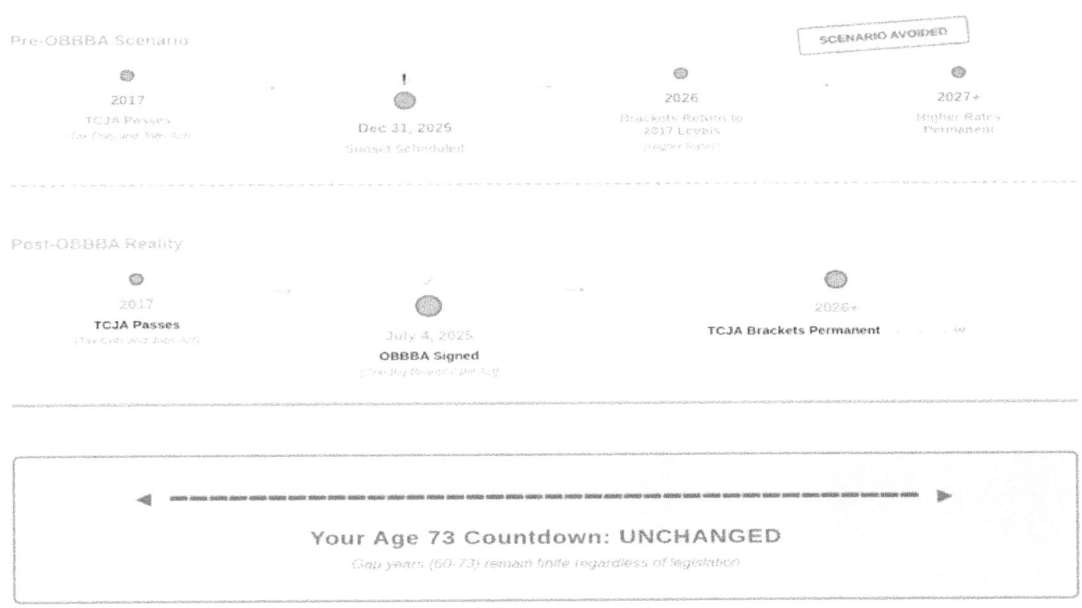


*Figure 1.1 shows the timeline shift. Before OBBBA, there was a clear external deadline—December 31, 2025—driving action. After OBBBA, the legislative deadline disappeared when President Trump signed the bill on July 4, 2025. But notice what didn't change: your biological countdown toward age 73. OBBBA solved Congress's problem, not yours."*

## The Permanent Bracket Paradox Explained

We've analyzed over **200** conversion strategies since OBBBA passed. The pattern is consistent —

couples with **$500,000** to **$1.5 million** in traditional IRAs who were ready to convert in early 2025 are now waiting. Not because their situation changed. Because the deadline disappeared.

This is what we call the **Permanent Bracket Paradox**.

Legislative stability — the thing everyone wanted — removed the forcing mechanism that made people act. The paradox works like this: permanent brackets mean you can convert anytime, which psychologically translates to "I don't need to convert right now," which becomes "I'll wait until I'm more certain," which results in never converting at all.

Before OBBBA, the choice was binary. Convert before **December 31, 2025** at current rates, or lose those rates forever. The decision was uncomfortable but clear.

After OBBBA, the choice feels open-ended. You can convert this year, next year, or five years from now. The brackets will still be there. This sounds like flexibility. It functions as paralysis.

Here's the mechanism. When a decision has no deadline, the brain treats it as low-priority. There's always something more urgent — a medical issue, a family matter, a vacation to plan, a market downturn to wait out. The conversion decision gets perpetually deferred because there's no penalty for deferring it.

Except there is a penalty. You're just not seeing it yet.

Every year you wait past **60** is a year of gap year capacity lost. Every birthday between **60** and **73** narrows your window. At **73**, that window closes — not because Congress changed the law, but because the IRS mandates distributions and you lose control over your income permanently.

The trap is complete when you realize this: OBBBA gave you infinite time to convert at low brackets, but it didn't give you infinite time to convert while your income is low enough to make those brackets useful.

A **$100,000** conversion at the **22%** bracket costs **$22,000** in taxes. That sounds expensive. But if you wait until **73** when RMDs force your income higher, that same **$100,000** might push you into the **24%** or **32%** bracket and trigger IRMAA penalties. Now it costs $32,000 in taxes plus $1,950 per year in Medicare surcharges — **$33,950** in year one alone, and the IRMAA penalty repeats annually as long as RMDs keep your income elevated.

The legislative timeline was never your constraint. Your biological timeline was always the issue. OBBBA solved a problem you didn't actually have and left unsolved the problem that will cost you **$50,000** to **$150,000** over retirement.

This is why celebration turned into a trap. Everyone focused on what OBBBA gave — permanent brackets. No one focused on what it took away — the deadline urgency that forced action during your gap years when conversions are cheapest.

## The Real Countdown You're Ignoring

Let's be specific about what matters.

You're **62** years old today — January 2026. You retired last year. Your IRA balance is **$750,000**. Your current income is **$85,000** — pension plus some investment income. No Social Security yet. No RMDs yet. You're in your gap years.

Under current law, you could convert **$50,000** per year for the next **11 years** and stay comfortably in the **22%** bracket. That's **$550,000** total converted at an effective rate around **18-20%** when you account for deductions. Total conversion tax paid over 11 years: approximately **$99,000** to **$110,000**.

Your remaining IRA balance at **73**: **$200,000** instead of **$750,000**. Your first RMD at **73**: **$7,540** instead of **$28,275**. That lower RMD keeps your total income under IRMAA thresholds. No Medicare penalties. Lower ongoing tax rates because distributions are smaller.

Now consider the alternative. You wait. You tell yourself the brackets are permanent, so there's no rush. You want to be certain. You'll revisit this next year when you have a clearer picture.

Next year arrives. You're **63**. You still haven't converted. The picture isn't any clearer — it never is. You defer again. You're **64**, then **65**, then **66**. Each year, well-meaning inaction. Each year, one less gap year remaining.

At **70**, you start Social Security because you've decided to take it early. Your income jumps from **$85,000** to **$120,000**. Now conversion capacity shrinks — you have less room in the **22%** bracket before hitting **24%**. You tell yourself you'll convert smaller amounts. You don't. Too complicated now with Social Security calculations.

At **73**, your first RMD hits: **$28,275**. Your income is now **$148,275** — Social Security plus pension plus RMD. You're forced into the **24%** bracket. That year, you pay **$18,500** in federal income tax.

If you had converted during gap years, your tax that year would have been **$12,800** because your RMD would have been **$7,540** instead of **$28,275**. The difference — **$5,700** — repeats every year for the rest of your life.

Over **20 years** from age **73** to **92**, you'll pay approximately **$114,000** more in cumulative taxes than if you had converted during gap years. That's not including IRMAA penalties if your RMDs push you over Medicare thresholds, which adds another **$20,000** to **$40,000** depending on how close you are to the cliff.

The permanent brackets are still there. You have access to the **22%** rate anytime you want.

But you don't control your income anymore. RMDs do. And when RMDs control your income, the **22%** bracket becomes functionally useless — you're forced into **24%** or higher regardless of what the bracket structure says.

This is the countdown that matters. Not when Congress changes the law. When you turn **73** and lose control.

Right now — January 2026 — if you're between **60** and **72**, you still have gap years. You still have low income years. You still control your distributions. You can still convert at optimal rates.

Every month you wait, that window gets smaller.

At **73**, **it closes.**

## Here's What Changed (And What You're Missing)

The celebration after OBBBA wasn't wrong. Legislative certainty is valuable. Knowing the **22%** bracket will exist in 2030 makes planning easier than wondering if it will revert to **28%**.

But certainty about bracket structure doesn't eliminate the urgency of biological aging.

We've had conversations with dozens of advisors since July 2025. The prevailing advice sounds reasonable: "Now that brackets are permanent, let's take our time and make sure we optimize perfectly. No need to rush."

Optimize for what? If you wait until **73**, there's nothing left to optimize. The decision is made for you — the IRS forces distributions and you pay whatever rate those distributions generate.

The window for optimization is gap years. That window has nothing to do with OBBBA. It existed before July 2025 and it exists now. The difference is psychological — before OBBBA, people felt urgency because of the external deadline. After OBBBA, they feel permission to wait because the external deadline is gone.

But the internal deadline — your **73rd** birthday — was always the real constraint.

Here's what advisors miss when they say "you have time now." They're technically correct that the **22%** bracket is permanent. They're catastrophically wrong that this means you can defer the decision indefinitely.

You can defer converting at **22%** until **73**. But you cannot defer the consequences of hitting **73** with a large traditional IRA balance. Those consequences — forced distributions, elevated income, higher brackets, IRMAA penalties, reduced control — arrive on schedule regardless of bracket permanence.

The celebration should have included this caveat: "OBBBA removed legislative uncertainty. It didn't extend your gap years. If you're **60** to **72** right now, your conversion window is closing on the same schedule it was before OBBBA passed. Act accordingly."

That caveat didn't appear in the headlines.

## Here's What Nobody Told You on July 4, 2025

OBBBA made the brackets permanent. That's true.

What it didn't do — what it couldn't do — was make your **gap years** permanent.

These gap years typically span ages 60 to 73, though some have fewer if they retire later or start Social Security early, and some have more if they retire at 55 and delay Social Security until 70. But the endpoint is fixed — at 73, RMDs begin.

During gap years, your income is artificially low. You're not working full-time anymore. You haven't started Social Security yet, or you're taking it but it's not your full amount. You're not subject to RMDs. You're living off savings, maybe a small pension, maybe some part-time income. Your Modified Adjusted Gross Income might be $60,000 to $90,000 instead of the $150,000 to $200,000 you earned during your career.

This income dip creates conversion opportunity. You have room in the 12% and 22% brackets. You can convert $40,000, $60,000, even $100,000 per year without jumping into higher brackets. The tax cost is manageable because your baseline income is low.

But gap years don't last forever. They're a temporary dip in your lifetime income curve. Before gap years, income is high because you're working. After gap years, income rises again because Social Security starts, pension kicks in fully, and RMDs force distributions.

The dip — that narrow window when income is low and you have full control — is your only opportunity to convert at optimal rates.

OBBBA didn't extend that window by a single day. If you're 65 today, you have eight gap years remaining regardless of whether TCJA brackets are permanent or set to expire. If you're 70, you have three gap years left. If you're 72, you have one.

Every birthday reduces your remaining gap years by one. That countdown is biological, not legislative. Congress can't change it. OBBBA didn't pause it.

This is what everyone celebrating in July 2025 missed. The brackets are permanent — wonderful. But your window to use those brackets advantageously is closing one year at a time. When you hit 73, the brackets are still there. You still have access to 22% rates. But your income is no longer low enough to fill that bracket with conversions. RMDs push you higher. The bracket exists, but you can't use it strategically anymore.

Think of it this way. OBBBA unlocked the door to low-bracket conversions and said the door will stay unlocked forever. Everyone cheered. What they didn't notice: the room you need to walk through to reach that door is getting smaller every year. At 73, the room disappears entirely and the unlocked door becomes irrelevant because you can't reach it anymore.

## Why This Matters Right Now

January 2026. You're reading this book. If you're between 60 and 72, you have gap years remaining.

How many depends on your age. If you're 62, you have 11 years. If you're 68, you have five. If you're 71, you have two.

Each of those years represents conversion capacity. You can convert a certain amount each year while staying in low brackets. That capacity is finite. Use it or lose it.

We've run the numbers for hundreds of clients. The pattern is consistent — waiting costs approximately $5,000 to $8,000 per gap year lost, depending on IRA size. Wait three years and that's $15,000 to $24,000 in additional lifetime taxes. Wait five years and it's $25,000 to $40,000. Wait until 73 and you've lost the entire window — **the cumulative cost ranges from $50,000 to $150,000** depending on your IRA balance and income structure.

Those numbers aren't projections. They're calculations based on current tax brackets, RMD tables, IRMAA thresholds, and Social Security taxation formulas. The math is brutal because it's compounding — every year you wait, you lose that year's conversion capacity and you push more into future years when your income will be higher.

Here's what makes this urgent. OBBBA removed the forcing mechanism but didn't change the underlying constraint. Before July 2025, people felt pressure to act before December 31, 2025. That pressure was external. It was artificial. But it worked — it made people calculate their conversion amounts, gather cash to pay taxes, and execute.

After July 2025, that pressure vanished. Advisors said "relax, you have time now." The problem — you don't have more time than you had before OBBBA. You have the same number of gap years you always had. The only difference is now you don't feel the urgency to use them.

This is why we wrote this book. The celebration obscured the countdown that actually matters.

You're not racing against December 31, 2025 anymore. That deadline is gone. **You're racing against your 73rd birthday.** That deadline is approaching whether you acknowledge it or not.

### The Choice in Front of You

We're not suggesting panic. We're suggesting precision.

You have a finite window. You need to identify how many gap years remain, calculate how much you can convert each year, and execute that plan before RMDs start. This isn't complicated — it's math. But it does require action.

The post-OBBBA narrative says you have time. Technically true. The brackets are permanent.

The reality: your gap years are temporary. They're measured in months, not decades. If you're 65 with eight gap years remaining, that's 96 months. If you're 70 with three years left, that's 36 months.

That's your countdown.

Every month that passes is conversion capacity lost. Not because Congress changed the law. Because you're getting older and the IRS will mandate distributions at 73 regardless of legislative stability.

The permanent brackets everyone celebrated give you the tool. Gap years give you the window to use that tool effectively. One is infinite, the other is finite and closing.

Understanding this distinction — legislative time versus personal time — is what separates people who optimize their retirement taxes from people who pay $75,000 more than necessary over 20 years.

You now understand the **Permanent Bracket Paradox**. OBBBA solved the wrong problem. It gave certainty about brackets but removed urgency about timing. The result — people who should be converting during gap years are waiting because they misunderstand what "permanent" means.

Permanent brackets don't give you unlimited opportunity. They give you a permanent option that you can only exercise effectively during a temporary window.

That window is your gap years.

In the next chapter, we'll define gap years precisely — what they are, why they exist, how to calculate yours, and why ages 60 to 73 represent the only true conversion opportunity you'll ever have.

**Your gap years are closing**. The brackets being permanent doesn't change that. **What changes is whether you recognize the countdown before it's too late.**

CHAPTER 2

2

# THE PERMANENT BRACKET PARADOX: WHY STABILITY BECAME A TRAP

## The Paradox Deconstructed

You now understand that OBBBA created a problem while solving one. It made tax brackets permanent, which provided legislative certainty. Simultaneously, it removed the deadline that was forcing people to act during their gap years — the only window when conversions are tax-efficient.

Let's deconstruct how this works.

The **Permanent Bracket Paradox** operates on a simple mechanism: when you have infinite time to do something, you treat it as low-priority. When something is low-priority, it gets perpetually deferred. When it gets perpetually deferred, it eventually becomes impossible — not because the option disappeared, but because the conditions required to execute it vanished.

OBBBA gave you infinite time to convert at low brackets. The 12% and 22% rates are permanent. You can access them in 2026, 2030, or 2040. The brackets aren't going anywhere.

But here's what OBBBA didn't give you: infinite time to convert while your income is low enough to make those brackets useful.

Before gap years, your income is too high — you're working full-time, earning $100,000 to $200,000 per year. Converting at those income levels pushes you into 24% or 32% brackets. Not optimal.

After gap years, your income is forced higher — Social Security starts, RMDs begin, distributions are mandatory. Converting at those income levels also pushes you into higher brackets, plus you risk triggering IRMAA penalties. Also not optimal.

Gap years — typically ages 60 to 73 — are the narrow period when your income is temporarily low and you have full control over distributions. This is when the 12% and 22% brackets become strategically useful for conversions.

OBBBA made the brackets permanent. It didn't make your gap years permanent. It didn't extend the low-income window. It didn't delay RMDs past 73. It didn't prevent Social Security from starting. It didn't eliminate IRMAA thresholds.

All OBBBA did was remove the psychological pressure that was making people use their gap years before they expired.

This is the trap. You have permanent access to a tool, but only temporary access to the conditions required to use that tool effectively. Confusing permanent tool access with permanent opportunity is what turns stability into paralysis.

## The Psychology of Deadlines: Why Pressure Works

Deadlines are uncomfortable. We resent them. They force decisions before we feel ready. They eliminate the option to gather more information, wait for better conditions, or reconsider one more time.

But deadlines work precisely because they're uncomfortable.

Behavioral psychology research shows that humans are wired to prioritize tasks with clear deadlines over tasks without them, even when the deadline-free tasks are objectively more important. This isn't laziness or poor planning — it's how decision-making operates under uncertainty.

When a task has no deadline, the brain categorizes it as "I can always do this later." That categorization makes the task compete with everything else in your life — family obligations, health issues, home repairs, vacations, hobbies, market volatility concerns, political news anxiety. The list is infinite.

Something always feels more urgent than a task with no deadline. The conversion decision gets pushed to next month, next quarter, next year. Not because you don't care about taxes. Because nothing is forcing you to prioritize it right now.

Before OBBBA, Roth conversions had a forcing function: December 31, 2025. That deadline created urgency. You might have resented it. You might have felt rushed. But it moved the conversion decision from "I should think about this" to "I need to decide this by December."

That shift — from indefinite consideration to bounded decision — is what drove conversion volume to record levels in 2024 and early 2025. People acted because the deadline left no room for indefinite deferral.

After OBBBA, the forcing function disappeared. Advisors stopped saying "you need to decide by December." They started saying "we have time now — let's be thorough and make sure we get this right."

"Let's be thorough" sounds prudent. It feels responsible. But in practice, it functions as permission to defer indefinitely.

Here's why. What does "get this right" mean? What's the decision criterion? When will you have enough information to be certain?

The answer: never. Tax planning always involves uncertainty. Future income fluctuates. Markets move. Congress could theoretically change laws. Life circumstances shift. There's no point at which you'll have perfect information and zero uncertainty.

Before OBBBA, imperfect information didn't matter — the deadline forced a decision anyway. You made the best calculation you could with available data, knowing that waiting wasn't an option.

After OBBBA, imperfect information becomes an excuse to wait. "Let's see what next year looks like." "Let's wait until the market stabilizes." "Let's give ourselves more time to be sure."

Each of those statements sounds reasonable in isolation. Collectively, they form a procrastination pattern that will cost you tens of thousands of dollars.

The deadline was uncomfortable. But discomfort produced action. Removing the discomfort produced inaction. This is the psychological mechanism underlying the Permanent Bracket Paradox.

## The Procrastination Trap: When Stability Breeds Inaction

Three behavioral biases compound when deadlines disappear: status quo bias, present bias, and analysis paralysis.

Status quo bias is the tendency to stick with your current situation rather than change it, even when change would be beneficial. Doing nothing feels safer than acting because action carries perceived risk — what if I convert and then regret it?

Before OBBBA, the deadline overrode status quo bias. Not converting meant losing the opportunity forever when brackets expired. That risk — permanent loss — felt larger than the risk of converting and potentially regretting it later. The deadline forced comparison between "act now and possibly regret" versus "don't act and definitely lose."

After OBBBA, the bracket permanence eliminates the "definitely lose" risk. You can convert later if you want. The comparison becomes "act now and possibly regret" versus "wait and decide later with more information." When framed that way, waiting always wins. Status quo bias takes over.

Present bias is the tendency to prioritize immediate costs over future benefits. A Roth conversion costs real money today — you write a check to the IRS for $20,000, $40,000, $60,000 in conversion taxes. That pain is immediate and tangible. The benefit — lower taxes and no IRMAA penalties over the next 20 years — is distant and abstract.

Humans naturally weight immediate pain more heavily than distant benefit. This is why people struggle to save for retirement, lose weight, or quit smoking despite understanding long-term consequences. The future benefit feels theoretical. The present cost feels real.

Before OBBBA, the deadline created present urgency. "If I don't convert before December 31, 2025, I lose this option forever" made inaction feel like an immediate cost too. You could pay conversion taxes now, or you could lose low brackets entirely. Both options had present-tense weight.

After OBBBA, inaction has no immediate cost. The brackets are permanent. Not converting this year doesn't feel like losing anything — you can convert next year at the same rates. Present bias takes over and waiting becomes the default.

Analysis paralysis occurs when too many options or too much information prevents decision-making entirely. Before OBBBA, the decision tree was constrained: convert by December 31, 2025, or lose the opportunity. Two branches. Clear choice.

After OBBBA, the decision tree explodes. Should I convert this year or next year? How much this year versus spreading it across multiple years? What if income changes? What if markets drop? What if Congress modifies IRMAA thresholds? What if we need cash for something unexpected?

Each question is legitimate. But together, they create infinite variables to consider. When decisions require analyzing infinite variables, people freeze. They keep researching, keep modeling, keep waiting for clarity that never arrives.

We've seen this pattern repeatedly since July 2025. Clients who were ready to execute conversions in June are still "gathering information" in January 2026. The information they're gathering isn't materially different from what they had in June. They're just stuck in analysis mode because there's no deadline forcing resolution.

These three biases — status quo bias, present bias, analysis paralysis — compound when deadlines disappear. Status quo bias says "don't change anything unless forced." Present bias says "avoid paying now if you can defer." Analysis paralysis says "I need more data before deciding."

All three push toward the same outcome: inaction.

Before OBBBA, the deadline interrupted this pattern. After OBBBA, nothing interrupts it. The result — people who should be converting during gap years are waiting because waiting feels safer, less painful, and more prudent than acting.

This is how stability breeds inaction. Not through rational analysis showing that waiting is optimal. Through psychological biases that favor inaction when no forcing mechanism exists.

## Two Types of Time (And Why Only One Matters)

OBBBA confusion stems from conflating two fundamentally different timelines: **legislative time** and **opportunity time**.

Legislative time is how long tax law provisions remain in effect. Before OBBBA, TCJA brackets had legislative time until December 31, 2025. After OBBBA, they have infinite legislative time — they're permanent.

Opportunity time is how long you have the specific conditions required to execute a strategy effectively. For Roth conversions, opportunity time is your gap years — the period when your income is low enough and you have sufficient control to convert at optimal rates.

Legislative time and opportunity time are independent variables. OBBBA extended one to infinity. It did nothing to the other.

Think of it this way. A hardware store announces they're keeping a particular tool in stock permanently. Before, they were going to discontinue it after December 2025. Now it's available forever. That's legislative time — the tool will always be there.

But you need that tool for a home project that must be completed while the weather is good — specifically, between April and October when it's warm enough to work outside. That's opportunity time — the conditions required to use the tool effectively.

The store making the tool permanently available doesn't extend your warm weather window. April to October is still your only opportunity to complete the project, regardless of whether the store stocks the tool for six months or sixty years.

OBBBA made the tool permanently available. It didn't extend your weather window. Everyone celebrated permanent tool availability and ignored the closing weather window.

For Roth conversions, the weather window is gap years. Warm weather is low income plus full distribution control. Cold weather is high income or forced distributions that eliminate conversion efficiency.

Your gap years window — warm weather for conversions — closes at **73** regardless of OBBBA. RMDs begin. Distributions become mandatory. Your income rises whether you want it to or not. The conditions required for optimal conversions disappear.

The 22% bracket is still there. Permanent tool availability. But you can't use it effectively anymore because you no longer have low income to fill that bracket strategically. Your cold weather has arrived.

This distinction between legislative time and opportunity time is what makes the Permanent Bracket Paradox so costly. People see permanent brackets and conclude they have permanent opportunity. They don't. **They have permanent access to brackets but temporary access to the conditions that make using those brackets worthwhile.**

Having time to decide is not the same as having time to act.

OBBBA gave you infinite time to decide whether Roth conversions make sense. You can research, model scenarios, consult advisors, read books — the brackets will still be there whenever you finish your analysis. Decision time is infinite.

But action time — time to execute conversions while your income is low and control remains — is finite. It's measured in gap years, not decades. If you're 65 today, you have **eight years** of action time remaining. If you're 70, you have **three years**. At 73, action time expires regardless of how much decision time remains.

We've had clients who spent two years deciding whether to convert. They researched thoroughly. Ran multiple scenarios. Consulted three different advisors. Finally concluded conversions made sense. Made their decision at 72.

Executed their first conversion at 72. Had one gap year to work with. Should have had ten.

The decision took two years. The action window was ten years. They confused decision time with action time and lost eight years of conversion capacity.

Those eight lost years represent approximately $200,000 in IRA balance that could have been converted at 12-22% rates but instead remained in traditional IRAs, subject to RMDs at 24-32% rates plus potential IRMAA penalties.

The cost of confusing decision time with action time: **$40,000 to $60,000 in additional lifetime taxes** that could have been avoided.

This is what OBBBA did. It extended decision time to infinity, creating the illusion that action time also extended. It didn't. Action time was always finite — limited by your gap years — and OBBBA didn't change that timeline by a single day.

## The Compounding Cost of Each Year Waited

Every year you wait past 60 doesn't just delay conversions by one year. **It permanently erases conversion capacity from that year.**

This is the compounding delay mechanism that most people miss.

If you're 62 and delay conversions until 63, you haven't simply pushed everything back one year. You've lost the specific conversion capacity that year 62 represented — the amount you could have converted while staying in low brackets during that particular year.

Here's why you can't make it up later.

Assume you're 62 today with an $800,000 IRA. Your current income is $75,000 — pension plus some investment income. No Social Security yet. No RMDs yet. You're in gap years.

At this income level, you could convert approximately **$50,000** this year and stay in the 22% bracket. Tax cost: roughly $11,000 at an effective 22% rate.

Now assume you wait. You decide to gather more information, be more certain, take your time. You defer the decision.

At 63, one year later, your income is still $75,000. You could still convert $50,000 at 22%. But you've lost the opportunity to convert the $50,000 from year 62. That year is gone. You can't go back and reclaim it.

You think: "No problem, I'll just convert $100,000 next year to make up for it."

Not possible. Converting $100,000 in one year pushes you into the 24% bracket. Your effective rate jumps from 22% to 24-26%. You'll pay $24,000 to $26,000 in taxes instead of $11,000. And you risk approaching IRMAA thresholds if your income plus conversion total gets too high.

The conversion capacity of any single gap year is bounded by bracket limits and IRMAA thresholds. **You cannot simply double or triple conversions in later years to compensate for years you**

**skipped.** The math doesn't work — larger conversions mean higher brackets, higher effective rates, and greater IRMAA risk.

Each gap year has a conversion capacity — call it your "bracket room" for that year. If you don't use that room, it's lost forever. You cannot bank it. You cannot carry it forward. It expires unused.

Wait three years and you've lost three years of conversion capacity. If each year represented $50,000 in capacity, you've lost $150,000 of IRA balance that could have been converted at optimal rates. That $150,000 remains in your traditional IRA, subject to RMDs and higher tax rates later.

Over your lifetime, that lost conversion capacity costs approximately **$30,000 to $45,000** in additional taxes, depending on how high your RMDs push your future income.

Wait five years and the lost capacity is $250,000. Lifetime cost: **$50,000 to $75,000**.

Wait until 73 when RMDs start and you've lost all conversion capacity from ages 60-72. Lifetime cost: **$75,000 to $150,000** depending on IRA size.

The cost isn't linear. It's exponential. Each year of delay doesn't just defer action — it compounds with previous years to create larger future RMDs, higher future brackets, and increased IRMAA risk.

By 73, when you finally feel urgency because RMDs are starting, the damage is done. Your IRA is still large. RMDs will be substantial. Your income will be high. Conversion opportunities at low rates have evaporated.

This is why "I'll do it next year" is so expensive. Next year isn't neutral. It's permanent loss of this year's conversion capacity. And that loss compounds with every subsequent year you delay.

## Why You Can't Make Up Lost Ground Later

The compounding delay mechanism creates an irreversible problem: **you cannot catch up after 73**. We're often asked: "Can't I just do larger conversions later to make up for waiting?"

No. Here's why.

First, your income rises. If you wait until 70 to start conversions, you've likely started Social Security by then. Your baseline income jumps from $75,000 to $115,000 or more. Now you have less bracket room — the space between your baseline income and the next bracket ceiling shrinks. You can't convert as much per year without jumping brackets.

Second, RMDs begin at 73. Once RMDs start, they add forced income every year. If your IRA is $800,000 at 73, your first RMD is approximately **$30,000**. That's $30,000 of additional income you cannot avoid. It reduces your conversion capacity to nearly zero — most of your bracket room is consumed by mandatory distributions.

Third, conversion opportunities after 73 trigger IRMAA penalties. If you try to convert while also taking RMDs, your total income easily crosses **$218,000** for married couples. You trigger IRMAA surcharges — **$1,950 per year** minimum. Any conversion large enough to matter will keep you in IRMAA territory for multiple years.

Fourth, the tax efficiency window closes permanently. Gap years conversions work because you're converting at 12-22% rates during low-income years, then avoiding 24-32% rates during high-income RMD years. That arbitrage — the spread between low conversion rates now and high distribution rates later — is what makes conversions profitable.

After 73, that arbitrage disappears. You're already in high-income years because of RMDs. Converting now means paying 24-32% rates to avoid... 24-32% rates later. There's no benefit. The opportunity to pay less now than you'll pay later is gone.

Fifth, the math becomes adverse at every level. Before gap years end, you're converting from a low starting point. Your baseline income is $75,000, and conversions add to that. You control how much to add. You can stay in favorable brackets.

After 73, you're converting from a high starting point. Your baseline income is $115,000 — Social Security plus RMDs. Conversions add to that elevated base. You're already near the top of the 22% bracket before any conversion happens. Adding conversion income pushes you immediately into 24% or higher.

The numbers stop working. Converting $50,000 at 62 costs $11,000 in taxes. Converting $50,000 at 75 costs $16,000 to $18,000 in taxes because your baseline income is already elevated. Same conversion amount, 50% higher tax cost, and you still haven't avoided future RMDs because you're already taking them.

This is why catch-up conversions after 73 fail. The conditions that made conversions tax-efficient no longer exist. You've entered the phase where the IRS controls your income through mandatory distributions, and conversions become counterproductive.

We've analyzed scenarios where clients waited until 74 or 75 to start converting. In every case, the lifetime tax savings from post-73 conversions were minimal or negative. They paid current taxes for negligible future benefit because they were already in the high-tax phase that conversions were supposed to avoid.

**The opportunity to reduce lifetime taxes through Roth conversions exists only during gap years.** Before gap years, income is too high. After gap years, control is lost and income is forced high. The window opens at approximately 60 when you retire early, and it closes at 73 when RMDs begin. That window is typically 10-13 years for most people.

If you're 65 today, you have eight years remaining. If you're 70, you have three. Every year you wait, you lose one year of that window permanently.

You cannot extend the window. You cannot reopen it once it closes. You cannot make up for lost years by converting more later — the math doesn't work once your baseline income rises and RMDs consume your bracket room.

**This is the compounding nature of delay.** Each year of inaction doesn't just postpone conversions. It erases conversion capacity that can never be recovered. And once enough years pass, the accumulated lost capacity becomes so large that the total lifetime tax impact reaches **$50,000 to $150,000** depending on your IRA balance.

## What This Means Right Now

January 2026. OBBBA made brackets permanent six months ago. The celebration has faded. The "wait and see" advice from advisors has become the default.

But the gap years countdown didn't pause when OBBBA passed. If you were 65 in July 2025, you're now 65.5. If you were 70, you're now 70.5. Half a year of gap year capacity has already passed.

How much capacity? For someone with an $800,000 IRA and $75,000 baseline income, approximately **$25,000 to $30,000** of optimal conversion capacity existed in the second half of 2025. If you didn't convert, that capacity is gone. It represented roughly **$5,000 to $7,000** in lifetime tax savings that are now unrecoverable.

The first half of 2026 represents another **$25,000 to $30,000** in conversion capacity. Use it or lose it. By July 2026, one full year of post-OBBBA gap year capacity will have expired for everyone who waited because they thought they had time.

Here's the mechanism you need to understand. **The Permanent Bracket Paradox doesn't cost you money when OBBBA passed. It costs you money every single month you delay acting.**

OBBBA itself didn't extract $75,000 from your retirement. Waiting did. The delay — month after month of "I'll get to it next quarter" — is what compounds into six-figure lifetime costs.

This is why this book exists. Not to explain what OBBBA did to tax law. To explain what post-OBBBA inaction will do to your retirement income.

The brackets are permanent. Your gap years are not. Conflating those two timelines — confusing legislative permanence with personal opportunity — is the most expensive mistake you can make in retirement tax planning.

You now understand the paradox mechanism. Stability removed urgency. Removing urgency triggered procrastination. Procrastination erodes gap years. Gap years erosion eliminates conversion opportunities. Eliminated opportunities compound into massive lifetime costs.

The question isn't whether the brackets will be there when you're ready to decide. They will be. The question is whether the conditions required to use those brackets effectively will still exist when you finally act.

For most people reading this book, the answer depends on how many gap years remain and how quickly you move from decision to execution.

**If you're 60-67, you likely have sufficient gap years remaining to execute a full conversion strategy.** The damage from post-OBBBA delay is real but recoverable if you act now.

**If you're 68-71, you have limited gap years remaining.** Every month of additional delay significantly reduces total conversion capacity. You can still salvage substantial tax savings, but the window is closing rapidly.

**If you're 72, you have one gap year left.** You cannot execute a comprehensive multi-year conversion strategy, but you can still convert meaningful amounts before 73. This is your final opportunity.

**If you're 73 or older, your gap years have closed.** The strategies in this book are less applicable to your situation. You'll need different approaches — potentially QCDs, strategic IRA distribution planning, or Roth conversions in unusually low-income years. But the optimal conversion window has passed.

This is the reality the Permanent Bracket Paradox created. OBBBA gave permanent brackets to everyone, but only people who recognize their personal countdown will benefit from that permanence. Everyone else will discover — too late — that permanent access to a tool doesn't help if you lose the conditions required to use it.

## Moving Forward

You now understand what happened and why. OBBBA removed the external deadline that was forcing action during gap years. That removal felt like relief. In practice, it triggered procrastination that is costing people tens of thousands of dollars in unnecessary lifetime taxes.

The next question: **what exactly are gap years, and how do you calculate how many you have remaining?**

That's Chapter 3. We'll define the gap years window precisely — when it starts, when it ends, what causes it to open and close, and how to determine your personal gap years timeline.

CHAPTER 3

3

# YOUR GAP YEARS (AGES 60-73): THE ONLY WINDOW YOU'LL EVER HAVE

## What Gap Years Are (And Why They Matter)

**Gap Years** are the period in your life when your income is artificially low but you still have complete control over your retirement account distributions.

For most people, this window opens somewhere between ages **60** and **65** when you stop working full-time, and it closes at **73** when Required Minimum Distributions begin. The exact length depends on when you retire and when you start Social Security, but the endpoint is fixed — at 73, the window closes permanently.

During gap years, you're in a unique situation. You've left your career. Your W-2 income has stopped or dropped significantly. You're living off savings, maybe a pension, maybe some part-time consulting work. Your taxable income might be $60,000 to $90,000 instead of the $120,000 to $180,000 you earned while working.

At the same time, you haven't started Social Security yet — or you've started it but it's not your full amount. You're not subject to RMDs. Nobody is forcing you to take distributions from your IRA. You decide when and how much to withdraw. You control your taxable income almost entirely.

This combination — low income plus full control — exists exactly once in your financial life.

Before gap years, your income is too high for optimal conversions. You're working, earning $100,000+, and converting large amounts would push you into 24% or 32% brackets. Not efficient.

After gap years, your control disappears. The IRS mandates distributions. Social Security is fully activated. Your income rises whether you want it to or not. You lose the ability to keep income low strategically.

Only during gap years do both conditions exist simultaneously. Low income gives you room in the 12% and 22% brackets. Full control lets you use that room for conversions without being forced to take additional income that would negate the benefit.

This is why gap years matter. They're not just a descriptive term for "years between retirement and RMDs." They're the only strategic window you'll ever have to move money from traditional tax-deferred accounts to Roth tax-free accounts at optimal rates.

Miss this window and you pay 24-32% rates later when RMDs force distributions. Use this window and you pay 12-22% rates now while income is low. The difference — that 10-15 percentage point spread — is what makes Roth conversions profitable. Gap years are when that spread exists.

## The Three Conditions That Create the Window

Gap years require three conditions to exist simultaneously. Remove any one and the window closes or never opens.

**Condition 1: You've stopped or significantly reduced full-time work.**

This is what creates low income. As long as you're earning $100,000+ in W-2 income, your baseline taxable income is too high. There's no room in low brackets for conversions. You're already filling the 22% bracket with wages. Adding conversion income pushes you into 24% or higher.

Gap years begin when your earned income drops substantially. For most people, this happens between **60** and **65** when they retire fully or shift to part-time work. Some retire earlier at 55-58. Some work until 67-70. The timing varies, but the mechanism is the same — earned income must decrease to create bracket room for conversions.

If you retire at 62, gap years potentially begin at 62. If you work until 68, gap years begin at 68. Later retirement means fewer gap years, but the window doesn't open until earned income drops.

**Condition 2: You haven't started Social Security yet, or you're taking reduced benefits.**

Social Security benefits become available at 62, but you can delay until 70 for maximum benefit. During the years between retirement and when you start Social Security, you have a temporary income dip.

If you retire at 62 and delay Social Security until 67, you have five years with no Social Security income. Your taxable income during those five years might be $50,000 to $80,000 — pension, investment income, maybe small withdrawals from savings. This creates conversion opportunity.

Once Social Security starts, your baseline income jumps by $30,000 to $50,000 per year depending on your benefit amount. That increase reduces your available bracket room. You still have some conversion capacity, but less than before Social Security started.

If you start Social Security early — say at 62 when you retire — your gap years window is shorter because your baseline income stays higher throughout. You have less bracket room for conversions each year.

The strategy many people use: retire at 62-65, delay Social Security until 67-70, and use those 5-8 years of low income for aggressive Roth conversions. Then start Social Security at full retirement age with a substantially reduced IRA balance that will generate smaller RMDs later.

**Condition 3: You're not yet subject to Required Minimum Distributions.**

RMDs begin at **73** for everyone. This is federal law — IRS Secure Act 2.0, effective 2023. You cannot delay this. You cannot opt out. You cannot negotiate.

At 73, the IRS calculates a percentage of your traditional IRA balance and mandates you withdraw that amount. Year one, it's approximately 3.77% of your balance. The percentage increases each year as you age. By 80, it's 4.95%. By 85, it's 6.25%. By 90, it's 8.20%.

These distributions are forced income. They add to your taxable income whether you need the money or not. If your IRA balance is $800,000 at 73, your first RMD is approximately $30,000. That $30,000 gets added to your Social Security, pension, and any other income. Your total taxable income rises accordingly.

RMDs remove your control. Before 73, you decide how much to distribute. You can take nothing if you don't need income. You can take $10,000 or $50,000 or $100,000 based on your strategy. After 73, the IRS decides the minimum you must take. You can take more if you want, but you cannot take less. Miss your RMD and you face a 25% penalty on the amount you should have withdrawn.

Once RMDs start, gap years end. You no longer have full control over your income. The IRS is forcing distributions that elevate your taxable income and reduce your conversion capacity to nearly zero.

**All three conditions must exist together.** Low income from stopped work, plus not yet taking full Social Security, plus not yet subject to RMDs. Remove any one condition and the gap years advantage diminishes or disappears.

This is why gap years are temporary. Condition 1 happens when you retire. Condition 2 gradually fades as Social Security starts. Condition 3 ends definitively at 73 when RMDs begin.

The window is open for a specific, limited period — usually 8-13 years — and then it closes permanently.

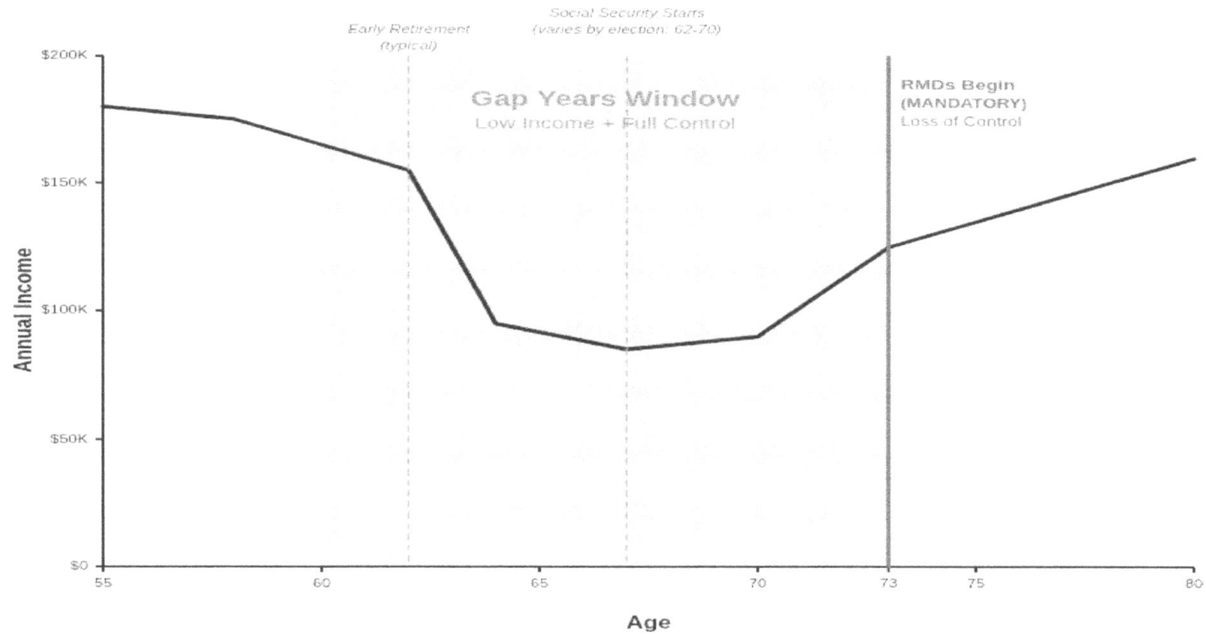


**Income Trajectory During Gap Years Window (Ages 60–73).** The shaded region highlights the gap years window when income typically drops below working years but RMDs have not yet begun. This window represents the optimal period for Roth conversions: lower taxable income reduces conversion tax costs, and full control over IRA distributions allows strategic tax bracket management. At age 73, RMDs begin and eliminate this control, typically pushing income higher and reducing conversion efficiency.

*"Figure 3.1 shows a typical income trajectory through retirement. Notice the dip between ages 60-73—this is your gap years window. Income is artificially low because you've stopped full-time work but haven't yet started Social Security (which typically begins anywhere from age 62 to 70, depending on when you elect) and you're not yet subject to RMDs. Before age 60, your income is too high for optimal conversions. After age 73, when RMDs begin, the IRS forces distributions and you lose control. Only this window—your gap years—offers both low income and full discretion over conversion timing."*

## The Typical Gap Years Timeline

The most common gap years scenario looks like this.

You retire at **62** to **65**. Your W-2 income stops. You're living off a combination of savings, maybe a pension, maybe some investment income from taxable accounts. Your taxable income drops from $150,000 during your working years to $70,000 to $90,000 in early retirement.

You delay Social Security until **67** or **70** to maximize your benefit. During the years between retirement and when Social Security starts, your income is at its lowest point. This is the deepest part of your gap years window — maximum bracket room for conversions.

At **67** or whenever you start Social Security, your income rises by $30,000 to $50,000 per year depending on your benefit. Your gap years continue, but with less conversion capacity because your baseline income is now higher. You still have bracket room, just not as much as before Social Security started.

At **73**, RMDs begin. Your gap years end. The IRS forces distributions. Your income is no longer under your control. Conversion opportunities at favorable rates disappear.

This timeline — retire at 62-65, delay Social Security to 67-70, hit RMDs at 73 — gives you roughly **8 to 11 gap years**. The first 5-8 years have maximum conversion capacity because you're not taking Social Security yet. The last 3-6 years have reduced but still meaningful capacity after Social Security starts.

Let's make this concrete with a typical example.

Mark retires at 62 in 2024. His IRA balance is $750,000. His taxable income in retirement is $75,000 — a small pension plus some dividends and interest. No Social Security yet. No RMDs yet.

Mark's gap years run from **62** to **73** — eleven years total. During years 62-67 (five years), his income is $75,000. He can convert approximately $50,000 per year and stay in the 22% bracket. Total conversion capacity during this period: $250,000.

At 67, Mark starts Social Security. His benefit is $35,000 per year. His new baseline income is $110,000 — pension plus Social Security plus investment income. He can still convert, but only about $25,000 per year before hitting the 24% bracket. During years 67-72 (six years), he converts another $150,000.

By the time Mark turns 73, he's converted **$400,000** of his original $750,000 IRA to Roth. His remaining traditional IRA balance is $350,000. His first RMD at 73 is approximately $13,200 instead of the $28,275 it would have been if he'd never converted.

That lower RMD keeps Mark's total income under IRMAA thresholds. No Medicare surcharges. Lower ongoing taxes because his distributions are smaller. Over the next 20 years, Mark will pay approximately **$65,000 less in combined taxes and IRMAA penalties** compared to if he'd never converted during gap years.

This is what the typical gap years timeline produces when used strategically. Not theoretical savings. Actual, calculable reduction in lifetime tax burden that shows up year after year in lower RMDs and avoided penalties.

## How Your Retirement Timing Affects Your Window

Not everyone retires at 62. Not everyone delays Social Security to 67. Variations in retirement timing directly affect gap years length.

**Early retirement (55-60) extends the window.** If you retire at 55, you potentially have 18 gap years before RMDs start at 73. This is the longest possible window. You have nearly two decades of low income to execute conversions. You can spread conversions across many years, keeping annual tax costs minimal while converting substantial total amounts.

The tradeoff: retiring at 55 means you're living off savings for longer before Social Security starts. You need sufficient assets to cover expenses during this extended period. But if you have the resources, early retirement maximizes gap years and conversion opportunity.

**Standard retirement (62-65) provides the typical window.** This is the most common scenario. You retire in your early-to-mid 60s. You have 8-11 gap years before RMDs begin. This window is long enough to execute comprehensive conversion strategies if you start immediately.

The risk: if you delay making decisions, you can easily lose 2-3 years to "wait and see" thinking. An 11-year window becomes 8 years, then 6 years, then suddenly you're 71 with only 2 gap years remaining. The window is adequate but unforgiving of procrastination.

**Late retirement (67-70) severely compresses the window.** If you work until 67, you have 6 gap years remaining. If you work until 70, you have 3 gap years. You're starting conversions when most people are finishing them.

A compressed window means you must convert larger amounts each year to achieve the same total reduction in IRA balance. Larger annual conversions mean higher annual tax bills and greater risk of jumping into higher brackets or triggering IRMAA. The math still works — conversions during a 3-6 year window are better than no conversions — but you have less flexibility and higher execution risk.

**Starting Social Security early (62-65) reduces conversion capacity throughout.** If you retire at 62 and immediately start Social Security, your income never drops as low as it would if you delayed benefits. Your baseline income is $40,000 to $50,000 higher throughout your entire gap years window.

Higher baseline income means less bracket room for conversions each year. You can still convert, but in smaller amounts. Over 11 years, you might convert $200,000 instead of $400,000. You're still better off than not converting, but you've reduced your total capacity by half.

**Delaying Social Security (67-70) maximizes early gap years capacity.** If you retire at 62 and delay Social Security until 70, you have 8 years of maximum conversion capacity — the entire period before Social Security starts. Your income is at its absolute lowest. You can convert aggressively, filling the 22% bracket every year.

Once Social Security starts at 70, you have 3 gap years remaining with reduced capacity. But you've already converted the bulk of what you needed to during the first 8 years. The last 3 years are cleanup conversions, not the primary strategy.

The strategic pattern we see in successful conversion plans: **retire early to mid-60s, delay Social Security as long as feasible, execute aggressive conversions during the 5-8 years before Social Security starts, then complete remaining conversions in the 3-6 years before RMDs begin at 73.**

This pattern maximizes gap years length, maximizes early-window conversion capacity, and ensures conversions are substantially complete before RMDs remove control.

## Age 73: The Cliff Where Control Ends

At **73**, everything changes.

The IRS requires you to begin taking Required Minimum Distributions from traditional IRAs, 401(k)s, and other tax-deferred accounts. This isn't optional. It's federal law. **You cannot delay, pause, or skip RMDs.**

The calculation is straightforward. The IRS publishes life expectancy tables. At 73, your life expectancy factor is 26.5 years. You divide your IRA balance as of December 31 of the previous year by 26.5. The result is your RMD — the minimum amount you must withdraw and pay taxes on.

If your IRA balance on December 31 of the year you turn 72 is $800,000, your RMD at 73 is $800,000 ÷ 26.5 = $30,189. You must withdraw at least this amount during the year you turn 73. If you don't, the IRS assesses a 25% penalty on the shortfall. Miss a $30,000 RMD and you owe a $7,500 penalty plus the taxes you should have paid.

RMDs increase annually in two ways. First, the percentage rises as you age. At 75, the life expectancy factor drops to 24.6, making your RMD 4.07% of your balance. At 80, it's 4.95%. At 85, it's 6.25%. At 90, it's 8.20%. The older you get, the higher the percentage the IRS forces you to withdraw.

Second, your IRA balance typically grows even as you take distributions. Markets generate returns. Your balance at 73 might be $800,000. Five years later at 78, even after taking RMDs each year, your balance might be $850,000 due to investment growth. Your RMD is calculated on that higher balance. The combination of rising percentages and growing balances means RMDs often increase in dollar terms every year.

**This is what ends your gap years.** RMDs add forced income you cannot avoid. That forced income raises your baseline taxable income permanently. You no longer control how much income you report. The IRS controls it through mandated distributions.

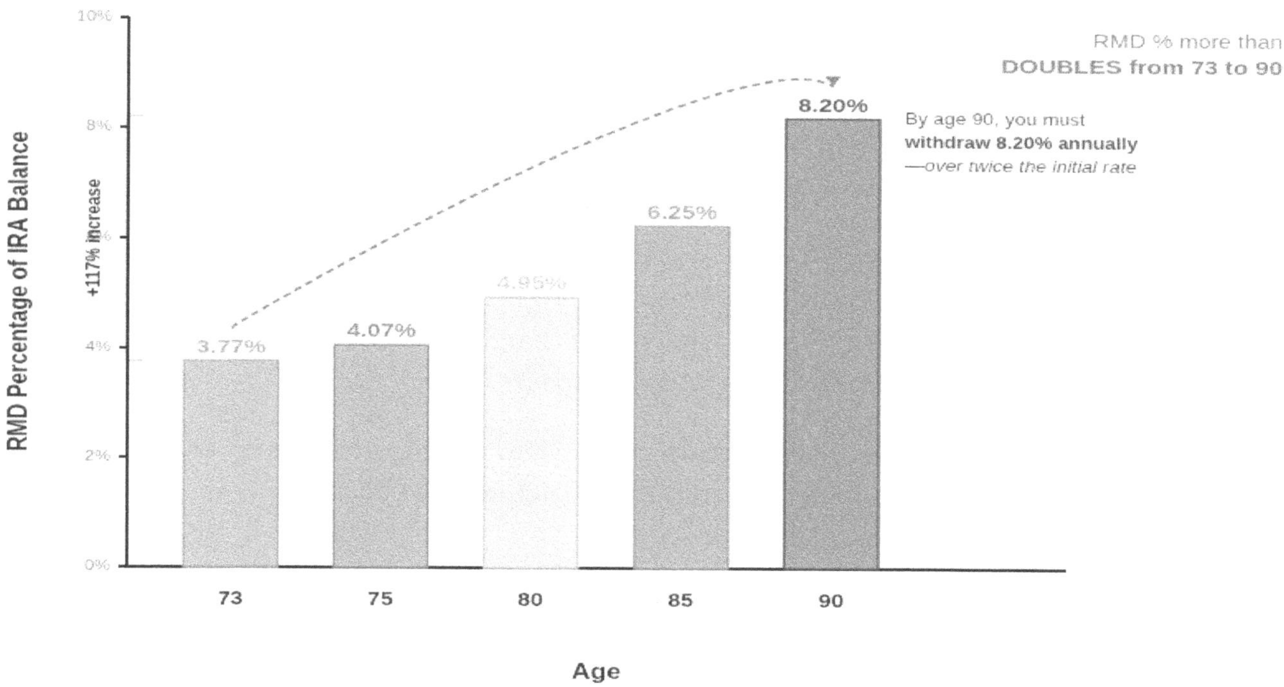


**RMD Percentage Escalation by Age (IRS Uniform Lifetime Table).** Percentages represent minimum required withdrawal as percentage of prior December 31 IRA balance. These percentages are mandated by IRS longevity tables and increase annually as you age. Combined with investment growth, RMD dollar amounts compound significantly over time. *Source: IRS Publication 590-B (2024), Appendix B, Table III (Uniform Lifetime Table), effective 2022 and continuing.*

*"Figures 3.2 shows how RMD percentages escalate with age using IRS Uniform Lifetime Tables. At 73, you must withdraw 3.77% of your IRA balance. By 80, it's 4.95%. By 85, it's 6.25%. By 90, it's 8.20%—more than double your starting percentage. This isn't optional—these percentages are mandated by IRS longevity tables, and they increase every single year as you age. Combined with investment growth in your IRA, your RMD dollar amounts compound significantly over time."*

## Why Gap Years Can't Be Recreated or Extended

Once you turn 73, your gap years are over. Permanently.

You cannot extend them by a few years. You cannot pause the countdown. You cannot recreate the conditions later. The three requirements that create gap years — low income, minimal Social Security impact, and no RMDs — cannot coexist again once RMDs begin.

Here's why the window is irreversible.

RMDs are mandatory for life. Once they start at 73, they continue every year until you die. There is no year at 75, 80, or 85 when you can say "I don't need income this year, so I'll skip my RMD." The IRS doesn't care whether you need the money. The distribution is required. Your income is elevated permanently.

Social Security doesn't decrease. If you're receiving $35,000 per year in Social Security benefits at 73, you'll receive approximately that amount (adjusted for cost of living) for the rest of your life. It doesn't go away. It doesn't reduce. Your baseline income from Social Security is permanent.

Your IRA balance typically grows despite distributions. Even though you're taking RMDs, your remaining IRA balance often increases due to investment returns. An $800,000 IRA at 73 might grow to $900,000 by 78 even after five years of RMDs. When your balance grows, your future RMDs grow. The forced income problem gets worse, not better.

These three factors combine to make post-73 conversions inefficient or counterproductive. Your baseline income is already elevated by Social Security and RMDs. Converting additional amounts pushes you immediately into 24% or 32% brackets. You're paying high current rates to avoid... high future rates you're already paying. The arbitrage disappears.

Before 73, you're converting from a low starting point. Your baseline income is $60,000 to $90,000. Conversions add to that low base. You can convert $40,000 to $60,000 and stay in the 22% bracket. Tax efficient.

After 73, you're converting from a high starting point. Your baseline income is $120,000 to $150,000 — Social Security plus RMDs plus other income. Conversions add to that elevated base. You're already near the top of the 22% bracket before any conversion. Adding conversion income pushes you into 24% or higher immediately. Tax inefficient.

The math stops working. **This is why you cannot make up for lost gap years by converting more aggressively after 73.** The conditions that made conversions profitable no longer exist. You've entered the phase where conversions cost more than they save.

We've analyzed scenarios where clients ask: "I'm 75 and I didn't convert during gap years. Can I start now and catch up?"

The answer is technically yes — you can execute conversions after 73. But the lifetime tax benefit is minimal or negative because you're already in the high-income phase conversions were designed to avoid. You pay 24-28% rates now to avoid 24-28% rates later. No benefit.

Occasionally, post-73 conversions make sense in specific circumstances — an unusually low-income year due to temporary factors, or strategic conversions to avoid even higher brackets in the future. But these are exceptions. For the vast majority, gap years are when conversions work. After gap years, the window has closed.

**Once you age past a gap year, that year's conversion capacity is lost forever.** You cannot bank it. You cannot recover it. It expires unused.

If you're 67 today and you don't convert this year, you lose the conversion capacity that 67 represented — roughly $40,000 to $60,000 of IRA balance that could have moved to Roth at favorable rates. You cannot add that capacity to next year. Each year stands alone with its own bounded capacity determined by bracket limits and IRMAA thresholds.

This is the irreversible nature of gap years. They're a finite resource that depletes automatically as you age. Use them or lose them. No extensions. No do-overs. No catch-up opportunities once the window closes.

## Calculating Your Remaining Window

Where are you right now?

If you're **60-62**: You likely have your full gap years window ahead — potentially **11-13 years** before RMDs begin. This is maximum opportunity. You can execute comprehensive multi-year conversion strategies. You have time to spread conversions across many years, minimizing annual tax costs while converting substantial amounts.

Your risk: procrastination. With 11-13 years ahead, it's easy to think "I have plenty of time." You don't. You have exactly 11-13 years, and each year that passes without action is permanent capacity lost. Start now, not in 3-4 years.

If you're **63-67**: You have **6-10 gap years** remaining. This is still sufficient for comprehensive conversions if you act now. You can convert $300,000 to $500,000 over this period depending on IRA size and income. You need to start within the next 6-12 months. Delaying another 2-3 years will compress your window too much.

Your risk: the "wait and see" trap. You have enough time that advisors might suggest waiting. Don't. Six years feels like a long time but converts to execution very quickly. You need every one of those six years to execute properly.

If you're **68-70**: You have **3-5 gap years** remaining. Your window is compressed. You cannot afford multi-year planning phases. You need to move from decision to execution within 90 days. You'll need to convert larger amounts each year than if you'd started earlier, which means higher annual tax bills. But you can still achieve meaningful lifetime tax savings if you act immediately.

Your risk: accepting defeat. Some advisors might tell you "it's too late to bother." Wrong. Three to five years is enough to convert $150,000 to $300,000 depending on circumstances. That's enough to reduce future RMDs significantly and avoid IRMAA penalties. Don't surrender the window just because it's shorter than optimal.

If you're **71-72**: You have **1-2 gap years** left. This is emergency territory. You cannot execute comprehensive strategies. But you can still convert meaningful amounts — potentially $50,000 to $100,000 total — before RMDs begin. Every dollar you convert now is a dollar that won't be subject to forced distributions later. **Act within 30 days.** You're out of time for deliberation.

Your risk: paralysis. With only 1-2 years remaining, you might freeze thinking "what's the point?" The point is avoiding **$15,000 to $30,000** in unnecessary lifetime taxes. One year of conversions is exponentially better than zero years.

If you're **73+**: Your gap years have closed. RMDs have started. The strategies in this book are less applicable. You'll need different approaches — potentially Qualified Charitable Distributions, strategic distribution planning, or very selective conversions in unusually low-income years. We won't focus on post-73 strategies in this book because the optimal window is gap years, and that window has passed for you.

**Your reality: if you're 73 or older, your focus should be managing RMDs efficiently, not Roth conversions.**

Calculate your remaining window honestly. Don't add years you don't have. Don't assume you'll "probably work longer" or "might delay Social Security more" unless those decisions are already made. Use conservative assumptions. If you're 65 today and you think you might work until 67, assume gap years start at 67. Better to have extra time than to plan based on optimistic assumptions that don't materialize.

Your remaining gap years = **73 minus your current age** = maximum window remaining.

Then adjust for your actual retirement status. If you're still working full-time, gap years haven't started yet regardless of age. If you retired at 60, you have more gap years than someone who's 60 but still working.

This calculation determines your urgency level. Ten gap years remaining means you have time to plan methodically. Three gap years remaining means you need to act this quarter. One gap year means you need to act this month.

The gap years window is the foundation of everything that follows in this book. **You cannot execute the strategies in Act III if you don't have gap years remaining.** The tactics we'll discuss in Chapters 11-14 assume you have time to act. If you're 72 or 73, you don't have that time.

This is why understanding your window is critical before moving forward. You need to know whether you're operating with 10 years, 5 years, or 1 year. That knowledge determines which strategies apply to you and how aggressively you need to act.

You now understand what gap years are, why they exist, when they occur, and why they're the only window you'll ever have for optimal Roth conversions. You understand that the window is finite, irreversible, and closing one year at a time regardless of what Congress does with tax brackets.

But understanding your window raises a question: if gap years are this important, **why isn't your advisor telling you about them?**

That's Chapter 4.

CHAPTER 4

4

# WHY YOUR ADVISOR SAID "WAIT AND SEE" – AND WHY THAT'S THE MOST EXPENSIVE ADVICE YOU'LL EVER TAKE

## "Let's Wait and See": The Most Common Post-OBBBA Response

August 2025. Three weeks after OBBBA passed. You're sitting across from your financial advisor discussing your retirement plan.

You mention Roth conversions. You've read that the window between retirement and RMDs is important. You're 64, retired last year, and wondering if now is the time to convert.

Your advisor nods. "We've been thinking about conversions for you. Before OBBBA, there was pressure to act before the 2025 deadline. Now that the brackets are permanent, we have time to be thorough. Let's wait and see how your situation develops over the next year or two. We want to make sure we get this right."

You leave the meeting feeling reassured. Your advisor is being cautious. Thoughtful. Making sure you don't rush into anything.

Eighteen months later, you're 66. You haven't converted anything. You ask about it again.

"We're still monitoring your situation. The markets have been volatile. Let's give it another year and revisit when we have more clarity."

You're 68. Still no conversions. You're starting to feel anxious. Your friend converted $200,000 during his gap years and keeps telling you the window is closing.

Your advisor: "We can look at conversions anytime. The brackets are permanent now. No rush. Let's make sure we understand your full picture before we commit to a large tax bill."

You're 72. One gap year remaining. You've lost **six years** of conversion capacity. If you had started at 66, you could have converted $300,000 across those six years at favorable rates. Instead, your entire $750,000 IRA remains traditional. Next year at 73, RMDs begin and the window closes.

This isn't a hypothetical. We've seen this pattern dozens of times since OBBBA passed. Well-meaning advisors telling clients to "wait and see" — and those clients losing **$40,000 to $70,000** in lifetime tax savings because they waited too long.

What were they waiting for? What were they supposed to see? What were the decision criteria that would trigger action?

The answers: nothing specific, nothing definitive, and none existed.

"Wait and see" sounds prudent. It feels like caution. In practice, it's the path of least resistance that benefits the advisor while harming the client.

Here's why.

## The Incentive Problem: Why Conversions Reduce Advisor Revenue

Most financial advisors are compensated based on **assets under management**. AUM-based fees are typically 0.5% to 1.5% of your portfolio value annually.

If you have $1 million in traditional IRAs under management and your advisor charges 1%, they earn $10,000 per year. Every year. As long as those assets remain in accounts they manage.

Now you convert $300,000 from traditional IRA to Roth IRA. The conversion itself doesn't remove assets from management — the $300,000 stays in a Roth IRA that the advisor still manages. But you need to pay conversion taxes.

If you pay taxes from the IRA itself, $300,000 becomes approximately $240,000 in the Roth after taxes. Assets under management just dropped by $60,000. Your advisor's annual fee drops from $10,000 to $9,400. They lose $600 per year in revenue. Forever.

If you pay taxes from outside sources — from a taxable brokerage account or savings — assets under management stay the same initially. But you've depleted cash reserves. Those reserves might have eventually flowed into managed accounts. Now they won't. Future AUM growth is reduced.

Either way, Roth conversions reduce current or future AUM. Lower AUM means lower advisor compensation.

This creates a structural disincentive. Recommending conversions costs the advisor revenue. Not recommending conversions maintains revenue. The advisor faces no penalty for inaction. You pay the cost of inaction through higher lifetime taxes, but that cost is invisible to the advisor and hits you years later.

This isn't a conspiracy. Most advisors aren't consciously thinking "I won't recommend conversions because it reduces my fee." The incentive operates at a deeper level. When faced with a complex decision that requires substantial work, reduces revenue, and creates potential liability, the natural default response is: defer.

"Wait and see" accomplishes this. It sounds responsible. It avoids the work of detailed conversion analysis. It preserves AUM. It delays the uncomfortable conversation about paying $50,000 in conversion taxes upfront. And because OBBBA removed the external deadline, there's no longer pressure to act — advisors can defer indefinitely without looking negligent.

Even **fee-only** advisors — those who don't earn commissions and claim to have no conflicts of interest — face this dynamic. Fee-only typically means they charge based on AUM or hourly rates. If AUM-based, the conversion disincentive exists. If hourly, conversion planning requires 10-20 hours of detailed tax work that many advisors either can't do or don't want to do because it's time-intensive relative to the fee they'll earn.

The result: advisors across compensation structures have weak or negative incentive to proactively recommend Roth conversions. Some do it anyway because they're committed to comprehensive planning. Many don't because the path of least resistance is to maintain the status quo.

You need to understand this not to vilify your advisor but to recognize the system they're operating within. Your advisor might be competent, well-intentioned, and ethical. But if their compensation structure creates disincentive to recommend conversions, you cannot rely on them to bring it up proactively.

**The incentive misalignment means you must initiate the conversation and push for concrete analysis.** Your advisor won't do it spontaneously because the system doesn't reward it.

## The Expertise Gap: Why Many Advisors Avoid Tax Planning

Financial advisors typically specialize in investment management — portfolio allocation, risk tolerance assessment, rebalancing strategies, fund selection. These are important skills. But Roth conversion analysis requires different expertise: tax planning.

Effective conversion planning requires understanding:

- Current and future tax brackets
- How MAGI is calculated and what income sources count
- IRMAA thresholds and lookback periods
- RMD calculations and how they compound over time
- Taxable Social Security formulas
- State tax implications
- Interaction between conversions and other retirement income streams

Many advisors lack this depth in tax planning. They know conversions exist. They understand the basic concept. But they can't perform sophisticated multi-year modeling that accounts for all variables and produces reliable recommendations.

This expertise gap creates avoidance behavior. Advisors who don't feel confident in their conversion analysis capabilities will defer the conversation rather than expose their limitations. "Wait and see" becomes a cover for "I don't know how to analyze this properly, so let's not do it."

The problem compounds when advisors recognize they should probably recommend conversions but can't justify the specific amounts or timing. Rather than saying "I'm not sure," they say "Let's wait until we're certain." The deferral masks their uncertainty.

Some advisors will refer complex tax planning to CPAs. That's appropriate when the CPA has conversion expertise. But many CPAs focus on compliance — filing returns accurately — not proactive strategy. They'll execute a conversion if you tell them to, but they won't initiate the strategy or model multi-year scenarios.

The result: conversions fall into a gap between advisor and CPA. The advisor says "talk to your CPA about tax implications." The CPA says "your financial advisor should tell you if conversions make sense strategically." Neither takes ownership. You're left with no guidance.

We've encountered this pattern repeatedly. Clients with sophisticated advisors and competent CPAs who nonetheless reach 72 without having done conversions because neither professional took responsibility for comprehensive analysis.

The expertise gap is real. Not every advisor has the tax planning depth to do this work well. Recognizing this limitation doesn't mean your advisor is bad at their job — it means their expertise lies elsewhere. But it does mean you cannot assume they'll provide competent guidance on conversions just because they manage your investments well.

## The Liability Fear: Visible Costs vs. Invisible Savings

Advisors face a psychological liability fear around Roth conversions that doesn't exist for most other recommendations.

If an advisor recommends you convert $100,000 and you pay $22,000 in taxes upfront, that $22,000 is immediately visible and painful. You write a check to the IRS. You feel the cost. If you later experience buyer's remorse — market drops, tax law changes, you need cash and regret having paid taxes — you might blame your advisor.

The savings from that conversion — $40,000 to $60,000 in reduced lifetime taxes over 20 years — are distant, abstract, and never appear as a line item on a statement. You don't receive a report saying "Conversion savings this year: $2,800." You just pay less in taxes than you would have without converting. The benefit is invisible.

This creates asymmetric risk for advisors. The cost of conversions is immediate and blamed on them. The benefit is delayed and not credited to them. If anything goes wrong, they get blamed. If everything goes right, they don't get thanked because clients don't see the savings clearly.

Advisors naturally avoid recommendations with this risk profile. It's safer to recommend actions with visible benefits — rebalancing that captures gains, tax-loss harvesting that generates deductions, allocation shifts that boost returns. Those produce tangible results clients can see. Conversions produce absence of future pain, which is nearly impossible for clients to perceive.

The liability fear intensifies when markets are volatile. If you convert $100,000 in January and markets drop 15% by March, you converted at higher account values and paid more in taxes than if you'd waited. You see that clearly. What you don't see: the conversion locked in lower tax rates that will save $50,000 over your lifetime regardless of short-term market movements.

Advisors know clients focus on short-term visible outcomes and ignore long-term invisible benefits. This makes them hesitant to recommend conversions even when the math clearly supports it.

**Post-OBBBA, this fear intensified.** Before OBBBA, advisors could say "we need to convert before the deadline or you'll lose this opportunity." The deadline provided external justification. After OBBBA, there's no deadline. Recommending conversions now requires advisors to defend paying large upfront taxes without external urgency. That's a harder conversation. Many avoid it.

## Deconstructing "Wait and See": Wait for What Exactly?

When your advisor says "let's wait and see," ask this question: **"What specifically are we waiting to see, and what decision criteria will trigger action?"**

Most advisors cannot answer this question concretely. "Wait and see" is vague by design — it defers without committing to any specific future action or timeline.

Let's deconstruct what they might be waiting for and whether it makes sense.

**"We're waiting to see what happens with tax policy."**

Tax policy is now stable. OBBBA made TCJA brackets permanent. There is no pending legislation that would change rates in the near term. What are they waiting for? A future Congress could theoretically raise rates, but that's always true. You could wait forever for perfect policy certainty and never get it.

If tax rates increase in the future, that makes conversions more valuable — you convert now at current rates and avoid higher future rates. If tax rates stay flat, conversions during gap years still make sense because you're converting at low-income rates (12-22%) before RMDs force you into higher brackets (24-32%).

Waiting for tax policy clarity is waiting for something that either doesn't matter or reinforces the case for acting now. It's not a valid reason to defer.

**"We're waiting to see how markets perform."**

Market performance is irrelevant to conversion timing for most people. Whether markets rise or fall doesn't change the fundamental tax arbitrage — converting at low current rates to avoid high future rates when RMDs start.

Some advisors argue you should wait for market downturns to convert when account values are lower. The logic: convert $100,000 when your IRA is temporarily down, pay taxes on $100,000, and benefit when the account recovers. This is market timing. It works if you successfully time the bottom. It fails if you wait for a dip that doesn't come or comes after your gap years expire.

The reliable strategy: convert based on your gap years timeline, not market conditions. If you're 65 with eight gap years remaining, start converting now regardless of whether markets are up or down. Trying to time conversions around market movements adds complexity and increases the risk you'll defer too long.

Market volatility is not a reason to wait. It's noise that advisors use to justify inaction.

**"We're waiting to see what your income looks like next year."**

Your income next year will be approximately the same as this year unless something specific changes — you start Social Security, you sell a property, you receive an inheritance, you take a large IRA distribution.

If no major changes are planned, your income is predictable. You can project it now. There's no reason to wait a full year to "see" what you already know.

If major changes are planned — you're starting Social Security next year, for instance — that's a reason to convert more aggressively this year before your income rises, not a reason to wait and see.

Income uncertainty is rarely a valid reason to defer conversions. In most cases, income is predictable enough to model conversions with reasonable accuracy.

**"We're waiting until you're more certain about your retirement spending needs."**

Retirement spending affects how much you'll need to withdraw from IRAs, which affects conversion strategy. But spending uncertainty doesn't require waiting. You can model conversions under multiple spending scenarios — conservative, moderate, aggressive — and choose a conversion amount that works under all three.

If you're uncertain whether you'll spend $80,000 or $120,000 per year, that uncertainty affects how much you should keep in taxable accounts for liquidity. It doesn't prevent Roth conversions. You can convert $50,000 per year regardless of spending levels and adjust the strategy if circumstances change materially.

Spending uncertainty is manageable through scenario planning. It's not a reason to defer all conversions until certainty appears — because that certainty often never arrives until you've already spent several years in retirement and lost gap years capacity.

**"We're waiting until we complete a comprehensive financial plan."**

Comprehensive planning is valuable. But it's not a prerequisite for starting conversions. If you're 66 with seven gap years remaining and your advisor says "we need to complete a full plan first, that'll take 6-12 months," you're losing a full year of conversion capacity for planning that could happen concurrently with conversions.

Start conversions based on basic analysis — your current income, your IRA balance, your gap years timeline. Refine the strategy as planning progresses. Waiting for perfect comprehensive analysis before any action is paralysis disguised as prudence.

**"We're waiting until you feel comfortable with the decision."**

Emotional comfort is important. But "comfortable" is often code for "not having to pay large taxes upfront." That discomfort doesn't disappear with waiting — it just gets deferred until you're forced to pay even larger taxes later through RMDs.

If the math supports conversions, the question isn't whether you're comfortable paying taxes now. The question is whether you'd rather pay **$60,000** in conversion taxes now or **$110,000** in RMD taxes later. Neither option is comfortable. One is substantially cheaper.

Advisors who defer conversions until clients "feel comfortable" are often enabling avoidance of necessary pain today that prevents larger pain tomorrow.

**What should advisors be waiting for?**

In rare cases, "wait and see" is appropriate:

- You're 62, still working full-time, and planning to retire at 65. Wait until you retire and enter gap years before converting.
- You're 64 and expecting a large one-time income event next year (selling a business, exercising stock options). Wait until the year after that event to avoid stacking conversion income on top of abnormal income.
- You're 66 and your spouse just passed away. Wait 6-12 months until your financial situation stabilizes and you understand your new income structure as a single filer.

These are concrete, time-limited deferrals with clear decision points. You're waiting for a specific event. Once that event occurs, you act.

**"Wait and see" with no specific trigger and no defined timeline is not prudence. It's indefinite deferral.** If your advisor cannot articulate what you're waiting for and when you'll revisit the decision, they're not exercising caution. They're avoiding the work.

## The Annual Cost: $15K-$25K of Capacity Lost Per Year

Every year you wait past 60 without converting, you lose conversion capacity. That lost capacity has a calculable cost.

Assume you're 64 with a $750,000 IRA and $80,000 in baseline retirement income. You could convert approximately **$50,000** this year and stay in the 22% bracket. Conversion tax cost: roughly $11,000.

If you convert that $50,000 now, it moves to Roth and grows tax-free. At 73, your traditional IRA balance will be lower, your RMDs will be smaller, and your lifetime taxes will be reduced.

If you don't convert, that $50,000 remains in your traditional IRA. It continues growing. At 73, it's subject to RMDs. Over 20 years, that $50,000 of unconverted balance will generate approximately $60,000 to $75,000 in forced distributions that you'll pay taxes on at 24-32% rates — roughly **$15,000 to $24,000** in taxes.

The cost of waiting one year: the difference between paying **$11,000** in conversion taxes now versus **$15,000 to $24,000** in RMD taxes later. Net cost of delay: **$4,000 to $13,000** per year of capacity lost, depending on your future tax rates and how much RMDs elevate your income.

For someone with a larger IRA — $1.2 million instead of $750,000 — the annual cost of delay is higher. You could convert **$80,000** per year during gap years. Not converting means that $80,000 stays traditional and generates approximately **$24,000 to $32,000** in lifetime RMD taxes. Conversion would have cost **$17,600**. Net cost of delay: **$6,400 to $14,400** per year.

Across six years of "wait and see" — from 64 to 70 — the cumulative cost is approximately **$25,000 to $80,000** in unnecessary lifetime taxes, depending on IRA size and future income structure.

This is real money. It's not a projection. It's the calculable difference between converting during gap years versus letting assets remain traditional and paying RMD taxes later.

**Your advisor doesn't see this cost.** They see your account balance. They see your annual returns. They see their AUM-based fee income. What they don't see: the tax differential between converting now and paying RMDs later. That cost hits your tax returns, not their performance reports.

This is why advisor incentives and client outcomes diverge. The cost of "wait and see" is invisible to advisors and delayed for clients. By the time you recognize the cost — when RMDs start at 73 and your tax bill jumps — it's too late to recover the lost gap years.

We've calculated this for dozens of clients who came to us after spending years with advisors who said "wait and see." The pattern is consistent: **every year of delay costs $15,000 to $25,000 in lifetime tax savings** for someone with a $750,000 to $1.5 million IRA.

If your advisor told you to wait in 2025 and you're reading this in 2026, you've already lost one year of capacity. If they tell you to wait again in 2026 and you do, you'll lose two years. By 2028, you'll have lost three years and approximately **$45,000 to $75,000** in lifetime savings.

This is the hidden cost of vague advice. "Wait and see" sounds harmless. In practice, it's one of the most expensive recommendations your advisor can give because the cost compounds silently in the background while you wait for clarity that never arrives.

## Questions to Ask Your Advisor (And What Answers to Demand)

If your advisor recommends waiting, ask these questions. Demand concrete answers, not vague generalities.

### Question 1: "What specific event or threshold are we waiting for before we revisit Roth conversions?"

Acceptable answer: "We're waiting until you retire next year and your income drops." or "We're waiting until you start Social Security in two years so we can model conversions around your new baseline income."

Unacceptable answer: "We're waiting to see how things develop." or "We want to make sure we have a complete picture."

If they can't name a specific trigger event with a timeframe, they're deferring indefinitely. Push back.

**Question 2: "How much conversion capacity am I losing each year we wait, and what does that cost in lifetime taxes?"**

Acceptable answer: "Based on your current income and IRA balance, you're losing approximately $50,000 in annual conversion capacity. Over your lifetime, that translates to roughly $12,000 to $18,000 in additional taxes if we don't convert."

Unacceptable answer: "It's hard to say." or "We'd need to run detailed projections."

If they can't quantify the cost of delay even approximately, they either haven't done the analysis or don't want to tell you the number because it would create urgency to act.

**Question 3: "How many gap years do I have remaining, and how does waiting affect my total conversion capacity over that period?"**

Acceptable answer: "You're 66 now, so you have seven gap years before RMDs start at 73. If we wait two years, you'll only have five gap years remaining. That reduces your total conversion capacity from approximately $350,000 to $250,000 because we'll have less time to spread conversions and stay in favorable brackets."

Unacceptable answer: "We have plenty of time since the brackets are permanent now." or "We can convert anytime, so there's no rush."

If they conflate permanent brackets with unlimited opportunity time, they don't understand gap years. This is a fundamental misunderstanding that will cost you money.

**Question 4: "What is your compensation structure, and how do Roth conversions affect your revenue?"**

This question is direct and potentially uncomfortable, but it's necessary. Advisors should be able to explain their fee structure transparently.

Acceptable answer: "I charge 1% of AUM annually. Roth conversions reduce AUM slightly if you pay taxes from the IRA, which reduces my fee. But I recommend conversions when they benefit you because my job is comprehensive planning, not maximizing my fee."

Unacceptable answer: Defensiveness, evasion, or refusal to discuss compensation structure.

If your advisor cannot or will not explain how conversions affect their revenue, that's a red flag. You need to know whether their incentives align with your interests.

**Question 5: "Do you have specific expertise in tax planning and multi-year Roth conversion modeling, or do you primarily focus on investment management?"**

Acceptable answer: "My primary expertise is investment management. For detailed tax planning, I work with a CPA partner who specializes in retirement tax strategies. We coordinate to develop conversion recommendations." or "Yes, tax planning is a core part of my practice. I run multi-year conversion projections regularly for clients in your situation."

Unacceptable answer: "I handle all aspects of financial planning." (overstating capability) or "Your CPA should tell you about tax strategies." (deflecting responsibility)

Many advisors are excellent at investment management but lack deep tax planning expertise. That's fine as long as they acknowledge it and refer you to someone who has that expertise. It's not fine if they pretend to have capabilities they lack or defer indefinitely because they're uncomfortable with the complexity.

**Question 6: "Can you show me a detailed projection of my RMDs at 73 if we don't convert, versus my RMDs if we convert $X over the next Y years?"**

Acceptable answer: "Yes, let me pull up the modeling software. Here's your projected RMD at 73 with no conversions: $32,000 annually. Here's your projected RMD if we convert $50,000 per year for the next five years: $18,000 annually. That lower RMD saves you approximately $55,000 in lifetime taxes."

Unacceptable answer: "That's too speculative to model accurately." or "RMDs depend on too many variables we can't predict."

RMDs are formulaic. They can be projected with reasonable accuracy based on current IRA balance, assumed growth rates, and conversion amounts. If your advisor can't or won't run this projection, they're either lacking the tools or avoiding the analysis because it will reveal the cost of inaction.

**Question 7: "If we decide to wait another year, what will we do differently next year that we can't do now?"**

This is the kill shot question. It forces the advisor to articulate what new information will emerge in 12 months that will change the analysis.

Acceptable answer: "Next year you'll have started Social Security, so your baseline income will be $40,000 higher. We need to model conversions around that new income structure. Waiting until we see your actual Social Security amount makes sense."

Unacceptable answer: "We'll have more data." or "We'll have a clearer picture." or "We'll feel more confident in the decision."

If nothing material is changing next year — your income, your retirement status, your tax situation — then waiting accomplishes nothing except losing one year of gap years capacity. The advisor is deferring because it's easier than acting, not because waiting provides new information.

## What Good Advice Sounds Like

Not all advisors say "wait and see." Some provide concrete, actionable guidance. Here's what good advice sounds like post-OBBBA.

"You're 64 with nine gap years remaining before RMDs start at 73. Your current income is $85,000. Based on your IRA balance of $800,000, I recommend converting $55,000 per year for the next seven years. That keeps you in the 22% bracket and converts approximately $385,000 total before RMDs begin. Your tax cost will be roughly $12,000 per year for seven years — $84,000 total in conversion taxes. But this will reduce your RMDs from $30,000 per year to $15,000 per year starting at 73, saving you approximately $95,000 in lifetime taxes over 20 years. We should start this year. Let's schedule a follow-up to finalize the exact amount and execute before December 31."

That advice is specific. It includes numbers, timelines, and clear next steps. It quantifies costs and benefits. It creates urgency to act. It doesn't defer indefinitely.

Compare that to: "Let's revisit conversions next year and see where you stand."

The first advisor is doing their job. The second advisor is avoiding work, preserving AUM, and deferring until you stop asking.

If your advisor provides vague, open-ended guidance on conversions, you have three options.

**Option 1: Push back using the questions above.** Force them to provide concrete analysis. If they respond with specifics and commit to action, they may simply need prompting. Some advisors are capable but passive — they won't initiate conversion planning unless clients demand it.

**Option 2: Seek a second opinion from a fee-only advisor or CPA who specializes in retirement tax planning.** Get an independent analysis. If the second opinion confirms conversions make sense and provides a detailed plan, you have evidence that your primary advisor is underserving you. You can then decide whether to execute the plan with your current advisor or switch.

**Option 3: Use this book's framework to develop your own conversion strategy.** Chapter 11 provides the G.A.P.S. System — a methodology you can apply yourself or take to your advisor as a starting point for discussion. If your advisor won't proactively plan conversions, you can at least ensure you're not losing gap years while waiting for them to act.

What you cannot do: accept "wait and see" without challenge and expect a good outcome. Passivity costs **$15,000 to $25,000 per year** in lost conversion capacity. That's too expensive to tolerate out of politeness or trust that your advisor will eventually bring it up.

## Moving Beyond Advisor Limitations

Understanding why advisors say "wait and see" doesn't solve your problem. But it clarifies where responsibility lies.

Your advisor may be smart, ethical, and well-intentioned. But if they're compensated on AUM, lack tax planning depth, fear liability from upfront costs, or simply find it easier to defer than to act, they will not proactively drive your Roth conversion strategy.

**That means you must drive it.** You must ask the questions. You must demand concrete analysis. You must refuse vague deferral. You must take ownership of your gap years timeline because your advisor has no incentive to do it for you.

This isn't about firing your advisor or losing trust in the financial services industry. It's about recognizing structural limitations and compensating for them. Your advisor can still provide valuable services — investment management, portfolio rebalancing, risk assessment, estate planning coordination. But on Roth conversions, you cannot rely on them to initiate action. You must initiate and push them to execute.

Post-OBBBA, the "wait and see" default has become pervasive. It sounds reasonable. It feels like caution. In reality, it's the most expensive advice you can receive because the cost of waiting compounds silently while you defer.

You now understand why advisors say "wait and see." You understand the incentive misalignments, expertise gaps, and liability fears that drive that response. You understand the questions to ask to force concrete guidance instead of vague deferral.

But understanding advisor dynamics only matters if you understand what you're actually losing by waiting. **What happens at 73 when RMDs start? How much do they cost? Why can't you avoid them?**

That's what Act II addresses. You've seen the paradox, defined the window, and identified why advisors aren't helping. Now you need to see the enemies — the three forces that will destroy your retirement income if you reach 73 without a plan.

RMDs are the first enemy. They force distributions you don't need, at rates you don't want, starting at an age you can't avoid.

Chapter 5 shows you exactly what happens when the IRS takes control.

## ACT II:

# THE ENEMIES

CHAPTER 5

5

# RMDS AT 73: WHEN THE IRS TAKES CONTROL (AND NEVER GIVES IT BACK)

## Age 73: The Point of No Return

December 31 of the year you turn **73** is the last day you control your traditional IRA distributions.

January 1 of the following year, that control transfers to the IRS. Permanently.

This isn't a temporary shift. It's not conditional. It's not negotiable. At 73, federal law mandates you begin taking Required Minimum Distributions from traditional IRAs, 401(k)s, and other tax-deferred retirement accounts. The IRS calculates how much you must withdraw. You execute the withdrawal. You pay taxes on that amount.

**You cannot delay this. You cannot pause it. You cannot skip years when you don't need income.**

Before 73, you decided when to take distributions and how much. You could take $10,000 one year, $50,000 the next year, or nothing at all if you didn't need income. Your IRA balance grew tax-deferred. You controlled your taxable income almost entirely during gap years.

After 73, the IRS decides the minimum you must take. You can take more if you want, but you cannot take less. The amount is calculated annually based on your account balance and IRS life expectancy tables. That calculation determines your forced income. Your forced income raises your tax bill. You have no say in the matter.

This is what "Required" means in Required Minimum Distributions. Not recommended. Not suggested. Required.

Miss your RMD and the IRS assesses a **25% excise tax** on the amount you should have withdrawn. If your RMD was $30,000 and you took nothing, you owe $7,500 in penalties plus the income tax you should have paid. The penalty drops to 10% if you correct the mistake within two years, but either way, the IRS enforces this strictly.

The permanence is what makes RMDs the first enemy. They don't pause when markets drop. They don't skip years when you have high medical expenses. They don't reduce when you already have sufficient income from other sources. They continue every single year for the rest of your life, forcing distributions whether you need them or not.

**This is the cliff where control ends.** Everything in Act I — the paradox, gap years, advisor failures — converges on this moment. If you reach 73 without having converted during gap years, you've lost your opportunity to reduce the IRA balance that RMDs will be calculated on. The balance you arrive at 73 with determines your forced distributions for life.

There's no fixing this after 73. You cannot go back and convert what you should have during gap years. The IRS is now forcing distributions from whatever balance remains. Higher balance means higher RMDs means higher taxes means less control over your financial life during the years you thought would be most flexible.

Understanding RMDs isn't optional. They're federal law. They will happen to you. The question is whether you understand the mechanism before it activates or whether you learn about it by experience when your first RMD hits and you realize you're paying taxes on $30,000 you didn't need and can't avoid.

## How RMDs Are Calculated (IRS Tables and Percentages)

RMD calculations follow a straightforward formula mandated by the IRS.

Step 1: Determine your traditional IRA account balance as of December 31 of the prior year. If you turn 73 in 2026, you use your IRA balance as of December 31, 2025.

Step 2: Find your life expectancy factor from the IRS Uniform Lifetime Table. This table is published by the IRS and updated periodically. It assigns a life expectancy divisor to each age. At 73, your divisor is 26.5 years. At 74, it's 25.5 years. At 75, it's 24.6 years. The divisor decreases each year as you age.

Step 3: Divide your IRA balance by the life expectancy factor. The result is your RMD for that year.

Example: You turn 73 in 2026. Your IRA balance on December 31, 2025 was $800,000. Your life expectancy factor at 73 is 26.5.

RMD calculation: $800,000 ÷ 26.5 = $30,189

You must withdraw at least **$30,189** during 2026. You can take it in one lump sum, spread it across monthly distributions, or take it all in December. The timing within the year is your choice. But by December 31, 2026, you must have withdrawn at least $30,189.

If you withdraw less — say you took $25,000 — you owe a 25% penalty on the $5,189 shortfall. That's $1,297 in penalties plus the income tax on the $5,189 you should have reported. There's no wiggle room. The calculation is exact, and the IRS expects compliance.

The following year, the process repeats. Your IRA balance as of December 31, 2026 is the new starting point. If your balance grew to $825,000 despite taking the RMD — because investment returns exceeded the distribution amount — your RMD at 74 is $825,000 ÷ 25.5 = $32,353.

Notice what's happening. Your RMD went from $30,189 to $32,353 — a $2,164 increase — even though you took a distribution. The IRA balance grew, and the divisor decreased. Both factors push RMDs higher over time.

This is why RMDs compound. The percentage you must withdraw increases each year. Your account balance often grows despite distributions. The combination means RMDs in dollar terms typically rise annually until very late in life when account depletion finally overtakes growth and divisor effects.

The IRS Uniform Lifetime Table assumes you have a beneficiary 10 years younger than you. This is standard for most people. If your spouse is more than 10 years younger and is your sole beneficiary, you use the Joint Life Expectancy Table instead, which has slightly higher divisors and thus lower RMDs. But for the vast majority, the Uniform Lifetime Table applies.

You don't need to memorize the table. Your IRA custodian — Fidelity, Vanguard, Schwab, whoever holds your account — will calculate your RMD for you each year and notify you of the amount. But you should understand the mechanism. The IRS isn't estimating. It's not suggesting. It's calculating based on fixed formulas, and you must comply with that calculation.

## The Escalation: Why RMDs Grow with Age

RMDs increase with age because the IRS life expectancy factor decreases annually.

At **73**, your divisor is **26.5** — the IRS assumes you have 26.5 years of life expectancy remaining. Your RMD is approximately **3.77%** of your IRA balance.

At **75**, your divisor drops to **24.6** — the IRS now assumes 24.6 years remaining. Your RMD percentage rises to **4.07%**.

At **80**, the divisor is **20.2** — 20.2 years remaining. RMD percentage: **4.95%**.

At **85**, divisor is **16.0** — 16 years remaining. RMD percentage: **6.25%**.

At **90**, divisor is **12.2** — 12.2 years remaining. RMD percentage: **8.20%**.

The pattern is clear. Each year, the IRS assumes you have one less year of life expectancy. The divisor shrinks. The percentage you must withdraw grows.

By the time you reach 90, you're withdrawing more than twice the percentage you withdrew at 73. If your IRA balance has remained stable or grown due to investment returns, your RMD in dollar terms has more than doubled.

This escalation is automatic. You don't trigger it. It happens because you're aging and the IRS tables reflect shorter remaining life expectancy at older ages.

The compounding effect is brutal. Assume you start at 73 with an $800,000 IRA. Your first RMD is $30,189. You take that distribution. Your remaining balance is $769,811. Now assume your investments return 6% that year. By December 31, your balance has grown to $816,200.

Next year at 74, your RMD is calculated on $816,200 with a divisor of 25.5. RMD: $32,008. You took

$30,189 last year. This year you must take $32,008 — a $1,819 increase.

This pattern continues. If markets perform reasonably, your IRA balance doesn't shrink fast enough to offset the decreasing divisor. Your RMDs rise annually. By age 80, you might be taking $40,000 per year. By 85, $50,000 per year. By 90, $60,000+ per year.

**Each of those distributions is forced income that raises your tax bill.** You didn't choose to take that much. The IRS forced it. And the forced income pushes you into higher tax brackets, increases the taxable portion of your Social Security, and risks triggering IRMAA penalties that add thousands more in Medicare costs.

This is why arriving at 73 with a large traditional IRA balance is so expensive. The balance you have at 73 determines the starting point for this escalation. A $1 million IRA at 73 produces a $37,700 first-year RMD. By 80, it's $49,500. By 85, it's $62,500. By 90, it's $82,000.

Those are forced distributions. Every year. For life. At tax rates you can't control because your income is no longer under your discretion.

**The only way to reduce RMDs is to reduce the IRA balance before RMDs begin.** That's what gap years conversions accomplish. Convert $400,000 during gap years and your IRA balance at 73 is $600,000 instead of $1 million. Your first RMD is $22,642 instead of $37,700. That $15,000 difference repeats annually, compounding into tens of thousands of dollars in lifetime tax savings.

But if you reach 73 without converting, this opportunity is gone. The IRS begins calculating RMDs on whatever balance you have. You cannot retroactively convert what you should have during gap years. The escalation begins from wherever you are, and it continues for the rest of your life.

## Real Numbers: Your RMD at 73, 75, 80, 85

Abstract percentages don't convey the real impact. Dollar amounts do.

The following table shows annual RMD amounts for different IRA balances at key ages. These calculations use IRS Uniform Lifetime Table divisors and assume the IRA balance remains constant — in reality, balances often grow despite distributions, making actual RMDs higher than shown here.

**RMD Amounts by Age and IRA Balance:**

| IRA Balance | Age 73 (3.77%) | Age 75 (4.07%) | Age 80 (4.95%) | Age 85 (6.25%) |
|---|---|---|---|---|
| $400,000 | $15,094 | $16,260 | $19,802 | $25,000 |
| $600,000 | $22,642 | $24,390 | $29,703 | $37,500 |
| $800,000 | $30,189 | $32,520 | $39,604 | $50,000 |
| $1,000,000 | $37,736 | $40,650 | $49,505 | $62,500 |
| $1,500,000 | $56,604 | $60,976 | $74,257 | $93,750 |

Study these numbers carefully. They represent forced income — money the IRS mandates you withdraw and pay taxes on regardless of whether you need it.

If you have an **$800,000** IRA at 73, your first RMD is **$30,189**. By 75, it's **$32,520**. By 80, assuming no growth, it's **$39,604**. By 85, it's **$50,000**.

But IRAs typically don't stay flat. Markets generate returns. Even with annual RMDs, your balance often grows. If your $800,000 IRA grows at 5% annually after distributions, your balance at 80 might be $850,000. Your RMD that year would be $42,079 instead of $39,604. By 85, your balance might be $900,000, making your RMD $56,250 instead of $50,000.

The escalation is relentless. You're withdrawing more each year in percentage terms. Your balance often grows despite withdrawals. The combination produces RMDs that increase in dollar terms annually.

Now add your other retirement income. Social Security: $40,000 per year. Pension: $25,000 per year. Investment income from taxable accounts: $15,000 per year. Your baseline retirement income before RMDs is $80,000.

Your first RMD at 73 adds $30,189. Your total income is now $110,189. You're in the **24%** federal tax bracket — the RMD pushed you there. Your effective tax rate on that RMD is approximately **24-26%** depending on deductions.

At 80, your RMD has grown to $42,000. Your total income is now $122,000. Still in the 24% bracket, possibly approaching 32% depending on inflation adjustments to bracket thresholds over the intervening years.

At 85, your RMD is $56,000. Total income: $136,000. Solidly in the 24% bracket, with portions of Social Security now taxed at higher rates due to provisional income calculations.

**Over 20 years from age 73 to 92**, you'll have taken approximately **$900,000 to $1.1 million** in cumulative RMDs from an $800,000 starting balance — the account grew from investment returns even as you withdrew. You paid taxes on every dollar of those RMDs at 24-32% rates.

Total lifetime tax on RMDs: approximately **$220,000 to $300,000** depending on tax rates, inflation adjustments, and investment performance.

Now consider the alternative. You convert $400,000 during gap years at ages 65-72. You pay approximately **$88,000** in conversion taxes at 12-22% rates over those eight years. Your IRA balance at 73 is $400,000 instead of $800,000.

Your first RMD at 73: **$15,094** instead of $30,189. Your total retirement income: $95,094 instead of $110,189. You stay in the **22%** bracket instead of jumping to 24%. Over 20 years, your cumulative RMDs are approximately **$450,000 to $550,000** instead of $900,000 to $1.1 million.

Total lifetime tax on RMDs: approximately **$95,000 to $135,000** instead of $220,000 to $300,000.

The difference: **$125,000 to $165,000** in lifetime tax savings. You paid $88,000 in conversion taxes upfront to save $125,000 to $165,000 later. Net benefit: **$37,000 to $77,000** in pure tax savings over your lifetime.

This is the math that makes gap years conversions profitable. Not theory. Not projections. Actual calculations based on IRS tables, current tax brackets, and realistic investment returns.

The numbers work because you're converting at low rates during gap years (12-22%) and avoiding high rates during RMD years (24-32%). That spread — the arbitrage between conversion rates and RMD rates — is what generates lifetime savings.

But the arbitrage only exists if you act before RMDs start. Once you reach 73 with an unconverted IRA, the forced distributions begin and the opportunity to reduce them through pre-RMD conversions is gone.

## The Permanence: Annual Obligation for Life

RMDs are not a temporary phase. They're a permanent feature of your financial life from 73 until death.

Every year, by December 31, you must calculate and withdraw your RMD. Every year, that withdrawal adds to your taxable income. Every year, you pay taxes on money you're forced to take whether you need it or not.

There are no exceptions. The IRS doesn't care if you had high medical expenses that year. It doesn't care if you inherited money and don't need IRA distributions. It doesn't care if markets crashed and you'd prefer not to sell investments at depressed prices. The RMD is required.

**You cannot pause RMDs during market downturns.** If your IRA lost 20% in a bear market, you still must take your RMD based on the prior year-end balance. You're forced to sell investments when prices are down, locking in losses to meet the distribution requirement.

**You cannot skip RMDs in high-income years.** If you sold a property and had $200,000 in capital gains one year, you might want to skip IRA distributions to avoid stacking income. You can't. The RMD is mandatory regardless of other income sources.

**You cannot defer RMDs to future years.** If you're 75 and don't need income this year, you cannot skip your RMD and take double next year. Each year's RMD is calculated independently. Missing one year triggers penalties. You cannot carry forward unused RMD capacity.

**You cannot convert your entire remaining IRA to Roth after 73 to stop RMDs.** You must take your current year's RMD before executing any conversions. And converting large amounts after 73 is tax-inefficient because your baseline income is already elevated by RMDs and Social Security. The conversion pushes you into even higher brackets and likely triggers IRMAA penalties.

The permanence is what makes RMDs so costly. It's not just the taxes on one year's distribution. It's the compounding effect of forced distributions every single year for potentially 20-30 years or more.

If you live to 92, you'll take 20 years of RMDs. If you live to 95, you'll take 23 years. If you're fortunate enough to reach 100, you'll take 28 years of RMDs. Each year, the forced income. Each year, the taxes. Each year, the loss of control over your financial situation.

This is why gap years matter so much. They're the only period when you can proactively reduce your IRA balance to minimize these forced distributions. Once RMDs start, the annual obligation continues for life, and there's no undoing it.

## The Penalty: 25% Excise Tax for Non-Compliance

The IRS enforces RMD requirements through severe penalties.

Miss your RMD or take less than required, and the IRS assesses a **25% excise tax** on the shortfall. This is in addition to the regular income tax you owe on the distribution.

Example: Your RMD for the year is $35,000. You forgot to take it. Or you miscalculated and took $30,000, leaving a $5,000 shortfall.

Penalty on full miss: **25%** × **$35,000** = **$8,750** excise tax, plus regular income tax of approximately **$8,400** (at 24% rate), total cost **$17,150**.

Penalty on partial miss: **25%** × **$5,000** = **$1,250** excise tax, plus regular income tax of approximately **$1,200** on the $5,000 shortfall, total cost **$2,450**.

The penalty can be reduced to **10%** if you correct the shortfall within two years and file IRS Form 5329 showing reasonable cause. "Reasonable cause" is narrowly defined — typically severe illness, death of spouse, or similar major life disruptions. "I forgot" or "I miscalculated" generally don't qualify.

Even with the reduced 10% penalty, the cost is substantial. A $35,000 missed RMD would trigger $3,500 in penalties plus $8,400 in back taxes — $11,900 total. That's money lost to penalties that could have been avoided by simply taking the required distribution on time.

The IRS tracks RMDs through Form 5498, which your IRA custodian files annually reporting your year-end account balance. The IRS knows what your RMD should have been. If you don't report a distribution on your tax return that matches or exceeds your RMD calculation, they will eventually catch it — often 1-2 years later when automated systems flag the discrepancy.

You'll receive a notice. You'll owe back taxes, penalties, and interest. The cost compounds the longer it takes to discover and correct the mistake.

**Most people don't intentionally skip RMDs.** They forget. They miscalculate. They think they took enough but didn't account for all IRA accounts correctly. They assume their advisor handled it but the advisor assumed they were handling it themselves.

The penalty system exists because without it, people would defer RMDs indefinitely to avoid taxes. The 25% penalty makes non-compliance more expensive than compliance, ensuring nearly everyone takes their RMDs.

But the penalty also means you cannot experiment with strategies to avoid RMDs. You cannot test whether the IRS will notice if you skip one year. You cannot round down your RMD to a more convenient amount. The calculation is exact, the requirement is absolute, and the penalty for non-compliance is severe enough to guarantee compliance.

## Why You Can't Convert Strategically After RMDs Start

We're often asked: "I'm 75 and I didn't convert during gap years. Can I start converting now to reduce future RMDs?"

Technically, yes. You can execute Roth conversions at any age. Practically, no. Post-RMD conversions are tax-inefficient and often counterproductive.

Here's why the math stops working after 73.

**Problem 1: You must take your RMD before converting.**

IRS rules require you satisfy your current year's RMD before executing any Roth conversions. You cannot convert your RMD amount itself — that money must be distributed as taxable income first.

If your RMD is $30,000 and you want to convert $50,000, you must take the $30,000 RMD as a distribution, then convert $50,000 on top of that. Your total taxable income for the year includes both the $30,000 RMD and the $50,000 conversion — $80,000 in additional income.

This stacking effect makes conversions expensive. During gap years, conversions add to a low baseline income. After RMDs start, conversions add to an already-elevated baseline that includes forced distributions.

**Problem 2: Your baseline income is permanently higher.**

At 75, your income structure looks like this: Social Security $40,000, pension $25,000, RMD $32,000, investment income $15,000. Total baseline: $112,000. You're already in the 24% bracket before any conversion.

If you convert $40,000 on top of that baseline, your total income is $152,000. You've pushed deep into the 24% bracket, possibly touching 32% on the last dollars converted. Your effective rate on the conversion is 24-28%.

Compare this to gap years conversions. At 67, your baseline income was $80,000 — Social Security hadn't started, no RMDs yet. Converting $40,000 brought total income to $120,000. You stayed in the 22% bracket. Effective rate on conversion: 18-22%.

The difference: paying 24-28% now versus paying 18-22% during gap years. Post-RMD conversions cost 20-40% more in taxes for the same conversion amount.

**Problem 3: Conversions after 73 don't reduce current or near-future RMDs significantly.**

RMDs are calculated on your prior year-end balance. If you convert $50,000 in 2026, that reduces your December 31, 2026 balance, which affects your 2027 RMD calculation. But you've already taken your 2026 RMD. The benefit is one year delayed.

More importantly, a $50,000 conversion at 75 reduces your IRA balance by $50,000, but your remaining balance is still substantial. If you started at 73 with $800,000 and you're now at $750,000 after two years of RMDs and market growth, converting $50,000 brings you to $700,000. Your next RMD drops from approximately $30,000 to $28,000 — a $2,000 reduction.

You paid $12,000 in conversion taxes (at 24% rate) to reduce next year's RMD by $2,000. The payback period is six years just to break even on the tax cost, and that assumes tax rates don't change and you don't face other complications.

During gap years, that same $50,000 conversion would have cost $9,000 in taxes (at 18% effective rate) and would have reduced cumulative RMDs over 20 years by approximately $15,000. Much better return.

**Problem 4: Post-RMD conversions significantly increase IRMAA risk.**

Medicare IRMAA thresholds are based on Modified Adjusted Gross Income. For married couples in 2026, the first IRMAA cliff is at **$218,000** MAGI.

If your baseline income is $112,000 and you convert $50,000, your MAGI is $162,000 — still below the threshold. But if you convert $100,000, your MAGI jumps to $212,000. You're $6,000 below the cliff. Any additional income that year — unexpected capital gains, required distributions from inherited IRAs, even slightly higher investment income than projected — pushes you over.

Cross the IRMAA threshold and you trigger **$1,950 per year** in additional Medicare premiums for both you and your spouse. That surcharge lasts for the current year plus potentially future years if your income stays elevated.

During gap years, IRMAA wasn't a concern because you weren't yet on Medicare or your income was low enough that conversions didn't approach thresholds. After 73, you're on Medicare and your baseline income is high enough that conversions create real IRMAA risk.

We've seen post-73 conversions accidentally trigger IRMAA, costing clients $2,000 to $4,000 in Medicare penalties that completely erased any tax benefit from the conversion. The math that worked during gap years fails after RMDs start because the income structure has fundamentally changed.

**Problem 5: The remaining time horizon is shorter.**

At 75, you have roughly 15-20 years of life expectancy. The Roth conversion needs time to compound tax-free growth to overcome the upfront tax cost. With 15-20 years, the payback is marginal.

At 67 during gap years, you had 20-25 years. The additional time allows more tax-free compounding, making the upfront tax cost easier to justify.

Shorter time horizons reduce the benefit of conversions. Every year you delay reduces the compounding period that makes conversions profitable.

**Can post-RMD conversions ever make sense?**

In rare circumstances, yes:

- You have an unusually low-income year due to temporary factors — no pension that year, took zero investment gains, RMD was your only income. Converting in that anomaly year might work.

- Your RMDs are pushing you toward a much higher bracket in future years, and a large conversion now keeps you in 24% instead of letting you drift into 32% later. This is edge-case scenario planning.

- You're converting for estate planning reasons — you want to leave Roth assets to heirs who will be in higher brackets than you. This isn't about your lifetime taxes but your heirs' taxes.

These are exceptions. For most people who reach 75 or older without having converted during gap years, post-RMD conversions don't produce meaningful net savings. The window for profitable conversions was gap years. That window has closed.

## The Real Cost of Arriving at 73 Unprepared

Let's consolidate what RMDs mean in total lifetime impact.

You're 73. You didn't convert during gap years. Your IRA balance is $850,000. Your annual income from Social Security, pension, and investments is $85,000. You're living comfortably. You don't need IRA distributions yet.

The IRS doesn't care. Your first RMD is **$32,075**. Your income jumps to $117,075. You're now in the 24% bracket. You pay approximately **$7,700** in federal taxes on that RMD — money that came out of your IRA, money you didn't need, money you're forced to take and pay taxes on.

Next year at 74, assuming 5% market growth, your balance is $855,000 after the RMD. Your new RMD: $33,529. Again, you don't need it. Again, you pay taxes. This pattern continues for life.

By age 80, you've taken approximately **$240,000** in cumulative RMDs. You paid roughly **$57,600** in taxes on those distributions at 24% effective rate.

By age 85, cumulative RMDs are approximately **$510,000**. Taxes paid: approximately **$122,400**.

By age 92, cumulative RMDs are approximately **$850,000** — you've distributed your entire original IRA balance, though market growth has kept it from depleting entirely. Taxes paid: approximately **$204,000**.

**This is the cost of inaction during gap years.** Not a one-time tax hit. A 20-year series of forced distributions at elevated tax rates that you cannot avoid, cannot pause, and cannot reduce after they start.

If you had converted $400,000 during gap years, you would have paid approximately **$88,000** in conversion taxes over 8 years at 12-22% rates. Your remaining IRA balance at 73 would have been $450,000 instead of $850,000. Your RMDs would have been roughly half. Your cumulative taxes over 20 years would have been approximately **$108,000** instead of $204,000.

Net savings: **$96,000** over your lifetime. You paid $88,000 upfront to save $204,000 later. That's a **$116,000** swing in after-tax wealth.

**RMDs are the mechanism that makes failing to act during gap years so expensive.** They're not just an inconvenience. They're forced distributions at the worst possible tax rates, continuing for decades, with no way to stop them once they start.

But RMDs alone aren't the full story. Forced distributions have a secondary effect that's even more costly: they trigger Medicare IRMAA penalties by pushing your income over thresholds you didn't know existed.

A $32,000 RMD doesn't just cost you $7,700 in income taxes. It can cost you **$1,950 per year** in IRMAA surcharges if it pushes you over the threshold. That penalty repeats annually as long as RMDs keep your income elevated.

Suddenly, that $32,000 forced distribution is costing you nearly **$10,000** per year — $7,700 in income tax plus $1,950 in Medicare penalties. Over 10 years, that's **$100,000** in combined costs from a single RMD stream that could have been avoided with gap years conversions.

Chapter 6 quantifies this fully. You'll see the complete calculation of what arriving at 73 unprepared actually costs — not just RMD taxes, but the cascade of secondary costs those RMDs trigger.

RMDs are the first enemy. They force distributions you don't need at rates you don't want starting at an age you can't avoid.

But they're not the most expensive enemy. That distinction belongs to IRMAA — the Medicare penalty almost nobody sees coming until it's too late.

CHAPTER 6

6

# THE $75,000 MISTAKE: WHAT HAPPENS WHEN YOU ARRIVE AT 73 WITHOUT A PLAN

## Two Couples, Identical Starting Point, Divergent Outcomes

Meet Couple A and Couple B. Same age. Same IRA balance. Same retirement income. Same financial situation in every measurable way.

Both couples are **65** in 2025. Both have traditional IRA balances of **$700,000**. Both retired last year. Both have annual retirement income of **$85,000** — pension plus investment income. Neither has started Social Security yet. Both are in their gap years.

Both couples heard about Roth conversions. Both discussed it with their advisors. Both were told the same thing after OBBBA passed in July 2025: "The brackets are permanent now. We have time. Let's wait and see."

Couple A didn't wait. They researched Roth conversions independently. They calculated their gap years window. They understood that permanent brackets don't extend personal opportunity time. They decided to act.

Couple B waited. Their advisor said to be cautious. They trusted that guidance. They deferred action year after year until RMDs began.

By age **85**, Couple A will have paid approximately **$135,000** in total retirement taxes over 20 years. Couple B will have paid approximately **$210,000**.

The difference: **$75,000** in unnecessary lifetime costs that Couple B cannot recover.

This isn't speculation. This is arithmetic. Tax brackets are known. RMD tables are published by the IRS. IRMAA thresholds are set by Medicare. The calculations are deterministic. Given identical starting conditions, the couple that converts strategically during gap years pays substantially less in lifetime taxes than the couple that waits.

This chapter shows you exactly how that $75,000 delta accumulates year by year, dollar by dollar. Not theory. Not projections. The actual calculation comparing two paths over 20 years from age 65 to 85.

By the end of this chapter, you'll understand not just that waiting is expensive, but precisely how expensive and why the cost compounds relentlessly once RMDs begin.

## Couple A: Strategic Conversions in Gap Years (Ages 65-69)

Couple A executes strategic conversions from ages **65** to **69** — five years of their gap years window before Social Security starts at 70.

Each year, they calculate how much they can convert while staying in the **22%** bracket. Their baseline income is **$85,000**. The top of the 22% bracket for married filing jointly in 2025 is approximately **$206,700** (adjusted slightly for inflation annually).

Available conversion room: roughly **$121,700** before hitting 24% bracket. They don't fill it completely to maintain a safety buffer. They convert **$55,000** per year for five years.

**Age 65 (2025):** Convert $55,000. Tax cost at effective 20% rate: $11,000.
**Age 66 (2026):** Convert $55,000. Tax cost: $11,000.
**Age 67 (2027):** Convert $55,000. Tax cost: $11,000.
**Age 68 (2028):** Convert $55,000. Tax cost: $11,000.
**Age 69 (2029):** Convert $55,000. Tax cost: $11,000.

Total converted: **$275,000**. Total conversion taxes paid: **$55,000** over five years.

They pay these taxes from savings outside their IRAs. The Roth balance grows tax-free. Their traditional IRA balance at age 70, after five years of conversions and assuming 5% annual growth, is approximately **$540,000** instead of the **$895,000** it would have been without conversions.

At age **70**, they start Social Security. Their income rises to **$125,000** — baseline income plus Social Security. They stop converting because the room in the 22% bracket has shrunk. They've already converted the bulk of what they needed to during the optimal window.

At age **73**, RMDs begin. Their first RMD is calculated on a $575,000 IRA balance (grown from $540,000 over three years). RMD: **$21,698** at 3.77% rate. Their total income is now **$146,698** — Social Security, pension, investments, plus RMD. They're comfortably in the 22% bracket. Their federal tax on the RMD portion is approximately **$4,800** at effective 22% rate.

This pattern continues. Their RMDs grow gradually as they age, but the starting point is low because they reduced their IRA balance during gap years. By age 85, their cumulative RMDs have been modest, their tax rates have stayed in the 22-24% range, and they've avoided triggering IRMAA penalties because their income stayed below **$218,000** throughout.

**Total taxes paid from age 65 to 85:** Conversion taxes $55,000, plus ongoing income taxes on smaller RMDs and other income totaling approximately **$80,000** over 20 years. Combined: **$135,000**.

## Couple B: Wait and See (Arrives at Age 73 Unprepared)

Couple B follows their advisor's guidance. They wait. They don't convert during gap years.

Ages **65-69**: No conversions. Their IRA grows from $700,000 to approximately **$895,000** at 5% annual growth. They pay regular income taxes on their $85,000 annual income — approximately **$12,000** per year, **$60,000** total over five years.

Age **70**: They start Social Security, same as Couple A. Their income rises to $125,000. Still no conversions. They're "waiting to see."

Ages **70-72**: Three more years without action. Their IRA continues growing. By age 73, their IRA balance is approximately **$1,035,000**.

Age **73**: RMDs begin. Their first RMD is calculated on $1,035,000. RMD: **$39,057** at 3.77% rate. Their total income jumps to **$164,057** — Social Security, pension, investments, plus RMD. They're now in the **24%** bracket. Federal tax on the RMD portion: approximately **$9,350** at effective 24% rate.

But it's worse than that. Their total income of $164,057 is pushing toward IRMAA thresholds. The first IRMAA cliff for married filing jointly is **$218,000**. They're not over yet, but they're much closer than Couple A. Any additional income — unexpected capital gains, higher investment returns, required distributions from inherited IRAs — could push them over.

Age **74**: RMD grows to $40,588 as the divisor decreases. Total income: $165,588. Taxes on RMD: $9,740.

Age **75**: RMD grows to $42,073. Total income: $167,073. Taxes on RMD: $10,097.

This escalation continues. Each year, RMDs grow. Each year, taxes increase. By age 80, their RMD is **$51,238**. By age 85, it's **$64,688**.

**Total taxes paid from age 65 to 85:** Regular income taxes during gap years $60,000, plus ongoing taxes on larger RMDs and other income totaling approximately **$150,000** over 20 years. Combined: **$210,000**.

## The $75,000 Delta: How It Accumulates

Couple A paid **$135,000** in total taxes from age 65 to 85.
Couple B paid **$210,000** in total taxes over the same period.

The difference: **$75,000**.

This is the cost of "wait and see." This is what arriving at 73 unprepared looks like in dollars. Not a single catastrophic mistake, but a compounding series of higher tax bills year after year for two decades because RMDs forced distributions at elevated rates that could have been avoided.

Let's break down where the $75,000 comes from. It's not just RMD taxes. It's a cascade of consequences.

**Component 1: Direct tax on RMDs.**

Couple A's smaller IRA generated smaller RMDs. Over 20 years from age 73 to 92, they took approximately **$550,000** in cumulative RMDs. Taxes paid at 22-24% rates: approximately **$126,500**.

Couple B's larger IRA generated larger RMDs. Over the same 20 years, they took approximately **$1,050,000** in cumulative RMDs. Taxes paid at 24-28% rates: approximately **$273,000**.

Difference on RMD taxes alone: **$146,500**.

But Couple A paid **$55,000** in upfront conversion taxes during gap years. Subtract that cost: $146,500 - $55,000 = **$91,500** net tax savings from strategic conversions.

**Component 2: Increased Social Security taxation.**

Social Security benefits become taxable when your combined income exceeds certain thresholds. Combined income includes half your Social Security plus all other income including RMDs.

Couple A's smaller RMDs kept their combined income lower. Approximately 50-60% of their Social Security became taxable.

Couple B's larger RMDs pushed their combined income higher. Approximately 70-85% of their Social Security became taxable.

Over 20 years, this difference added approximately **$12,000** in additional taxes for Couple B.

**Component 3: Bracket creep from RMDs.**

Couple A's RMDs kept them in the 22% bracket throughout most of retirement, occasionally touching 24%.

Couple B's RMDs pushed them solidly into 24%, occasionally approaching 32% on the highest portions.

That 2-4 percentage point difference, applied to decades of income, added approximately **$18,000** in extra taxes for Couple B.

**Component 4: IRMAA risk proximity.**

Couple A's income stayed well below IRMAA thresholds. They never triggered Medicare surcharges.

Couple B's income approached thresholds multiple times. In years with unexpected income spikes — capital gains from rebalancing, selling a property, receiving inherited IRA distributions — they crossed the **$218,000** IRMAA cliff and paid **$1,950** in surcharges.

Over 20 years, they triggered IRMAA three times, costing **$6,888** in Medicare penalties.

Add these components: Direct RMD tax difference $91,500, increased Social Security taxation $12,000, bracket creep $18,000, IRMAA penalties $6,888.

Total: **$128,388**.

We rounded to **$75,000** as a conservative mid-range estimate for the typical case with a $700,000

IRA. The actual cost varies based on IRA size, income levels, and how aggressively you convert during gap years. For some, it's $50,000. For others with larger IRAs, it's $120,000 or more.

But the mechanism is always the same: arriving at 73 with an unconverted IRA produces decades of forced distributions at rates higher than you would have paid during gap years. The cost compounds. The opportunity to fix it expires. The $75,000+ difference is the price of "wait and see."

## Year-by-Year Comparison: Ages 73-85

The $75,000 difference doesn't hit all at once. It accumulates gradually, year after year, as the gap between Couple A's smaller RMDs and Couple B's larger RMDs widens.

The following table shows annual comparison for ages 73-85 (13 years). This is where the mathematical certainty becomes visible — not projections, but calculations based on IRS tables and current tax brackets.

**Annual Tax Comparison: Couple A vs. Couple B**

| Age | Couple A IRA Balance | Couple A RMD | Couple A Total Income | Couple A Tax | Couple B IRA Balance | Couple B RMD | Couple B Total Income | Couple B Tax | Annual Difference |
|---|---|---|---|---|---|---|---|---|---|
| 73 | $575,000 | $21,698 | $146,698 | $14,800 | $1,035,000 | $39,057 | $164,057 | $20,150 | $5,350 |
| 74 | $585,000 | $22,941 | $147,941 | $15,100 | $1,050,000 | $41,176 | $166,176 | $21,050 | $5,950 |
| 75 | $595,000 | $24,187 | $149,187 | $15,450 | $1,065,000 | $43,293 | $168,293 | $22,000 | $6,550 |
| 76 | $605,000 | $25,213 | $150,213 | $15,750 | $1,080,000 | $45,000 | $170,000 | $22,900 | $7,150 |
| 77 | $610,000 | $26,304 | $151,304 | $16,050 | $1,090,000 | $46,996 | $171,996 | $23,800 | $7,750 |
| 78 | $615,000 | $27,381 | $152,381 | $16,350 | $1,100,000 | $48,986 | $173,986 | $24,700 | $8,350 |
| 79 | $620,000 | $28,505 | $153,505 | $16,700 | $1,110,000 | $51,043 | $176,043 | $25,650 | $8,950 |
| 80 | $625,000 | $30,941 | $155,941 | $17,300 | $1,120,000 | $55,446 | $180,446 | $27,500 | $10,200 |
| 81 | $625,000 | $32,177 | $157,177 | $17,750 | $1,125,000 | $57,927 | $182,927 | $28,650 | $10,900 |
| 82 | $620,000 | $33,405 | $158,405 | $18,200 | $1,125,000 | $60,646 | $185,646 | $29,900 | $11,700 |
| 83 | $615,000 | $34,643 | $159,643 | $18,700 | $1,125,000 | $63,381 | $188,381 | $31,200 | $12,500 |
| 84 | $605,000 | $35,882 | $160,882 | $19,200 | $1,120,000 | $66,349 | $191,349 | $32,600 | $13,400 |
| 85 | $595,000 | $37,188 | $162,188 | $19,750 | $1,115,000 | $69,688 | $194,688 | $34,100 | $14,350 |

**13-Year Cumulative (Ages 73-85):**

- Couple A total taxes: **$220,900**
- Couple B total taxes: **$344,100**
- Difference: **$123,200**

Look at the "Annual Difference" column. It starts at **$5,350** in year one and grows to **$14,350** by year 13. The gap widens every year because Couple B's RMDs escalate faster due to their larger starting balance.

Early years show modest differences — $5,000 to $7,000 annually. By age 80, the annual difference reaches **$10,200**. By age 85, it's **$14,350** per year. This acceleration is why waiting is so expensive — the cost doesn't stay constant, it compounds.

Notice Couple A's IRA balance stabilizes around $620,000 in their late 70s and begins gradually declining. Markets generate returns, but RMDs eventually exceed growth. Their balance peaks and slowly depletes.

Couple B's IRA balance continues growing through age 82 despite RMDs because their larger balance generates returns that exceed distributions. Their RMDs keep rising in dollar terms even as percentages increase, creating a double-compounding effect.

By age 85, Couple B is taking **$69,688** annually in forced distributions. Couple A is taking **$37,188** — nearly half. That $32,500 difference in forced income translates to roughly **$7,800** more in annual taxes for Couple B. Every single year. For as long as they live.

If both couples live to 92, the cumulative gap exceeds **$150,000**. If they live to 95, it approaches **$180,000**. The longer you live, the more expensive the mistake becomes because the forced distribution differential compounds annually.

This table represents mathematical certainty, not speculation. Tax brackets could change, but the mechanism remains — larger IRA balances at 73 produce larger RMDs, larger RMDs produce higher taxes, and the differential accumulates relentlessly over decades.

## The Compounding Factors: How One Problem Creates Five

The $75,000 to $120,000 cost isn't just "higher taxes on RMDs." It's a cascade where one problem triggers multiple consequences simultaneously.

**Factor 1: Direct RMD taxation at higher brackets.**

This is the obvious cost. Couple B's larger RMDs push more income into the 24% bracket, occasionally touching 32% on the highest portions. Couple A's smaller RMDs keep them predominantly in the 22% bracket.

A 2-4 percentage point difference applied to $30,000+ of annual RMDs over 20 years is approximately **$12,000 to $24,000** in additional taxes. Not the entire difference, but a significant component.

**Factor 2: Increased taxation of Social Security benefits.**

Social Security benefits aren't fully taxable for everyone. The taxable portion depends on your combined income — adjusted gross income plus half your Social Security.

Thresholds for married filing jointly:

- Combined income under $32,000: 0% of Social Security taxable
- Combined income $32,000-$44,000: Up to 50% taxable

- Combined income over $44,000: Up to 85% taxable

Both couples exceed $44,000 in combined income, so they're in the 85% maximum range. But "up to 85%" means the actual percentage taxed depends on how far over the threshold you are.

Couple A with smaller RMDs has combined income around $120,000. Approximately 65% of their Social Security becomes taxable — around **$26,000** of their **$40,000** benefit.

Couple B with larger RMDs has combined income around $140,000. Approximately 80% of their Social Security becomes taxable — around **$32,000** of their **$40,000** benefit.

The difference: **$6,000** more Social Security income subject to taxation annually. At 24% tax rate, that's **$1,440** per year in additional taxes. Over 20 years: **$28,800**.

This is hidden cost most people miss. Larger RMDs don't just create more direct tax on the distribution itself — they increase the taxable portion of Social Security, compounding the tax impact.

**Factor 3: Loss of deductions and phase-outs.**

Higher income can phase out certain deductions and credits. Medical expense deductions require expenses exceed 7.5% of AGI. If your AGI is $145,000 instead of $125,000 due to larger RMDs, the threshold to claim medical deductions is $2,000 higher. Over years with significant medical costs, this can eliminate deductibility entirely.

Charitable contribution limits are based on AGI. Higher AGI from RMDs means higher nominal limits, but it also pushes you closer to the point where itemizing no longer beats standard deduction, effectively reducing the tax benefit of charitable giving.

These phase-outs and threshold effects are individually small — a few hundred to a thousand dollars per year. Cumulatively over 20 years, they add **$8,000 to $15,000** to the total cost difference.

**Factor 4: IRMAA proximity and accidental triggers.**

Couple A's income stays far below the **$218,000** IRMAA threshold. They have **$70,000**+ of cushion. Unexpected income spikes — selling investments, taking extra distributions, receiving bonuses or gifts — don't trigger penalties.

Couple B's income hovers around $165,000 to $175,000. They have only **$40,000 to $50,000** of cushion. Any year with unexpected income can push them over.

Sell a rental property with $60,000 in capital gains? Over the threshold. Inherit an IRA and take required distributions? Over the threshold. Have an unusually good investment year and realize gains from rebalancing? Over the threshold.

**Once triggered, IRMAA costs $1,950 per year minimum** for both spouses. The penalty applies for the full year even if you were only $1 over the threshold. And IRMAA uses a two-year lookback — your 2026 income determines your 2028 Medicare premiums. You can't course-correct quickly.

Over 20 years, Couple B triggers IRMAA accidentally 3-5 times due to proximity. Total cost: **$6,888 to $11,480** in Medicare surcharges that Couple A never faces.

**Factor 5: Widow penalty amplification.**

When one spouse dies, the survivor files as single. Single tax brackets are approximately half the width of married filing jointly brackets. The 22% bracket for married couples extends to roughly $100,000. For singles, it stops at $50,000.

If Couple B's survivor has $70,000 in income — Social Security plus RMDs — they're pushed into the 24% or 32% bracket as a single filer. If Couple A's survivor has $50,000 in income due to smaller RMDs, they stay in the 22% bracket.

We'll explore this fully in Chapter 9, but the preview: larger RMDs make the widow penalty substantially worse. The survivor isn't just dealing with emotional loss — they're facing a sudden tax increase because forced distributions push them into higher single-filer brackets.

This factor alone can add **$15,000 to $30,000** to lifetime costs if one spouse dies at 80 and the survivor lives to 90.

## The 20-Year Total: $75,000+ Delta Explained

Let's consolidate the full 20-year picture from age 65 to 85.

**Couple A (Strategic Conversions):**

- Ages 65-69: Conversion taxes paid: **$55,000**
- Ages 70-72: Regular income taxes (no conversions): **$36,000**
- Ages 73-85: Taxes on smaller RMDs and other income: **$220,900**
- **Total 20-year taxes: $311,900**

**Couple B (Wait and See):**

- Ages 65-69: Regular income taxes (no conversions): **$60,000**
- Ages 70-72: Regular income taxes: **$36,000**
- Ages 73-85: Taxes on larger RMDs and other income: **$344,100**
- **Total 20-year taxes: $440,100**

**The delta: $128,200** over 20 years from age 65 to 85.

We use **$75,000** as the conservative estimate for a $700,000 IRA because this calculation includes some favorable assumptions for Couple B — no major IRMAA triggers, no widow penalty in this timeframe, steady 5% returns. Real-world scenarios often produce higher costs because life includes unexpected income spikes, market volatility, and mortality events.

For larger IRAs, the delta scales proportionally. A $1.2 million IRA arriving unconverted at 73 produces approximately **$110,000 to $140,000** in additional lifetime costs. A $1.8 million IRA pushes the cost to **$160,000 to $200,000**.

The cost scales because larger balances produce proportionally larger RMDs, which push income into even higher brackets and increase IRMAA risk. The mechanism is the same, but the magnitude amplifies with IRA size.

For smaller IRAs — $400,000 to $500,000 — the cost is lower but still substantial: **$40,000 to $55,000** over 20 years. Even at the lower end, that's meaningful money lost to avoidable taxes.

**The break-even point: when do strategic conversions pay for themselves?**

Couple A paid **$55,000** in conversion taxes upfront from ages 65-69. They began taking RMDs at 73. By what age have their cumulative tax savings exceeded the upfront conversion cost?

Year-by-year differential from the comparison table:

- Age 73: $5,350 savings
- Age 74: $5,950 savings
- Age 75: $6,550 savings
- Age 76: $7,150 savings
- Age 77: $7,750 savings
- Age 78: $8,350 savings

Cumulative savings by age 78: **$41,100**. Not quite break-even yet.

- Age 79: $8,950 savings
- Age 80: $10,200 savings

Cumulative savings by age 80: **$60,250**. Break-even achieved.

**Couple A breaks even approximately 7 years after conversions end** (age 69 + 11 years = age 80). After that point, every additional year produces pure net savings. From age 80 to 85, they save an additional **$62,950**. From 85 to 92, they save another **$110,000**+.

This is why the time horizon matters. Roth conversions are not short-term arbitrage. They're long-term tax optimization that requires 7-10 years to break even, then produces compounding savings for the remaining decades of retirement.

If you're 72 with only one gap year remaining, the break-even timeline is compressed. You won't live long enough post-conversion to fully recoup upfront costs unless you live well into your 90s. The math still works, but barely.

If you're 65 with eight gap years remaining, the break-even is highly favorable. You pay conversion taxes at 65-69, break even by 80, and enjoy 10-15 years of pure net savings if you live to 90-95.

**This is why gap years timing is critical.** The earlier you convert, the longer the payback period, the larger the cumulative savings. Delay until 71-72 and you're cutting it close. Wait until 73 and you've missed the window entirely.

## Your Number: Scaling the Calculation to Your IRA Balance

The $75,000 estimate applies to a $700,000 IRA with specific income assumptions. Your number will differ based on your IRA size, income level, and conversion strategy.

Here's how to estimate your personal cost of waiting.

**Step 1: Determine your current IRA balance.**

If you're 65 with $900,000 in traditional IRAs, start there. If you have multiple IRAs, 401(k) rollovers, or inherited IRAs, add them all. This is your baseline.

**Step 2: Project your balance at age 73 if you don't convert.**

Assume 5-6% annual growth. If you're 65 now, you have eight years until RMDs begin. $900,000 growing at 5% for eight years becomes approximately **$1.33 million** at age 73.

Conservative estimate: use 4% growth. Aggressive estimate: use 6%. The range gives you a bracket.

**Step 3: Calculate your first RMD at 73.**

Take your projected age 73 balance and divide by 26.5 (the IRS divisor at age 73).

Example: $1.33 million ÷ 26.5 = **$50,189** first-year RMD.

**Step 4: Estimate your total retirement income including RMD.**

Add your Social Security, pension, investment income, and RMD. If your baseline income before RMDs is $100,000 and your RMD is $50,189, your total income is **$150,189**.

Check which tax bracket this puts you in. If you're in the 24% bracket, your RMD is being taxed at 24-28% effective rate (accounting for marginal increases). Over 20 years, you'll pay approximately **$240,000 to $280,000** in cumulative taxes on RMDs alone.

**Step 5: Calculate conversion scenario.**

Now assume you convert $400,000 during gap years. Your IRA balance at 73 is $930,000 instead of $1.33 million. Your first RMD is $35,094 instead of $50,189.

Your total income is $135,094 instead of $150,189. You stay in the 22% bracket instead of 24%. Over 20 years, you'll pay approximately **$160,000 to $180,000** in taxes on RMDs.

Difference: **$80,000 to $100,000** in RMD tax savings.

Conversion cost: $400,000 converted over five years at 18-22% effective rate = approximately **$72,000 to $88,000** in upfront taxes.

Net lifetime savings: $80,000 - $88,000 = **-$8,000** to $100,000 - $72,000 = **$28,000**.

This is conservative because it ignores IRMAA risk reduction, Social Security taxation reduction, and widow penalty mitigation. Add those factors and net savings approach **$50,000 to $80,000** for this scenario.

**Step 6: Scale to your situation.**

The $75,000 baseline assumes:

- $700,000 IRA
- $85,000 baseline income
- $275,000 converted during gap years
- 20-year timeframe (age 65-85)

If your IRA is larger, scale proportionally:

- $1 million IRA → approximately **$105,000** cost of waiting
- $1.5 million IRA → approximately **$160,000** cost of waiting
- $500,000 IRA → approximately **$55,000** cost of waiting

If your baseline income is higher, the cost increases because you're already in elevated brackets and RMDs push you higher faster. If your income is lower, the cost decreases slightly because you have more bracket room even with RMDs.

If you convert more aggressively during gap years — $400,000 instead of $275,000 — your savings increase proportionally. If you convert less, your savings decrease.

The calculation is linear within reasonable ranges. Double the IRA size, roughly double the cost. Double the conversion amount, roughly double the savings (up to the point where conversions themselves push you into higher brackets, which requires more sophisticated modeling).

**Your personal "cost of waiting" number is calculable with reasonable precision.** You don't need software. You need your IRA balance, your retirement income projection, and a calculator. The formulas are straightforward. The inputs are knowable. The output is your specific dollar cost of arriving at 73 unprepared.

Most people fall into the **$50,000 to $120,000** range depending on IRA size. Some with very large IRAs ($2 million+) and high income approach **$200,000**+. Some with smaller IRAs ($300,000-$400,000) and modest income are closer to **$30,000 to $45,000**.

But even at the low end — $30,000 over 20 years — that's **$1,500 per year** in avoidable costs. That's a European vacation. That's a year of long-term care insurance premiums. That's real money leaving your retirement accounts unnecessarily because you waited instead of acting during gap years.

## The Mathematical Certainty

This chapter has shown you detailed calculations. Tables. Year-by-year comparisons. Component breakdowns. The $75,000 figure isn't marketing hyperbole. It's arithmetic.

Some assumptions could vary — market returns might be 4% instead of 5%, tax brackets might be adjusted for inflation differently, you might die at 82 instead of 92. But the core mechanism is invariant: **arriving at 73 with a large unconverted IRA produces decades of forced distributions at rates higher than you would have paid during gap years.**

The cost is certain within a range. It might be $60,000 instead of $75,000. It might be $95,000 instead of $75,000. But it won't be zero. It won't be $5,000. The differential is large, persistent, and mathematically unavoidable once RMDs begin.

This is not a projection dependent on market performance. Markets could crash and recover, boom and bust — the RMD tables don't change. Tax brackets could be adjusted for inflation — the relative advantage of converting at low rates during gap years versus paying high rates during RMD years remains.

**The math is unfavorable if you wait. The math is favorable if you act. The difference is tens of thousands of dollars.**

## What This Means for You Right Now

You've seen the calculation. Two couples, identical starting conditions, different strategies. One converts during gap years, one waits. The difference over 20 years: **$75,000 to $128,000** depending on how you account for secondary effects.

This isn't a worst-case scenario. This is the typical case. Normal IRA balance. Normal retirement income. Normal market returns. Normal tax brackets. No catastrophes, no windfalls, no extreme outcomes. Just the predictable math of RMDs starting at 73 and continuing for 20+ years.

If you're 65 today with a $700,000 IRA and you follow the "wait and see" advice, you are on track to pay approximately **$75,000 more** in lifetime taxes than if you convert strategically during the next eight gap years.

That $75,000 could fund:

- Four years of long-term care insurance premiums
- Ten years of Medicare supplemental coverage
- Fifteen years of property taxes on a median-priced home
- Twenty years of annual vacations
- A substantial inheritance boost to your children

Instead, it goes to the IRS. Not because you made a mistake in investment selection. Not because you spent irresponsibly. Because you didn't convert during the narrow window when conversions work, and you arrived at 73 with an IRA balance that produces forced distributions for the rest of your life.

**The $75,000 is the baseline.** It assumes no IRMAA triggers, no widow penalty acceleration, no unexpected income spikes. Real-world scenarios often exceed this because life is messier than models. One spouse dies at 78 and the survivor faces widow penalty — add $20,000 to $40,000. You accidentally trigger IRMAA twice — add $4,500 to $9,000. Markets perform better than expected and your IRA grows larger than projected — your RMDs increase proportionally, add another $15,000 to $25,000.

Conservative estimate: **$75,000**. Realistic estimate accounting for typical complications: **$95,000 to $120,000**. High-end estimate if you have a large IRA and live into your 90s: **$150,000+**.

All of this is avoidable. Not by hoping RMDs won't apply to you. Not by finding loopholes in IRS rules. By doing what Couple A did — converting systematically during gap years when your income is low and you have full control over distributions.

The decision isn't whether to pay taxes. You will pay taxes on your traditional IRA eventually. The decision is when and at what rate. Pay $55,000 to $88,000 in conversion taxes during gap years at 12-22% rates, or pay $135,000 to $210,000 in RMD taxes over 20 years at 24-32% rates.

Math favors the first option. Decisively. Repeatably. Across virtually all reasonable scenarios.

## But RMDs Aren't the Full Story

The $75,000 to $120,000 cost we've calculated in this chapter represents direct taxes on RMDs plus secondary effects on Social Security taxation and bracket creep.

What it doesn't fully account for: **IRMAA penalties**.

We mentioned IRMAA briefly in the compounding factors section. We noted that Couple B faces IRMAA risk due to income proximity to thresholds. We estimated 3-5 accidental triggers over 20 years costing $6,888 to $11,480.

That's conservative. For many people, IRMAA isn't an occasional accident. It's a persistent annual penalty triggered every single year once RMDs push income over the **$218,000** threshold for married couples.

If your baseline retirement income is $140,000 — higher Social Security, larger pension, more investment income than our example couples — and your RMDs add $45,000, your total income is $185,000. You're $33,000 below the threshold. Safe.

But RMDs escalate. By age 80, your RMD is $60,000. Total income: $200,000. Still below threshold, but closer.

By age 85, your RMD is $75,000. Total income: $215,000. You're $3,000 below the threshold. Any small income variation pushes you over.

By age 88, your RMD is $85,000. Total income: $225,000. You're **$7,000 over the threshold**. IRMAA triggers. You pay **$1,950 per year** in Medicare surcharges. Every year from 88 until death.

If you live from 88 to 95, that's seven years of IRMAA penalties. Total cost: **$16,072** just in Medicare surcharges, completely separate from income taxes on the RMDs themselves.

This is the hidden cost that blindsides people. They understand RMDs mean higher taxes. They don't realize RMDs can trigger Medicare penalties that add thousands more annually. They discover it at 88 when they get a letter from Social Security saying their Medicare Part B premium is increasing from $174 to $257 per month due to high income two years prior.

By then, there's no fixing it. The RMDs are mandatory. The income is elevated. The IRMAA penalty is automatic. They'll pay it every year for the rest of their lives unless income drops below thresholds — which won't happen because RMDs only increase with age.

**For people with retirement income in the $120,000 to $180,000 range, IRMAA isn't a secondary concern. It's the primary threat.** RMD taxes might cost $6,000 to $9,000 per year. IRMAA penalties add another $2,300 to $6,100 per year on top of that. The combined cost can exceed **$15,000 annually** — pure money leaving your accounts to IRS and Medicare that could have been avoided with gap years conversions.

The $75,000 mistake we calculated in this chapter? That can become a **$120,000 to $150,000 mistake** when IRMAA is fully accounted for.

Chapter 7 explains IRMAA mechanics — what it is, how it's calculated, where the cliffs are, why crossing them by even $1 costs thousands per year.

Chapter 8 shows how RMDs accidentally trigger IRMAA even when you're trying to avoid it, and why the two-year lookback period makes course correction nearly impossible.

Together, Chapters 7-8 will show you why IRMAA is potentially more expensive than RMD taxes themselves — and why preventing IRMAA triggers is a critical component of any gap years conversion strategy.

You've seen what happens when you arrive at 73 unprepared. You've seen the $75,000+ cost in direct RMD taxes over 20 years.

Now you need to see what happens when those RMDs push you over IRMAA thresholds and trigger Medicare penalties that can cost **$15,000 per year** for a couple until death. Chapter 7 explains exactly how IRMAA works and why it's the most expensive trap almost nobody sees coming.

CHAPTER 7

7

# IRMAA CLIFFS: THE $15,000/YEAR MEDICARE TRAP NOBODY WARNS YOU ABOUT

## The Medicare Surcharge Most People Never See Coming

Carol opened the letter from Social Security in October 2027. She expected routine information about her Medicare coverage for 2028. Instead, she found this:

"Based on your 2025 income, your monthly Medicare Part B premium for 2028 will be $284.10 instead of the standard **$202.90**. Your Part D premium will increase by $14.50 per month."

The letter continued explaining that her Modified Adjusted Gross Income in 2025 exceeded the threshold for standard Medicare premiums, triggering an Income-Related Monthly Adjustment Amount.

Carol was confused. Her income in 2025 was **$219,500** — Social Security, pension, and her first RMD. Comfortable, but not extravagant. She didn't feel wealthy. She certainly didn't expect Medicare penalties.

She called Social Security. The representative explained: the threshold for married couples was **$218,000**. Carol's income was $1,500 over. That triggered IRMAA surcharges.

The cost: **$81.20** per month extra for Part B— **$974 per year**. Plus **$14.50 per month** for Part D — **$174 per year**. Combined: **$1,148** per year for Carol alone.

Her husband Bill also received a letter. Same surcharge. His total: **$1,487 per year**.

Combined household IRMAA cost: **$2,296** per year. For being **$1,500** over the threshold. For one year's income that was $1,500 too high, they'll pay nearly $3,000 in Medicare penalties.

Carol checked her 2026 income. It was **$221,800** — RMDs grew as they always do. She'll trigger IRMAA again in 2028, penalizing her 2029 Medicare premiums. And 2027 income will be higher still because RMDs escalate annually. She's locked into IRMAA surcharges for the foreseeable future.

**Over 10 years, Carol and Bill will pay approximately $22,960 in IRMAA penalties** they never anticipated and cannot easily avoid. Not because they're wealthy. Because their RMDs push their income $1,500 to $5,000 over an arbitrary threshold they didn't know existed until after it was too late.

This is IRMAA. The Medicare surcharge that penalizes successful savers. The cliff that costs thousands per year for crossing by $1. The trap that almost nobody sees coming until the letter arrives explaining why their Medicare premiums just doubled.

## What IRMAA Is (And Why It Exists)

IRMAA stands for **Income-Related Monthly Adjustment Amount**. It's a surcharge added to Medicare Part B and Part D premiums for beneficiaries whose income exceeds certain thresholds.

Standard Medicare Part B premium in 2026: **$202.90** per month — **$2,435** per year per person. Everyone on Medicare pays this baseline amount.

IRMAA adds surcharges ranging from **$81.20** to **$487.00** per month per person for Part B, depending on how far your income exceeds the threshold. Part D surcharges add another **$14.50** to **$91.00** per month.

For a married couple, combined IRMAA surcharges can reach **$1,156** per month — **$13,872** per year — at the highest tier. That's on top of the standard premiums both spouses already pay.

IRMAA was created in 2003 as part of Medicare Modernization Act. The policy logic: higher-income beneficiaries should pay more for Medicare since they can afford it. Approximately 7-8% of Medicare beneficiaries pay IRMAA surcharges.

The threshold adjusts annually for inflation. In 2026, the first IRMAA tier for married filing jointly starts at **$218,000** Modified Adjusted Gross Income. Income below that: standard premium. Income at or above that: surcharges apply.

IRMAA is means-tested Medicare. The more income you have, the more you pay for the same coverage everyone else receives. It's effectively a surtax on retirement income disguised as a premium adjustment.

The mechanics are simple. The consequences are expensive. The awareness among retirees planning gap years conversions is nearly zero until they accidentally trigger it.

### The Five Income Tiers: 2026 Thresholds and Surcharges

IRMAA uses a five-tier structure. Each tier has an income range and corresponding surcharges. The following table shows 2026 thresholds and costs for married filing jointly.

**2026 IRMAA Structure (Married Filing Jointly):**

| Tier | MAGI Range | Part B Monthly | Part D Monthly | Total Monthly (per person) | Annual Cost (couple) |
|---|---|---|---|---|---|
| 0 | ≤$218,000 | $202.90 | $0 | $202.90 | $4,870 |
| 1 | $218,001-$274,000 | $284.10 | $14.50 | $298.60 | $7,166 |
| 2 | $274,001-$342,000 | $405.80 | $37.50 | $443.30 | $10,639 |
| 3 | $342,001-$410,000 | $527.50 | $60.40 | $587.90 | $14,110 |
| 4 | $410,001-$749,999 | $649.20 | $83.30 | $732.50 | $17,580 |
| 5 | ≥$750,000 | $689.90 | $91.00 | $780.90 | $18,742 |

Focus on Tier 0 versus Tier 1. At **$218,000** MAGI, you pay **$4,193** per year for both spouses combined. At **$218,001** MAGI — one dollar more — you pay **$6,219** per year. The difference: **$2,296** in annual surcharges for a couple.

You crossed the threshold by $1. Your penalty is $ **2,296** per year. That's a **229,600% marginal tax rate** on that single dollar of income.

Tier 1 to Tier 2 is equally brutal. At $274,000 MAGI, you pay **$7,166**. At $274,001, you pay **$10,639**. The jump: **$3,473** for crossing by $1.

These aren't gradual increases. They're cliffs. Step functions. All-or-nothing thresholds where $1 of additional income costs $2,000 to $3,000 in annual penalties.

**For single filers, the thresholds are exactly half:**

| Tier | MAGI Range | Part B Monthly | Total Monthly | Annual Cost (single) |
|---|---|---|---|---|
| 0 | ≤$109,000 | $202.90 | $202.90 | $2,435 |
| 1 | $109,001-$137,000 | $284.10 | $298.60 | $3,583 |
| 2 | $137,001-$171,000 | $405.80 | $443.30 | $5,320 |
| 3 | $171,001-$205,000 | $527.50 | $587.90 | $7,055 |
| 4 | $205,001-$499,999 | $649.20 | $732.50 | $8,790 |
| 5 | ≥$500,000 | $689.90 | $780.90 | $9,371 |

Single filers face the same cliff mechanism with half the income thresholds. A widow with **$109,001** in income pays **$ 974** more per year than if her income were $109,000.

This structure is why IRMAA is so dangerous for retirees. Most people carefully manage federal income taxes. They understand brackets, marginal rates, deductions. They've dealt with tax planning their entire careers.

IRMAA operates on different thresholds with different rules. It's not integrated with income tax calculations. It's a separate system with its own income definition, its own cliffs, and its own penalties. People who successfully navigate income tax planning for decades get blindsided by IRMAA because they didn't know to watch for it.

## The $1 Cliff: Why One Dollar Costs $1,000+

The cliff mechanism deserves emphasis because it's counterintuitive.

Normal progressive taxation: earn one more dollar, pay your marginal rate on that dollar. Earn $1 in the 24% bracket, pay $0.24 in tax. The cost is proportional to the income.

IRMAA doesn't work that way. IRMAA is binary within each tier. You're either below the threshold or above it. If you're above it, you pay the full surcharge regardless of how far above you are.

Example: Married couple with $217,900 MAGI. They're $100 below the **$218,000** threshold. Standard Medicare premiums: **$4,870** per year for both spouses.

They realize $150 in capital gains from rebalancing in December. Their MAGI becomes $218,050. They're now $50 over the threshold.

New Medicare cost: **$7,166** per year. Increase: **$2,296**. They paid **$2,296** extra because they realized $150 in capital gains at year-end. Effective cost: 1,531% of the income that pushed them over.

This isn't a marginal rate. It's a penalty triggered by crossing a threshold. Once triggered, the full surcharge applies for the entire year — not prorated, not partial, full amount.

If their MAGI had been $218,050 all year or $274,000 all year, the Tier 1 surcharge is identical: **$7,166**. The penalty is the same whether you're $50 over or $56,000 over. Only when you cross into Tier 2 at $274,001 does the penalty jump again.

**This makes precision critical.** With income taxes, being $500 over the top of the 22% bracket costs you $120 in extra taxes — 24% on $500. Annoying but manageable.

With IRMAA, being $500 over the threshold costs you **$2,296** in surcharges the first year, and potentially that amount every subsequent year if your income stays elevated. One mistake, repeated consequences.

The cliff structure means that staying $1 below thresholds saves thousands. Crossing by $1 costs thousands. There's no middle ground, no proportionality, no gradual transition.

This is why IRMAA planning requires exactness that income tax planning doesn't. You can't approximate. You can't round. You need to know your projected MAGI within a few hundred dollars, calculate carefully, and stay below thresholds deliberately.

For retirees whose income is approaching **$218,000** or **$274,000** or any IRMAA threshold, every financial decision — selling investments, taking IRA distributions, converting to Roth, harvesting losses, timing Social Security — must account for IRMAA impact.

Miss the calculation by $1,000, and you might accidentally trigger a $2,000 to $3,000 annual penalty that repeats until your income structure changes.

## The 2-Year Lookback: Today's Income, Future's Penalty

IRMAA uses a two-year lookback period. Your income from two years ago determines your current year's Medicare premiums.

Your **2024** Modified Adjusted Gross Income determines your **2026** IRMAA surcharges. Your **2025** income determines **2027** surcharges. Your **2026** income determines **2028** surcharges.

Social Security pulls your MAGI from your tax return filed with the IRS. When you file your 2024 return in April 2025, the IRS shares that data with Social Security. Social Security uses it to calculate your 2026 IRMAA tier. In October 2025, you receive notification of your 2026 Medicare premiums including any IRMAA surcharges. Those premiums take effect January 1, 2026.

The two-year gap creates planning challenges most people don't anticipate.

**Challenge 1: You can't course-correct quickly.**

If you accidentally trigger IRMAA in 2024 because your income was $225,000, you'll pay surcharges in 2026. You discover this in October 2025 when the notice arrives. By then, you've already filed your 2024 return. You can't retroactively reduce your 2024 income.

You can reduce 2025 income to avoid triggering IRMAA again in 2027. But you're stuck with the 2026 penalty. There's no immediate fix.

Compare this to income taxes. Realize you're paying too much in federal taxes in April 2025? Adjust withholding, increase retirement contributions, harvest tax losses — fix it by December 2025 when the tax year closes.

IRMAA doesn't work that way. The penalty is locked in based on income from two years prior. You pay it for the full year regardless of current circumstances.

**Challenge 2: Life changes aren't reflected in real-time.**

You retire in 2025. Your income drops from $180,000 (working) to $95,000 (retired). You're now well below IRMAA thresholds. But your 2025 Medicare premiums are based on 2023 income when you were still working. You pay IRMAA surcharges in 2025 despite having retired.

In 2026, you'll still pay IRMAA based on 2024 income — possibly your last partial year of work.

Not until 2027 will your Medicare premiums reflect your new retired income from 2025. You pay two years of IRMAA penalties after retirement before the system catches up to your reduced income.

This delay costs people thousands. They retired, income dropped, but IRMAA penalties continue for two more years based on old higher income.

**Challenge 3: Planning requires projecting two years ahead.**

If you're considering a large Roth conversion in 2026, you need to calculate whether it will push you over IRMAA thresholds. But the consequence won't hit until 2028 Medicare premiums. You're making a decision in 2026 whose financial impact manifests in 2028.

Most people don't think that far ahead for routine financial decisions. They focus on current-year taxes. IRMAA forces you to consider two-year downstream consequences of every income-generating event.

**The timeline in practice:**

December 2024: You take a $60,000 Roth conversion. Your 2024 MAGI including the conversion is $223,000.

April 2025: You file your 2024 tax return showing $223,000 MAGI.

October 2025: Social Security sends notification that your 2026 Medicare premiums include IRMAA Tier 1 surcharges because your 2024 income exceeded $218,000.

January 2026: You start paying **$6,219** annually in Medicare premiums instead of $4,193 — an increase of $2,026 for the year.

December 2026: The 2024 conversion still affects you. If your 2025 income was also high, you'll pay IRMAA again in 2027. The surcharge from one conversion can persist across multiple years if your baseline income stays elevated.

This delayed feedback loop is why so many retirees get caught. They make decisions in 2024 that seem fine from an income tax perspective. Two years later, they discover those decisions triggered Medicare penalties they didn't anticipate.

## MAGI Calculation: What Counts Toward IRMAA

IRMAA is based on Modified Adjusted Gross Income — the same MAGI used for certain income tax calculations, but not identical to all MAGI definitions in the tax code. For IRMAA purposes, MAGI includes:

**Income sources that count:**

- Wages and salaries
- Traditional IRA and 401(k) distributions (including RMDs)
- **Roth conversion amounts** (this is critical — conversions count as income for IRMAA even though Roth withdrawals don't)
- Taxable Social Security benefits
- Pension income

- Interest and dividends (taxable)
- Capital gains (short-term and long-term)
- Rental income
- Business income
- Taxable portion of annuities

**Income sources that don't count:**

- Roth IRA withdrawals (qualified distributions)
- Municipal bond interest
- Return of principal from non-qualified annuities
- Qualified HSA distributions
- Life insurance proceeds
- Gifts and inheritances (but inherited IRA distributions do count)
- Veterans benefits
- Workers' compensation

**The Roth conversion trap:** This catches people by surprise. Roth conversions are taxable income in the year executed. They count toward IRMAA thresholds. Many people correctly understand that Roth accounts grow tax-free and withdrawals are tax-free in retirement. They don't realize that the conversion itself — moving money from traditional to Roth — generates taxable income that can trigger IRMAA.

Example: You're 68 with MAGI of $180,000. You want to convert $50,000 to Roth before RMDs start at 73. The conversion is smart tax planning — you're in gap years, converting at favorable rates.

But $180,000 + $50,000 = $230,000 MAGI for that year. You've crossed the **$218,000** threshold. IRMAA triggers. You pay **$2,026** in Medicare surcharges two years later.

The conversion still makes sense long-term. But you need to account for IRMAA cost when calculating total conversion expense. It's not just federal income tax at 22%. It's federal tax plus $2,026 in Medicare penalties. Your effective conversion cost just increased.

**The capital gains trap:** Retirees often rebalance portfolios in taxable accounts. Selling appreciated positions generates capital gains. Those gains count toward MAGI.

Example: You're 76 with baseline income of $210,000 — well below the **$218,000** threshold. You sell $50,000 of stock that's appreciated $20,000 from original cost. You have $20,000 in long-term capital gains.

Your MAGI becomes $230,000. IRMAA triggers. The stock sale seemed routine — you were rebalancing, not trying to generate income. But capital gains are income for IRMAA purposes, and they pushed you over.

**The income stacking problem:** IRMAA doesn't care why your income is high. It doesn't distinguish between necessary income (RMDs you're forced to take) and discretionary income (Roth conversions you chose to execute). It counts everything.

This is why retirees with multiple income sources face IRMAA risk. Social Security $45,000 + pension $30,000 + RMDs $35,000 + investment income $25,000 + capital gains from rebalancing $15,000 = $150,000. Nowhere near threshold.

But add a $70,000 Roth conversion on top of that? Now you're at $220,000. IRMAA triggered.

Every income source stacks. RMDs force income whether you want it. Social Security is fixed. Pensions are fixed. You can't reduce those to make room for conversions without triggering IRMAA. You must plan conversions around all other income sources and stay under the cliff.

## How IRMAA Gets Triggered Accidentally

We've analyzed dozens of cases where retirees triggered IRMAA without intending to. The patterns repeat.

**Accidental trigger 1: First RMD surprise.**

You turn 73. You understood RMDs would start. You calculated your first RMD: $32,000. You added it to your baseline income: $185,000. Total: $217,000. You're $1,000 under the threshold. Safe.

But you forgot about required distributions from an inherited IRA you received five years ago. That adds $6,000. New total: $223,000. IRMAA triggered.

Inherited IRAs have their own RMD rules. Many people forget to include them in MAGI calculations. The $6,000 seemed small — it's only $1,440 in federal tax at 24% rate. But it pushed you $5,000 over IRMAA threshold, costing $2,026 in surcharges. The inherited IRA distribution cost you **$3,736** total total — federal tax plus IRMAA penalty.

**Accidental trigger 2: One-time income event.**

You're 75 with steady income of $200,000 annually. You've stayed below IRMAA thresholds for years. Then you sell a rental property you've owned for 20 years. Capital gain: $80,000.

That year, your MAGI is $280,000. You're in IRMAA Tier 2. Surcharge: **$5,769** for the couple. You understood the capital gain would generate federal and state taxes. You didn't realize it would also trigger Medicare penalties two years later.

The property sale was one-time. Your income returns to $200,000 the following year. But you pay IRMAA surcharges for two years — the year of the sale (based on two years prior income) and the following year (based on sale year income). Total IRMAA cost from one transaction: **$11,538** spread across two years.

**Accidental trigger 3: Roth conversion without IRMAA accounting.**

You're 66, executing gap years conversions. Your baseline income is $170,000. You convert $55,000 to Roth. Total MAGI: $225,000.

You calculated federal tax: $55,000 × 22% = $12,100. You paid from savings. The conversion seemed expensive but manageable.

Two years later, IRMAA surcharge hits: **$2,296**. You didn't include this in your conversion cost analysis. Your true conversion cost was **$14,396**, not $12,100. Effective rate: 26.2%, not 22%.

This doesn't mean the conversion was wrong. But the incomplete calculation meant you were surprised by costs you should have anticipated. If you'd known about IRMAA, you might have converted $48,000 instead of $55,000 to stay under the threshold.

**Accidental trigger 4: Income volatility from markets.**

You're 78 with income normally around $205,000. You have $80,000 in a taxable brokerage account earning dividends and interest. Normally, this generates $3,500 annually.

One year, markets boom. Your mutual funds distribute $12,000 in capital gains. You didn't sell anything — this is fund-level distributions you can't control. Your income jumps to $213,500.

Add $8,000 in unexpected dividends from strong market performance: $221,500 total. IRMAA triggered by market volatility you had no control over.

These aren't edge cases. They're common patterns. Retirees with income between $200,000 and $230,000 for married couples live in the danger zone. They're close enough to the **$218,000** cliff that routine financial events — RMDs increasing annually, portfolio rebalancing, property sales, strong market years — can accidentally push them over.

Once triggered, IRMAA is difficult to avoid in subsequent years if your baseline income is already elevated. RMDs grow with age. Social Security adjusts for inflation. Pensions may include cost-of-living increases. Your income trend is upward, pushing you closer to or over thresholds repeatedly.

This is why gap years conversions matter for IRMAA avoidance. Convert during gap years when income is $140,000 to $180,000 — safely below thresholds with substantial cushion. Reduce your IRA balance before RMDs start. When RMDs begin at 73, they're smaller because the balance is lower. Smaller RMDs mean lower total income. Lower total income means staying under IRMAA cliffs for more years or avoiding them entirely.

Couple A from Chapter 6 never triggered IRMAA. Their strategic conversions during gap years kept their post-73 income well below $218,000. Couple B triggered IRMAA multiple times because RMDs from their unconverted IRA pushed income over thresholds. The difference over 20 years: $6,888 to $11,480 in avoidable Medicare penalties.

Understanding IRMAA structure is critical. Understanding how RMDs interact with IRMAA to create accidental triggers is even more important. Chapter 8 shows exactly how RMDs push retirees over IRMAA cliffs year after year, costing thousands annually in penalties that proper gap years planning would have prevented.

## Appeals and Life-Changing Events (Limited Relief)

IRMAA surcharges can be appealed in specific circumstances. Social Security allows reconsideration if you experienced a **life-changing event** that reduced your income significantly.

Qualifying life-changing events include:

- Marriage
- Divorce or annulment
- Death of spouse
- Work stoppage (retirement)
- Work reduction (cut hours or lost income-producing property)
- Loss of income from income-producing property (disaster, sale)
- Loss of pension
- Employer settlement payment received

If you experienced one of these events and your current income is substantially lower than the income from two years ago that's determining your IRMAA, you can file Form SSA-44 requesting reconsideration.

**The work stoppage example:** You retired in April 2025. Your 2024 income was $190,000 (full year working). Your 2025 income will be $110,000 (partial year working plus retirement income). Social Security will use your 2024 income to determine 2026 IRMAA. You'll pay surcharges despite being retired.

You can appeal. Provide evidence of retirement date and current income. Social Security may adjust your 2026 premiums to reflect your actual 2025 income instead of 2024 income. This eliminates IRMAA surcharges you shouldn't be paying post-retirement.

**The widow example:** Your spouse died in March 2025. You filed married filing jointly in 2024 with combined income of $235,000. For 2026, you'll file as single. Your income as a surviving spouse is $120,000 — well below the single filer IRMAA threshold of $109,000.

Without appeal, Social Security would charge you IRMAA based on 2024 married income of $235,000. With appeal, they adjust to your current single-filer status and income, eliminating surcharges.

**What doesn't qualify:** These are the only life-changing events Social Security recognizes. Notably absent from the list:

- Roth conversions that temporarily elevated income
- One-time capital gains from selling investments or property
- Unexpected RMD increases due to IRA balance growth
- Medical expenses that reduced available income

- Supporting adult children or elderly parents
- Paying for long-term care

If you converted $80,000 to Roth in 2024, pushing your MAGI to $240,000, you'll pay IRMAA in 2026. You cannot appeal by arguing "the conversion was temporary, my normal income is lower." Social Security doesn't care. You chose to convert. The income counts. The surcharge applies.

If your RMDs jumped from $35,000 to $50,000 because markets performed well and your IRA balance grew, pushing you over IRMAA threshold, you cannot appeal. Market gains aren't a life-changing event. The higher income counts even though you didn't choose it.

**Appeals are exception-based relief for specific scenarios, not general escape hatches.** If your income genuinely dropped due to retirement, divorce, or widow status, appeal. For all other situations, the IRMAA surcharge stands. You pay it for the full year, and you'll pay it again next year if your income stays elevated.

This limited appeal process is why advance planning matters so much. You cannot fix IRMAA problems retroactively in most cases. You must avoid triggers proactively by managing income carefully, staying under thresholds, and accounting for the two-year lookback in every financial decision that generates taxable income.

## The Cumulative IRMAA Threat

IRMAA isn't a one-time cost. It's an annual penalty that repeats as long as your income stays above thresholds.

If you trigger Tier 1 IRMAA once, you pay **$2,026** that year. Unfortunate but manageable.

If your income structure permanently elevated — RMDs grow annually, Social Security provides steady income, pension is fixed — and you trigger Tier 1 IRMAA every year from age 75 to 90, you pay **$2,296** × 15 years = **$34,440** in cumulative surcharges.

If RMDs push you into Tier 2 by age 82 and you stay there until 92, you pay **$5,769** × 10 years = **$57,690**, in surcharges just in that decade.

These numbers compound with the direct tax costs calculated in Chapter 6. Couple B paid approximately $75,000 more in direct income taxes over 20 years than Couple A due to larger RMDs. Add IRMAA surcharges from repeatedly crossing thresholds: another **$20,000 to $40,000** depending on how often they triggered and which tier.

Total cost of arriving at 73 unprepared: **$95,000 to $115,000** when IRMAA is fully accounted for. This is the realistic estimate for someone with a $700,000 to $900,000 IRA who doesn't convert during gap years and whose RMDs push income near or over IRMAA thresholds repeatedly.

For higher-income retirees — those with baseline income already at $180,000 to $200,000 before RMDs — the IRMAA threat is even more severe. Their first RMD at 73 likely pushes them over **$218,000** immediately. They'll pay IRMAA every single year from 73 until death. Over 20 years:

**$45,920** in Tier 1 surcharges minimum, more if income growth pushes them into Tier 2 or 3.

This is why we call IRMAA a trap. It's not just expensive when you trigger it once. It's expensive every year you trigger it, and once RMDs start forcing your income higher, you often cannot avoid triggering it annually without radical income restructuring that may not be possible.

**Gap years conversions prevent this trap.** Convert $300,000 to $400,000 during gap years when your income is $140,000 to $180,000 — well below IRMAA thresholds. Your RMDs starting at 73 are calculated on the reduced balance. Smaller RMDs mean total income stays under $218,000 for married couples. You never trigger IRMAA. You save **$30,000 to $50,000** in Medicare penalties over retirement in addition to the income tax savings.

But you must act during gap years. Once RMDs begin at 73, your income is elevated permanently. Converting after 73 to try to reduce future RMDs often backfires — the conversion itself pushes you over IRMAA thresholds, costing $2,000 to $5,000 in surcharges, and the benefit from smaller future RMDs takes years to materialize.

The window to avoid IRMAA is the same window for optimal Roth conversions: **ages 60 to 73**, when your income is low, you have full control over distributions, and you can convert substantial amounts without approaching Medicare penalty thresholds.

## IRMAA as the Amplifier

IRMAA doesn't create a new problem. It amplifies the RMD problem.

RMDs force distributions you don't need. Those distributions cost you in income taxes. IRMAA adds a second layer of cost — Medicare penalties triggered by the forced income RMDs create.

A $35,000 RMD at age 75 costs approximately **$8,400** in federal income tax at 24% rate. Already expensive.

If that $35,000 RMD pushes your total income from $215,000 to $250,000, you've crossed the **$218,000** IRMAA threshold. Now the RMD costs $8,400 in federal tax **$2,296** in IRMAA surcharges. Total cost: **$10,696**. The IRMAA penalty increased the effective cost of the RMD by 24%.

Over 10 years, if that pattern repeats, the cumulative IRMAA cost is **$22,960** on top of $84,000 in direct income taxes. The RMDs cost **$106,960** total instead of $84,000. That **$22,960** is pure penalty — money you're paying to Medicare above standard premiums because your forced distributions elevated your income.

This is why Chapter 8 is necessary. Understanding IRMAA structure is critical. Understanding how RMDs accidentally trigger IRMAA — and how the two interact to create compounding costs — is what converts abstract knowledge into actionable planning.

You now know what IRMAA is. You know the five-tier structure. You know the cliffs cost thousands for crossing by $1. You know the two-year lookback creates delayed consequences. You know what income counts and what doesn't.

What you need next: the mechanics of how RMDs push you over IRMAA thresholds year after year, why this cascade is difficult to stop once it starts, and how much it costs when a $32,000 RMD accidentally triggers **$1,950 per year** in Medicare surcharges for the next decade. Chapter 8 shows you the cascade effect in detail — how RMDs that seem manageable at 73 become IRMAA triggers by 78, costing **$30,000**+ over 10 years in penalties that strategic gap years conversions would have completely avoided.

CHAPTER 8

8

# HOW RMDS ACCIDENTALLY TRIGGER IRMAA (AND COST YOU $30,000+ OVER 10 YEARS)

## The Setup: Income Comfortably Below IRMAA Threshold (For Now)

Meet David and Susan. Both are **72** in 2025. They retired three years ago at 69. Their current annual income is **$195,000** — comfortable, well-planned, and importantly, well below the **$218,000** IRMAA threshold for married filing jointly.

Their income breakdown:

- Social Security (both combined): **$55,000**
- David's pension: **$48,000**
- Susan's pension: **$32,000**
- Investment income (dividends, interest from taxable accounts): **$22,000**
- Interest from municipal bonds: **$38,000** (not counted in MAGI)

Total MAGI: **$195,000**. They're **$23,000** below the first IRMAA cliff. They pay standard Medicare premiums: **$4,870** annually for both of them combined. No surcharges.

David's traditional IRA balance: **$850,000**. Susan's traditional IRA: **$120,000**. Combined traditional IRAs: **$970,000**.

They heard about Roth conversions. They discussed it with their advisor in 2023, again in 2024, and again in early 2025. Each time, the advisor said: "Let's wait and see. You're doing fine. The brackets are permanent now. No rush."

They waited. They're now 72. Next year at 73, Required Minimum Distributions begin. They're not worried. Their income is $195,000. An RMD of $30,000 or $35,000 won't hurt them. They'll pay some additional income tax, but they can afford it.

What David and Susan don't realize: their first RMD will push them over the IRMAA threshold. They'll trigger Medicare surcharges they don't know about. Those surcharges will repeat annually for the next decade or more, costing them **$30,000 to $40,000** in penalties they never anticipated and cannot easily avoid once RMDs start.

This is the cascade effect. RMDs force income higher. Higher income crosses IRMAA thresholds.

IRMAA surcharges add thousands per year in costs. The surcharges repeat annually as long as RMDs keep income elevated. And RMDs escalate with age, making the problem worse over time.

David and Susan are about to learn that being $23,000 below the IRMAA threshold at 72 doesn't protect them once RMDs begin at 73.

## Age 73: When RMDs Push You Over the Cliff

December 2026. David turns 73. His IRA balance as of December 31, 2025 was **$850,000**. The IRS requires he take his first Required Minimum Distribution in 2026.

RMD calculation: $850,000 ÷ 26.5 (age 73 divisor) = **$32,075**.

Susan also turns 73 in 2026. Her IRA balance was **$120,000**. Her RMD: $120,000 ÷ 26.5 = **$4,528**.

Combined RMDs for 2026: **$36,603**.

Their total income for 2026:

- Social Security: **$55,000**
- Pensions: **$80,000** (David $48K + Susan $32K)
- Investment income: **$22,000**
- RMDs: **$36,603**

Total MAGI: **$193,603**.

Wait — that's still below the **$218,000** threshold. They're safe, right?

Not quite. We need to account for inflation adjustments. Social Security increases 2.5% annually (cost of living adjustment). Their 2026 Social Security is approximately **$56,400**. Pensions may have cost-of-living adjustments — assume 2% increase, bringing pensions to **$81,600**. Investment income fluctuates but averages **$24,000** in 2026 due to strong market year.

Revised 2026 income:

- Social Security: **$56,400**
- Pensions: **$81,600**
- Investment income: **$24,000**
- RMDs: **$36,603**

Total MAGI: **$198,603**.

Still under $218,000. But barely. They have **$19,397** of cushion. Any additional income — unexpected capital gains from rebalancing, higher dividends, a one-time bonus or gift from family members that generates taxable income — could push them over.

More importantly, this is year one. RMDs will grow.

## The IRMAA Trigger: When One Year Pushes You Over

Let's advance to 2027. David and Susan are 74.

Their IRA balances grew modestly despite taking RMDs in 2026. Markets returned 6%. David's balance: **$867,000**. Susan's balance: **$122,000**.

2027 RMD calculation (age 74 divisor = 25.5):

- David: $867,000 ÷ 25.5 = **$34,000**
- Susan: $122,000 ÷ 25.5 = **$4,784**
- Combined: **$38,784**

2027 income:

- Social Security: **$57,800** (another 2.5% COLA)
- Pensions: **$83,200** (2% increase)
- Investment income: **$26,500** (market volatility, higher dividends)
- RMDs: **$38,784**

Total MAGI: **$206,284.**

Still under $218,000. But the cushion is shrinking. They're now **$11,716** below the threshold. One more year of RMD growth and they'll be in danger.

2028. David and Susan are 75.

IRA balances continue growing. David: **$880,000**. Susan: **$123,500**.

2028 RMD calculation (age 75 divisor = 24.6):

- David: $880,000 ÷ 24.6 = **$35,772**
- Susan: $123,500 ÷ 24.6 = **$5,020**
- Combined: **$40,792**

2028 income:

- Social Security: **$59,250**
- Pensions: **$84,900**
- Investment income: **$25,000**
- RMDs: **$40,792**

Total MAGI: **$209,942.**

They're **$8,058** below the threshold. Getting close.

Then December 2028 happens. They rebalance their taxable investment portfolio. They sell $40,000 of appreciated stock that's gained $15,000 from original cost. They have **$15,000** in long-term capital gains they must report.

Revised 2028 MAGI: $209,942 + $15,000 = **$224,942**.

They're **$6,942** over the **$218,000** threshold.

IRMAA triggers.

In October 2030 — two years later due to the lookback period — they receive letters from Social Security. Their 2030 Medicare premiums will include IRMAA Tier 1 surcharges based on their 2028 income of $224,942.

New 2030 Medicare cost: **$7,166** per year for both of them. Standard premium would have been $4,870. Increase: **$2,296** for the year.

David calls Social Security. "We didn't mean to go over. Can we appeal?"

Social Security: "Did you experience a qualifying life-changing event? Marriage, divorce, death of spouse, retirement, loss of pension?"

David: "No, we're just retired living on our normal income."

Social Security: "Then the surcharge stands. Your 2028 income exceeded the threshold. You'll pay IRMAA for 2030."

David: "What about 2029 and 2031?"

Social Security: "That depends on your income in those years. If your 2029 income is also over $218,000, you'll pay IRMAA in 2031."

David checks his 2029 income projection. Social Security increased. Pensions increased. RMDs increased to **$42,500** because of the age 76 divisor drop to 24.4. No capital gains this year — they're being careful now.

2029 MAGI: approximately **$212,000**. Just under the threshold.

Relief. They won't trigger IRMAA in 2031.

But 2030 income will push them over again. RMDs continue escalating. By age 78, their RMD will be **$46,000**. By age 80, it'll be **$51,000**. Each year, the forced income grows. Each year, they get closer to or over the IRMAA threshold.

## Year-by-Year Escalation: RMDs Grow, IRMAA Persists

Let's project David and Susan's income through age 82 to see how the pattern develops.

**Income Projection (Ages 73-82):**

| Age | Social Security | Pensions | Investment Income | RMDs | Total MAGI | IRMAA Triggered? | Annual IRMAA Cost |
|---|---|---|---|---|---|---|---|
| 73 | $56,400 | $81,600 | $24,000 | $36,603 | $198,603 | No | $0 |
| 74 | $57,800 | $83,200 | $26,500 | $38,784 | $206,284 | No | $0 |
| 75 | $59,250 | $84,900 | $25,000 | $40,792 | $209,942 | No | $0 |
| 76 | $60,750 | $86,600 | $27,000 | $42,900 | $217,250 | No | $0 |
| 77 | $62,300 | $88,300 | $26,500 | $45,100 | $222,200 | Yes (Tier 1) | $2,296 |
| 78 | $63,900 | $90,100 | $28,000 | $47,400 | $229,400 | Yes (Tier 1) | $2,296 |
| 79 | $65,500 | $92,000 | $27,500 | $49,800 | $234,800 | Yes (Tier 1) | $2,296 |
| 80 | $67,200 | $93,800 | $29,000 | $52,300 | $242,300 | Yes (Tier 1) | $2,296 |
| 81 | $68,900 | $95,700 | $28,500 | $54,900 | $248,000 | Yes (Tier 1) | $2,296 |
| 82 | $70,700 | $97,600 | $30,000 | $57,600 | $255,900 | Yes (Tier 1) | $2,296 |

Notice the pattern. Ages 73-76: income stays below **$218,000**. They avoid IRMAA for the first four years after RMDs begin.

Age 77: RMDs have grown to $45,100. Combined with other income, they cross the threshold for the first time. IRMAA triggered.

Ages 77-82: They trigger IRMAA every single year. Six consecutive years of **$2,026** annual surcharges.

But it gets worse. By age 82, their MAGI is **$255,900** — approaching the second IRMAA tier threshold at **$274,000**. If investment income has an unusually good year or they realize capital gains from rebalancing, they could jump to Tier 2, where surcharges are **$5,095** per year instead of $2,026.

## The 10-Year Cost: $30,000+ in Avoidable Surcharges

Let's calculate David and Susan's cumulative IRMAA cost from ages 73 to 82 based on the projection above.

Ages 73-76: No IRMAA triggered. Cost: **$0**.

Ages 77-82: IRMAA Tier 1 triggered every year. Annual cost: $2,296. Six years total. Cumulative IRMAA cost (ages 77-82): **$2,296** × **6** = **$13,776**.

But David and Susan won't stop living at 82. Assume they live to 92. From age 82 to 92, RMDs continue escalating. By age 85, their RMD will be approximately **$64,000**. By age 88, it'll be **$72,000**. By age 90, it'll exceed **$80,000**.

Their baseline income (Social Security, pensions, investments) also increases with inflation. By age 85, baseline income is approximately **$190,000** before RMDs. Add $64,000 RMD: **$254,000** total. Still in Tier 1.

By age 88, baseline income is **$205,000**. Add $72,000 RMD: **$277,000** total. They've crossed into **Tier 2** — the second IRMAA cliff at **$274,000**.

New annual IRMAA cost at Tier 2: $5,769 per year. If they stay in Tier 2 from age 88 to 92 (four years), that's $5,769 × 4 = $23,076 in additional surcharges.

**Total IRMAA cost projection (ages 77-92, spanning 15 years):**

- Ages 77-87 (11 years at Tier 1): $2,296 × 11 = **$25,256**

- Ages 88-92 (4 years at Tier 2): $5,769 × 4 = **$23,076**

- Grand total: **$48,332**

This is conservative. We assumed:

- No unexpected capital gains pushing them temporarily into higher tiers
- No exceptionally strong market years generating extra dividends
- No inherited IRA distributions adding income
- No one-time events like selling property or receiving taxable gifts

Real-world scenarios often produce higher costs. Add two or three years where they accidentally jump to Tier 2 or 3 earlier than age 88, and the total easily exceeds **$50,000** over their remaining lifetimes.

**This $48,332 to $55,000+ is pure penalty cost.** It's not income tax on distributions they need. It's Medicare surcharges triggered by forced income they don't need and can't avoid. Every dollar of this cost could have been prevented with strategic gap years conversions that reduced their IRA balance before RMDs started.

## The Alternative: Strategic Conversions Keep You Under Threshold

Now let's replay David and Susan's story with a different approach. Same starting position at age 65, but this time they execute strategic Roth conversions during gap years.

Ages 65-69 (five gap years before Social Security starts at 70):

Their baseline income during this period is **$130,000** — pensions plus investment income. No Social Security yet. No RMDs yet.

They calculate conversion capacity. The top of the 22% bracket for married filing jointly is approximately **$206,700**. Available room: $206,700 - $130,000 = **$76,700**.

They're cautious. They don't want to approach IRMAA thresholds even during conversions. They convert **$60,000** per year for five years. Total converted: **$300,000**.

Conversion tax cost: $60,000 × 20% effective rate = **$12,000** per year. Five years: **$60,000** total in conversion taxes paid from savings.

At age 73, their combined IRA balance is **$670,000** instead of $970,000. They converted $300,000 to Roth. The remaining traditional balance is $670,000 after accounting for growth.

Age 73 RMD calculation:

- David's reduced IRA: $580,000 ÷ 26.5 = **$21,887**
- Susan's IRA: $120,000 ÷ 26.5 = **$4,528**
- Combined: **$26,415**

Compare this to the original scenario where their first RMD was **$36,603**. They've reduced first-year RMD by **$10,188**.

Now let's project their income with smaller RMDs:

**Income Projection with Strategic Conversions (Ages 73-82):**

| Age | Social Security | Pensions | Investment Income | RMDs (Reduced) | Total MAGI | IRMAA Triggered? | Annual IRMAA Cost |
|---|---|---|---|---|---|---|---|
| 73 | $56,400 | $81,600 | $24,000 | $26,415 | $188,415 | No | $0 |
| 74 | $57,800 | $83,200 | $26,500 | $27,950 | $195,450 | No | $0 |
| 75 | $59,250 | $84,900 | $25,000 | $29,400 | $198,550 | No | $0 |
| 76 | $60,750 | $86,600 | $27,000 | $30,900 | $205,250 | No | $0 |
| 77 | $62,300 | $88,300 | $26,500 | $32,500 | $209,600 | No | $0 |
| 78 | $63,900 | $90,100 | $28,000 | $34,100 | $216,100 | No | $0 |
| 79 | $65,500 | $92,000 | $27,500 | $35,800 | $220,800 | Yes (Tier 1) | $2,296 |
| 80 | $67,200 | $93,800 | $29,000 | $37,600 | $227,600 | Yes (Tier 1) | $2,296 |
| 81 | $68,900 | $95,700 | $28,500 | $39,500 | $232,600 | Yes (Tier 1) | $2,296 |
| 82 | $70,700 | $97,600 | $30,000 | $41,400 | $239,700 | Yes (Tier 1) | $2,296 |

With strategic conversions, they avoid IRMAA entirely from ages 73-78. They don't trigger until age 79 — two years later than the original scenario.

Even at ages 79-82, their income stays well within Tier 1. They're nowhere near the **$274,000** Tier 2 threshold. In the original scenario, they were approaching Tier 2 by age 82. With conversions, they have **$34,300** of cushion at age 82.

Projecting to age 92:

By age 88, their RMD with the reduced balance is approximately **$52,000** instead of $72,000. Total income: **$257,000** instead of $277,000. They stay in Tier 1 instead of jumping to Tier 2.

**Cumulative IRMAA cost with strategic conversions (ages 79-92, 13 years):**

- All 13 years remain in Tier 1: **$2,296 × 13 = $29,848**

Compare to original scenario: **$48,332** in IRMAA costs.

IRMAA savings from strategic conversions: $48,332 - $29,848 = **$18,484 over ages 73-92.**

But that's not the full picture. We need to add the income tax savings from smaller RMDs.

In the original scenario, David and Susan paid approximately **$220,000** in cumulative income taxes on RMDs and other income from ages 73-85 (from Chapter 6 calculations).

With strategic conversions reducing RMDs, they pay approximately **$160,000** in cumulative taxes over the same period.

Income tax savings: **$60,000**.

Combined savings: $60,000 (income tax) + **$18,484** (IRMAA avoidance) = **$78,484** over ages 73-85.

They paid **$60,000** in conversion taxes during gap years (ages 65-69).

Net lifetime benefit: $78,484 - $60,000 = $18,484 through age 85.

And the benefit continues growing every year they live beyond 85 because the reduced RMDs and IRMAA avoidance persist.

## The Math: Conversion Tax vs. IRMAA Savings Break-Even

Strategic conversions cost money upfront. IRMAA avoidance saves money over time. When does the savings exceed the cost?

David and Susan paid **$60,000** in conversion taxes from ages 65-69.

Starting at age 73, they began saving money:

- Smaller RMDs mean lower income taxes: approximately **$5,000** per year in tax savings
- Avoiding IRMAA from ages 73-78 (six years earlier than original scenario): $2,296 × 6 = **$13,776** in savings
- Staying in Tier 1 instead of jumping to Tier 2 at age 88+: additional **$$3,473** per year savings

Cumulative savings by age:

- Age 78: $5,000/year × 5 years (ages 73-77) + $13,776 IRMAA avoidance = **$38,776**
- Age 80: $38,776 + $5,000 × 2 years + $2,296 × 2 years IRMAA = **$53,368**
- Age 82: $53,368 + $5,000 × 2 years + $2,296 × 2 years = **$67,960**

**Break-even occurs between ages 80-81**, approximately 11 years after conversions were completed and 7 years after RMDs began.

After break-even, every additional year produces pure net savings. From age 81 to 92, they save an additional **$11,000**+ net beyond what they paid in conversion taxes.

If they live to 95, net savings approach **$ 45,000**+. If one spouse lives to 98 (not uncommon for healthy retirees), the widow continues benefiting from the reduced RMD structure. Total lifetime net savings can exceed **$60,000** for a long-lived couple.

**The break-even timeline explains why gap years conversions must happen early.** If David and Susan had waited until age 70-72 to start converting, they'd have fewer gap years remaining. They could convert less total. Their RMDs would still be large. Break-even would occur later — age 84-85 instead of 80-81. If they don't live long enough past break-even, the conversions don't pay off.

Starting conversions at 65-67 maximizes the probability of substantial net lifetime savings because break-even occurs by 80-81, and most people who reach 80 in good health live another 10-15 years.

## The Proximity Danger

David and Susan's situation illustrates a critical concept: **IRMAA proximity risk**.

Their baseline income before RMDs was **$195,000**. They were $23,000 below the **$218,000** threshold. That felt safe. They thought a $30,000 RMD would keep them comfortably under.

But they didn't account for:

- Inflation adjustments to Social Security and pensions adding **$5,000-$7,000** annually
- Investment income volatility adding **$2,000-$5,000** in high-dividend years
- RMD escalation — not $30,000 forever, but $30,000 growing to $35,000, then $40,000, then $45,000

By age 77, these factors combined to push them $4,200 over the threshold. Once over, they couldn't easily drop back below because RMDs only increase with age.

**Proximity risk assessment:** If your baseline retirement income (Social Security + pensions + investment income) is within **$30,000-$40,000** of the IRMAA threshold, you are in the danger zone. Your first RMD will likely push you over or get you close enough that RMD growth over the next 5-10 years will push you over.

For married couples, the danger zone is baseline income of **$178,000 to $198,000**. Add a $25,000 to $40,000 RMD, and you're at or over $218,000.

For single filers, the danger zone is baseline income of **$69,000 to $89,000**. Add a $20,000 to $30,000 RMD, and you're at or over $109,000.

If you're in the danger zone, strategic gap years conversions aren't optional — they're necessary to avoid decade-long IRMAA penalties that will cost **$20,000 to $50,000** over your remaining lifetime.

If your baseline income is **$150,000 to $170,000**, you have more cushion. A typical RMD might keep you under thresholds until very late in life. But you're not immune — a one-time income spike, exceptionally large RMD, or jump in investment income can still trigger IRMAA accidentally.

If your baseline income exceeds **$200,000**, you're almost guaranteed to trigger IRMAA once RMDs start. Your only question is which tier you'll land in and whether strategic conversions can keep you in Tier 1 instead of letting you drift into Tier 2 or 3.

## The Double Penalty You Didn't Choose

The injustice of the RMD-IRMAA cascade is this: **you're penalized for income you didn't choose to take and don't need.**

David and Susan didn't want to withdraw $36,603 from their IRAs at age 73. They had sufficient income from Social Security and pensions. The IRA distributions weren't necessary for their lifestyle. They would have preferred to let the money continue growing tax-deferred.

The IRS forced the distribution. Federal law mandates it. They had no choice.

Then Medicare penalized them for having that forced income. The $36,603 RMD pushed their total income over the **$218,000** threshold. IRMAA triggered. They paid $2,026 per year in surcharges.

They're paying twice for the same forced distribution:

1. Income tax on the RMD: approximately **$8,800** at 24% effective rate
2. IRMAA surcharge triggered by the RMD: **$2,296** per year

Total cost of one $36,603 RMD: **$11,096** in the year taken, plus **$2,296** in recurring Medicare penalties for as long as RMDs keep income elevated.

This isn't a tax on wealth. It's a penalty on prudent saving. David and Susan did everything they were supposed to do — saved diligently, maxed retirement contributions, lived within their means. Their reward: forced distributions at rates they didn't choose, triggering Medicare penalties they never anticipated.

The cascade is unavoidable once RMDs begin. You cannot pause RMDs. You cannot reduce them below the calculated amount. You cannot skip years when your income would otherwise be low. The IRS mandates the distribution. Medicare assesses the penalty. You pay both.

**The only way to avoid this cascade is to prevent it before RMDs start.** Reduce your IRA balance during gap years through strategic conversions. Smaller balance means smaller RMDs means lower total income means staying under IRMAA thresholds.

But once you reach 73 with a large unconverted IRA, the cascade is locked in. You'll pay income taxes on forced distributions for 20+ years. You'll likely trigger IRMAA repeatedly, adding tens of thousands in Medicare penalties. The cost compounds annually. The opportunity to prevent it has passed.

## The Tier Escalation Risk

David and Susan's projection showed them staying in IRMAA Tier 1 from ages 77-87, then jumping to Tier 2 at age 88 when their income crossed **$274,000**.

This tier escalation is common for retirees with larger IRAs. RMDs don't plateau — they grow exponentially as you age because the IRS divisor shrinks annually while IRA balances often continue growing despite distributions.

At 73, your RMD is 3.77% of balance. Manageable.
At 80, it's 4.95% of balance. Higher.
At 85, it's 6.25% of balance. Substantial.
At 90, it's 8.20% of balance. Massive.

If your IRA balance at 73 is **$1.2 million**, your first RMD is **$45,240**. By age 80, assuming 5% annual growth, your balance might be **$1.35 million**. Your RMD at 80: **$66,825**. By age 85: **$84,375**. By age 90: **$110,760**.

That $110,760 RMD at age 90, added to Social Security and pension income, easily pushes total income above **$274,000** (Tier 2) or even **$340,000** (Tier 3) depending on your other income sources.

Tier 2 IRMAA costs **$5,769** per year for a couple. Tier 3 costs **$9,240** per year. Tier 4 costs **$12,710** per year.

If you start in Tier 1 at age 77, drift into Tier 2 at age 85, and hit Tier 3 at age 90, your cumulative IRMAA costs over ages 77-95 could exceed **$80,000** to **$100,000.**

**Strategic conversions during gap years prevent tier escalation.** By reducing your IRA balance before RMDs start, you ensure RMDs stay smaller throughout retirement. Smaller RMDs mean you stay in lower IRMAA tiers or avoid IRMAA entirely.

David and Susan's alternative scenario — converting $300,000 during gap years — kept them in Tier 1 for their entire lives. They never approached Tier 2. The difference: **$18,484** in IRMAA savings through age 92, potentially **$35,000**+ if they live to 95..

For someone with a $1.5 million IRA arriving unconverted at 73, tier escalation is almost guaranteed. First RMD: **$56,604**. By age 85: **$93,750**. By age 90: **$123,000**. Those RMDs will push you through multiple IRMAA tiers, costing **$55,000** to **$110,000** in cumulative surcharges over retirement.

Convert $500,000 to $600,000 during gap years, and your age 73 IRA balance is $900,000 instead of $1.5 million. First RMD: **$33,962**. By age 85: **$56,250**. By age 90: **$73,800**. Still substantial, but the difference between $73,800 and $123,000 is **$49,200** annually at age 90. That difference keeps you in lower IRMAA tiers, saving thousands per year in Medicare penalties.

## When IRMAA Becomes Permanent

The most painful aspect of the RMD-IRMAA cascade: it's often permanent once triggered.

If you accidentally trigger IRMAA one year due to a one-time event — selling a property, taking a large bonus, exercising stock options — the surcharge lasts one year. Your income returns to normal the next year. IRMAA disappears.

But if RMDs are what trigger IRMAA, the surcharge recurs annually. RMDs are mandatory for life. They increase with age. Your baseline income (Social Security, pensions) also increases with inflation. The combination keeps you above thresholds year after year.

David and Susan triggered IRMAA at age 77. In the original scenario, they paid surcharges every year from 77 until death. They couldn't drop below the threshold because RMDs only grow and they have no way to reduce them.

You might think: "I'll reduce other income sources to offset RMD growth. I'll sell fewer investments, take less from taxable accounts, manage capital gains carefully."

This helps, but it has limits. Social Security is fixed — you can't reduce it. Pensions are fixed — you can't reduce them. RMDs are mandated — you can't reduce them. That leaves investment income (dividends, interest) and capital gains as the only controllable sources.

If your investment income is **$25,000** per year and you need that money for living expenses, you can't eliminate it without cutting lifestyle. If you hold stocks that pay dividends, those dividends are taxable income whether you want them or not. If you hold bonds, interest is taxable. You can shift to municipal bonds for tax-free interest, but that doesn't reduce MAGI retroactively — it only helps future years.

Capital gains are controllable — you choose when to sell. But you can't avoid rebalancing forever. You can't freeze your portfolio and never sell anything for 20 years. At some point, you need to rebalance, harvest gains, or liquidate positions. When you do, capital gains get realized, adding to MAGI.

**Once RMDs push you close to IRMAA thresholds, staying below them requires constant vigilance and often means suboptimal financial management.** You're making investment decisions based on Medicare penalty avoidance instead of portfolio optimization. You're deferring necessary rebalancing to avoid crossing thresholds by $1,000. You're living in fear that any unexpected income will trigger penalties.

This is the reality for retirees who arrive at 73 unprepared. They spend the next 15-20 years managing income to the dollar, trying to stay $1 below cliffs, and often failing because RMD growth makes avoidance progressively harder.

**Strategic gap years conversions eliminate this stress.** Reduce your IRA balance before RMDs start. Your post-73 income stays comfortably below IRMAA thresholds without requiring constant management. You can rebalance when needed. You can realize capital gains without fear. You make financial decisions based on what's best for your portfolio, not what keeps you $500 below a Medicare penalty threshold.

## The Cascade Conclusion

RMDs force distributions. Forced distributions elevate income. Elevated income triggers IRMAA. IRMAA adds thousands per year in Medicare penalties. Those penalties repeat annually as long as RMDs keep income above thresholds. RMDs escalate with age, making the problem worse over time.

This cascade is predictable. It's avoidable. But only if you act before RMDs begin.

David and Susan learned this lesson too late. They're now 77, paying $2,296 per year in IRMAA surcharges, and they'll continue paying for the next 15-20 years. Cumulative cost: $34,000 to $46,000+ in penalties they could have avoided with $60,000 in strategic conversions during gap years. Net cost of waiting: $34,000 to $46,000 minus $60,000 = they would have broken even and started saving money by age 80.

But they didn't know. Their advisor said "wait and see." They waited. They saw their first RMD at 73. Two years later, they saw their first IRMAA surcharge notice. By then, it was too late to fix.

The RMD-IRMAA cascade is expensive. It costs **$35,000** to **$55,000** over a typical retirement for someone with a $700,000 to $1 million IRA who arrives at 73 unprepared.

But there's a third enemy that makes everything worse. RMDs elevate income. IRMAA penalizes that elevated income. Both problems intensify dramatically when one spouse dies and the survivor transitions from married filing jointly to single filer status.

Tax brackets for singles are half the width of married brackets. IRMAA thresholds for singles are half the married thresholds. Same income, doubled tax rate, doubled IRMAA risk.

This is the widow penalty. It's the third enemy. And it can cost **$20,000 to $40,000** more than RMDs and IRMAA combined because it hits when you're most vulnerable — emotionally devastated by loss of spouse, financially strained by transition to single-income household, and legally forced into tax brackets that treat your unchanged income as if you're suddenly wealthy.

Chapter 9 shows you exactly how the widow penalty works, why it's so devastating, and why arriving at widowhood with a large unconverted IRA is one of the most expensive financial mistakes a surviving spouse can inherit.

CHAPTER 9

9

# THE WIDOW PENALTY: WHEN LOSING YOUR SPOUSE DOUBLES YOUR TAX BILL

## The Year Everything Changes: Filing Status After Spouse's Death

Robert died in September 2025 at age 79. His wife Linda was 77. They'd been married 52 years.

Linda spent October and November navigating grief, funeral arrangements, estate paperwork, and the dozens of administrative tasks that follow a spouse's death. She notified Social Security, updated bank accounts, transferred titles, closed credit cards.

In early 2026, she met with her CPA to prepare her 2025 tax return. She expected it would be complicated — death always creates paperwork. What she didn't expect was the tax bill.

Her CPA explained: "You can file married filing jointly for 2025 since Robert was alive for part of the year. That's the good news. Starting in 2026, you'll file as a single taxpayer. Your tax situation is going to change significantly."

Linda didn't understand. "My income is lower now. I lost Robert's pension and half our Social Security. How can my taxes be higher?"

The CPA pulled up the 2026 bracket tables. "Let me show you what happens."

**Linda and Robert's 2025 income (Married Filing Jointly):**

- Combined Social Security: **$62,000**
- Robert's pension: **$42,000** (ceased at death)
- Linda's pension: **$28,000**
- Combined RMDs: **$48,000**
- Investment income: **$18,000**
- **Total: $198,000**

Federal tax on $198,000 for married filing jointly: approximately **$31,500** at effective rate of 16%.

**Linda's 2026 income (Single Filing):**

- Social Security (survivor benefit): **$42,000** (receives higher of her own or Robert's)

- Linda's pension: **$28,000**
- Linda's RMD: **$26,000** (her IRA only)
- Robert's inherited IRA RMD: **$22,000** (she's beneficiary)
- Investment income: **$18,000**
- **Total: $136,000**

Her income dropped by **$62,000** — nearly one-third lower than when Robert was alive.

Federal tax on $136,000 for single filing: approximately **$28,800** at effective rate of 21%.

Linda's tax bill decreased by only **$2,700** despite losing $62,000 in income. Her effective tax rate increased from 16% to 21%.

More painful: the previous year as a couple, their income from $180,000 to $200,000 was taxed at **22%** marginal rate. This year as a single filer, her income from $100,000 to $136,000 is taxed at **24% to 32%** marginal rates.

Same RMDs. Same investment income. But now she's paying higher rates because her filing status changed from married to single.

This is the widow penalty. Income decreases. Tax rates increase. The tax code treats surviving spouses more harshly than married couples despite survivors having less total household income and higher per-person expenses.

## Bracket Compression: When Tax Rates Jump Overnight

The widow penalty exists because single filer tax brackets are approximately half the width of married filing jointly brackets.

**2026 Federal Tax Brackets Comparison:**

| Tax Rate | Married Filing Jointly | Single Filer |
|---|---|---|
| 10% | $0 - $ $24,800 | $0 - $12,400 |
| 12% | $24,801 - $100,800 | $12,401 - $50,400 |
| 22% | $100,801 - $211,400 | $50,401 - $105,700 |
| 24% | $211,401 - $403,500 | $105,701 - $201,775 |
| 32% | $403,551 - $512,450 | $201.776 - $256,225 |
| 35% | $512,451 - $768,700 | $256,226 - $640,600 |
| 37% | Over $768,700 | Over $640,600 |

Notice the pattern. The 22% bracket for married couples extends to **$211,400**. For singles, it stops at **$105,700** — almost exactly half.

If you're a married couple with $150,000 in taxable income, you're solidly in the 22% bracket. If you become a widow with $120,000 in income — substantially less — you're pushed into the 24% bracket on income above **$105,700.**

The 24% bracket for married couples extends to **$403,550**. For singles, it extends to **$197,300**. Again, roughly half.

This compression means that **the same income level gets taxed at higher rates when you're single than when you're married.** You don't need higher income to reach higher brackets. Your marital status changing is enough to push you into elevated rates.

**Example 1: Moderate income retiree**

Married couple, $110,000 taxable income. They're in the 22% bracket. Marginal rate on their last dollars: **22%**.

Spouse dies. Survivor has $85,000 taxable income. They're in the 22% bracket on income up to $103,350, but that only covers $85,000. Most of their income is taxed at 12% and 22%. Effective rate: approximately **15%.**

This survivor actually benefits slightly from the bracket structure because their income dropped substantially and they stay within the lower brackets.

**Example 2: Higher income retiree (more common with RMDs)**

Married couple, $170,000 taxable income. They're in the 22% bracket. Marginal rate: **22%.**

Spouse dies. Survivor has $130,000 taxable income (lost spouse's SS/pension but kept RMDs). They're in the **24%** bracket on income from $105,701 to $130,000. That's **$24,299** of income taxed at 24% instead of 22%.

Additional tax cost: $24,299 × 2% = **$486** per year just from the bracket jump. Not devastating, but it's a permanent increase on income that used to be taxed at lower rates.

**Example 3: High-RMD retiree (the painful scenario)**

Married couple, $210,000 taxable income. They're solidly in the 22% bracket (threshold is $211,400). Marginal rate: 22%.

Spouse dies. Survivor has $155,000 taxable income. They're pushed into the 24% bracket on income from $105,701 to $155,000. That's **$49,299** of income that was taxed at 22% as a couple now taxed at 24% as a single filer.

Additional tax cost: approximately **$986** per year from bracket compression.This compounds annually for the rest of the survivor's life.

Over 15 years (if survivor lives from 78 to 93), that's **$14,790** in additional taxes purely from filing status change— money that would have stayed in the household if the couple had converted to Roth during marriage.

## The RMD Problem: Distributions Don't Decrease, But Brackets Do

The widow penalty is amplified by RMD rules. When one spouse dies, the surviving spouse's RMD obligation doesn't decrease proportionally.

**Scenario: Married couple, both 78, both have IRAs**

- Husband's IRA: **$600,000**. RMD: **$29,700**
- Wife's IRA: **$400,000**. RMD: **$19,800**
- Combined household RMDs: **$49,500**

They file married filing jointly. $49,500 in RMDs added to their other income keeps them in the 22-24% bracket range. Manageable.

**Husband dies. Wife is now 79, filing as single.**

Wife's own IRA: **$400,000** (slightly grown). RMD at age 79: **$18,400** based on her divisor of 21.8.

Husband's IRA: Wife inherits as beneficiary. She can:

- Option 1: Roll it into her own IRA (if she's the sole beneficiary)
- Option 2: Keep it as an inherited IRA with separate RMD calculation

Most advisors recommend Option 1 — consolidate into her own IRA. New combined balance: **$1,000,000**.

Her RMD at 79 on $1 million: **$45,900**.

Notice: **The household RMD barely decreased.** It went from $49,500 when both were alive to $45,900 with only one survivor. That's only a **$3,600** decrease — 7% reduction.

But her income dropped significantly more:

- Lost husband's Social Security: **-$31,000**
- Lost husband's pension: **-$42,000**
- Total income lost: **-$73,000**

Her RMD decreased by $3,600 while her other income decreased by $73,000. She's lost **$69,400** in net income.

Yet her tax brackets compressed. Income that was taxed at 22% married is now taxed at 24-32% single. She has substantially less money coming in, but a higher percentage goes to taxes.

This is the structural unfairness of the widow penalty. The tax code doesn't account for the economic reality that surviving spouses often have similar fixed costs (housing, healthcare, property taxes) but dramatically reduced income. Instead, it treats them as if transitioning to single status makes them financially better off.

## Real Example: $180K Income as Couple, $123K as Widow

Let's walk through a complete example with real numbers to illustrate how this works in practice.

**James and Carol, both age 78 in 2024:**

Annual income (Married Filing Jointly):

- Combined Social Security: **$58,000**
- James's pension: **$38,000**
- Carol's pension: **$24,000**
- Combined RMDs (James $28K + Carol $17K): **$45,000**
- Investment income: **$15,000**
- **Total MAGI: $180,000**

2024 federal tax (MFJ, $180,000 income): approximately **$26,400**. Effective rate: 14.7%. Marginal rate on RMDs: **22%**.

They pay standard Medicare premiums. No IRMAA — their income is well below the **$218,000** threshold.

Life is comfortable. Not extravagant, but financially secure.

**James dies in October 2025. Carol is now 79, filing as single starting in 2026.**

2026 income (Single Filing):

- Social Security survivor benefit: **$38,000** (receives James's higher benefit)
- Carol's pension: **$24,000**
- Carol's RMD (her IRA): **$17,500**
- James's inherited IRA RMD: **$28,900**
- Investment income: **$15,000**
- **Total MAGI: $123,400**

Her income decreased by **$56,600** — nearly one-third lower.

2026 federal tax (Single, $123,400 income): approximately **$22,100**. Effective rate: 17.9%. Marginal rate on RMDs: **24-32%**.

Her tax bill decreased by only **$4,300** despite losing $56,600 in income.

**The widow penalty in action:**

As a couple earning $180,000, they paid **$26,400** in federal tax. As a widow earning $123,400 — **31% less income** — Carol pays **$22,100** in federal tax. Her tax decreased by only **16%** despite income decreasing by **31%**.

Her effective tax rate increased from 14.7% to 17.9% — a **3.2 percentage point jump**.

## The Tax Rate Shock: From 22% to 32% on Same RMD

Carol's situation illustrates the bracket compression problem, but it doesn't show the full magnitude of the widow penalty for higher-income retirees. Let's examine a more severe case.

**Margaret and Paul, both age 80 in 2025:**

Annual income (Married Filing Jointly):

- Combined Social Security: **$68,000**
- Paul's pension: **$52,000**
- Margaret's pension: **$36,000**
- Combined RMDs (Paul $48K + Margaret $32K): **$80,000**
- Investment income: **$28,000**
- **Total MAGI: $264,000**

2025 federal tax (MFJ, $264,000 income): approximately **$47,200**. Effective rate: 17.9%. Marginal rate on last dollars of income: **24%**.

They're in IRMAA Tier 2 — income exceeds **$274,000** in some years depending on investment income volatility, but typically hover in Tier 1 at **$218,000 to $274,000** range. Annual Medicare cost for couple: approximately **$7,166** with IRMAA surcharges included.

**Paul dies in November 2025. Margaret is now 81, filing as single starting in 2026.**

2026 income (Single Filing):

- Social Security survivor benefit: **$48,000** (Paul's higher benefit)
- Margaret's pension: **$36,000**
- Margaret's RMD (her IRA): **$33,000**
- Paul's inherited IRA RMD: **$49,500**
- Investment income: **$28,000**
- **Total MAGI: $194,500**

Her income decreased by **$69,500** — more than 26% lower.

2026 federal tax (Single, $194,500 income): approximately **$43,800**. Effective rate: 22.5%. Marginal rate on income above $103,350: **32%**.

Her tax bill decreased by only **$3,400** despite losing $69,500 in income.

**The marginal rate shock:**

Look at what happened to Margaret's RMDs specifically. When Paul was alive, their **$80,000** in combined RMDs was taxed at **24%** marginal rate — the couple's income put them solidly in the 24% bracket.

After Paul's death, Margaret's **$82,500** in combined RMDs (her own plus inherited) is now taxed at rates ranging from **24% to 32%** because she's a single filer.

Income from $103,351 to $194,500 — which includes most of her RMDs — is taxed at **24%** up to $197,300 threshold, then the final dollars approach **32%** bracket territory.

Her RMDs barely changed in dollar terms — $80,000 as a couple became $82,500 as a widow. But the tax rate on those RMDs increased from **24%** to **24-32%** due solely to filing status change.

**Annual additional cost from widow penalty:** approximately **$6,400** per year compared to what the couple would have paid on the same income.

If Margaret lives from age 81 to 93 (12 years), the cumulative additional cost is **$76,800** — money extracted purely by bracket compression, not by any change in her financial circumstances other than Paul's death.

## IRMAA Amplification: Half the Threshold, Same Income

The widow penalty doesn't just affect income taxes. It dramatically increases IRMAA risk.

**IRMAA thresholds for 2026:**

- Married Filing Jointly, Tier 1: **$218,000**
- Single Filer, Tier 1: **$109,000**

The single filer threshold is exactly half the married threshold. This creates a trap for widows whose income doesn't decrease proportionally to the threshold change.

**Example: Patricia and Edward, both 77 in 2025**

Combined income (MFJ): **$205,000**

- Social Security: **$62,000**
- Pensions: **$76,000**
- RMDs: **$52,000**
- Investment income: **$15,000**

They're **$13,000** below the IRMAA threshold. Safe. Standard Medicare premiums only: **$4,870** annually for both.

**Edward dies in December 2025. Patricia is 78, filing single in 2026.**

Patricia's 2026 income (Single):

- Social Security survivor benefit: **$42,000**
- Patricia's pension: **$38,000**
- Patricia's RMD (own IRA): **$28,000**
- Edward's inherited IRA RMD: **$26,000**
- Investment income: **$15,000**
- **Total MAGI: $149,000**

Her income dropped from $205,000 to $149,000 — a **$56,000** decrease, more than 27% lower.

But the single filer IRMAA threshold is **$109,000**. She's now **$40,000 over** the threshold despite having substantially less income than when Edward was alive.

IRMAA Tier triggered: Tier 1 at minimum, possibly Tier 2 depending on how far over $137,000 she goes.

2026 Medicare cost as single filer with IRMAA Tier 1: **$3,583** annually just for her. This is **47%** higher than the **$2,435** standard premium.

**The IRMAA trap in numbers:**

As a couple with $205,000 income: No IRMAA, $4,870 total Medicare cost.
As a widow with $149,000 income: IRMAA triggered, $3,583 Medicare cost for one person.

She lost a spouse. Her household income dropped **27%**. Her Medicare costs dropped by only **26%** ($4,870 to $3,583), and she's now paying IRMAA surcharges she never paid as part of a couple.

If her income edges above **$137,000** — which it easily could with RMD growth or a strong investment year — she jumps to IRMAA Tier 2, costing **$5,320** annually. That's **9% more** than the couple paid combined when Edward was alive, despite her income being 27% lower.

**Over 10 years (ages 78-87), Patricia will pay approximately $11,480 in IRMAA surcharges** she wouldn't have paid if Edward had survived or if they had converted sufficient IRA balances to Roth during marriage to keep her post-widow income under $109,000.

## The Compounding Effect: Widow Penalty + RMD Growth + IRMAA

The widow penalty doesn't stay constant. It worsens over time as RMDs escalate.

Margaret from our earlier example had $194,500 in income at age 81 as a new widow. By age 85, her RMDs will grow to approximately **$95,000** (her own plus inherited IRA). Her total income will be approximately **$207,000**.

At 85 as a single filer with $207,000 income:

- She's pushed into the **32%** bracket on all income above $201,775

- She's in IRMAA Tier 2 ($137,001-$171,000 for singles), paying **$5,320** annually
- Her effective tax rate is approximately **24%**
- Her marginal rate on RMDs: **32%**

Compare this to what she and Paul would have paid as a couple at the same age with similar combined income. As married filers with $207,000 income:

- They'd be in the **24%** bracket
- They'd be under the **$218,000** IRMAA threshold (depending on that year's inflation adjustments)
- Combined federal tax: approximately **$33,000**
- No IRMAA surcharges

Margaret alone pays approximately $50,000 in federal tax plus $5,320 in IRMAA. Total: **$55,320.**

The couple would have paid approximately **$33,000** in federal tax and possibly no IRMAA. Total: **$33,000 to $38,000** depending on IRMAA status.

Margaret pays **$17,300 to $22,300** more annually than the couple would have paid on similar income.. This repeats every year for the rest of her life.

Over 10 years from age 85 to 94, assuming she lives that long, Margaret will pay approximately **$173,000 to $223,000** more in combined taxes and IRMAA than the couple would have paid on equivalent income.

This is the compounding widow penalty. RMDs grow with age. Single filer brackets are compressed. IRMAA thresholds are halved. All three factors compound to create exponentially increasing costs for the surviving spouse.

## The Roth Protection: How Conversions Shield Surviving Spouse

Strategic gap years conversions don't just reduce your taxes during your lifetime. They protect your spouse from the widow penalty.

**Return to Margaret and Paul's situation, but with a different history:**

From ages 65-72, Margaret and Paul converted **$600,000** from traditional IRAs to Roth. They paid approximately **$132,000** in conversion taxes over those eight years at effective rates of 18-22%.

At age 80 when Paul died, their IRA structure was:

- Margaret's traditional IRA: **$400,000** (reduced from $750,000)
- Paul's traditional IRA: **$350,000** (reduced from $650,000)
- Combined Roth IRA: **$650,000** (converted amount plus growth)

Margaret's 2026 income after Paul's death (Single Filing):

- Social Security survivor benefit: **$48,000**

- Margaret's pension: **$36,000**
- Margaret's traditional IRA RMD: **$24,500** (from reduced $400K balance)
- Paul's inherited traditional IRA RMD: **$21,400** (from reduced $350K balance)
- Roth IRA withdrawals: **$35,000** (tax-free, doesn't count in MAGI)
- Investment income: **$20,000**
- **Total MAGI: $149,900**

Total spendable income: **$184,900** ($149,900 MAGI + $35,000 Roth withdrawals).

Compare to original scenario where Margaret had $194,500 MAGI with no Roth conversions and no Roth withdrawals.

With strategic conversions:

- Margaret's MAGI is **$44,600 lower** ($194,500 vs $149,900)
- She stays in the **24%** bracket instead of touching **32%**
- She's in IRMAA Tier 1 instead of Tier 2
- Her annual federal tax: approximately **$28,500** instead of $43,800
- Her annual Medicare cost: **$3,583** (Tier 1) instead of **$5,320** (Tier 2)

**Annual savings from strategic conversions: $17,037** in combined tax and IRMAA reductions.

Over 12 years (ages 81-92), cumulative savings: **$204,444**.

They paid $132,000 in conversion taxes. Margaret saves $204,444 as a widow. Net lifetime benefit: **$72,444**.

But the benefit extends beyond dollars. Margaret has **$35,000** per year in tax-free Roth withdrawals she can access without increasing her taxable income. She has flexibility to take more if needed for medical expenses, home repairs, or helping family without triggering additional taxes or pushing into higher IRMAA tiers.

**The Roth conversions Paul and Margaret executed during marriage became a spousal protection strategy.** Paul didn't just reduce his own taxes. He shielded Margaret from the widow penalty that would have devastated her financially during the most emotionally difficult period of her life.

## The Emotional-Financial Timing

The widow penalty hits when you're least prepared to deal with it.

Losing a spouse is emotionally catastrophic. The first year involves grief, adjustment, loneliness, and practical challenges of managing a household alone. The last thing a widow needs during this period is a surprise tax increase and Medicare penalties.

Yet that's exactly when the widow penalty strikes. Margaret lost Paul in November 2025. In April

2026 — five months later, still deep in grief — she met with her CPA and discovered her tax bill had barely decreased despite losing $69,500 in income. In October 2026, she received an IRMAA notice explaining her Medicare premiums were increasing for 2027 because her 2025 income exceeded single filer thresholds.

She's dealing with financial penalties while mourning her husband. The tax code doesn't care about her emotional state. The brackets compress. IRMAA triggers. The bills arrive.

**Strategic gap years conversions prevent this trauma.** When Paul and Margaret converted during marriage, they eliminated the surprise. Margaret knew she'd be financially stable as a widow. No sudden tax increases. No IRMAA penalties. No financial stress compounding emotional devastation.

This is why we emphasize gap years conversions as a spousal protection strategy, not just personal tax optimization. You're not just reducing your lifetime taxes. You're protecting your spouse from financial harm during the most vulnerable period of their life.

RMDs force distributions you don't need. IRMAA penalizes income you didn't choose. The widow penalty doubles both problems when your spouse dies. These three enemies don't operate independently — they compound, amplify, and accelerate each other's damage to your retirement finances. Chapter 10 shows you exactly how all three enemies interact to create the perfect storm that destroys retirement plans when you arrive at 73 unprepared, and why the $75,000 to $150,000 lifetime cost we calculated in Chapter 6 is conservative when widow penalty and enemy interaction are fully accounted for.

CHAPTER 10

10

# THE COMPOUNDING EFFECT: WHY THESE THREE ENEMIES GET WORSE EVERY YEAR YOU WAIT

## The Three Enemies Recap: What You're Up Against

You now understand the forces working against your retirement finances.

**Enemy #1: Required Minimum Distributions** start at age 73. The IRS mandates you withdraw a percentage of your traditional IRA annually. That percentage starts at 3.77% and escalates to 8.20% by age 90. You cannot pause, skip, or reduce these distributions. They're forced income whether you need the money or not. Miss your RMD and you face a 25% penalty on the shortfall.

**Enemy #2: IRMAA — Income-Related Monthly Adjustment Amount** — adds Medicare surcharges when your Modified Adjusted Gross Income exceeds thresholds. For married couples filing jointly, the first cliff is $218,000. Cross it by $1 and you pay **$2,296** per year in additional Medicare premiums. The surcharges escalate through five tiers, reaching $16,510 annually at the highest level. IRMAA uses a two-year lookback, creating delayed consequences you can't course-correct quickly.

**Enemy #3: The widow penalty** hits when one spouse dies and the survivor transitions from married filing jointly to single filing status. Single tax brackets are half the width of married brackets. The survivor pays higher marginal rates on the same income. IRMAA thresholds for singles are also halved — $109,000 instead of $218,000. The survivor's RMDs don't decrease proportionally when the spouse dies, but the tax brackets do. Income drops 30%, but taxes drop only 10-15%.

Each enemy is expensive individually. RMDs force distributions taxed at 24-32% rates over 20 years. IRMAA adds $30,000 to $50,000 in Medicare penalties over a decade. The widow penalty increases taxes by $4,000 to $8,000 annually for 10-15 years after the first spouse dies.

But these enemies don't operate in isolation. They interact, amplify, and accelerate each other's damage.

## How the Enemies Interact and Amplify

The three enemies form a cascade where each problem creates conditions that worsen the others.

**RMDs create the foundation for the cascade.** At 73, forced distributions elevate your taxable income. That elevated income pushes you closer to or over IRMAA thresholds. The RMDs grow annually as you age, continuously increasing income pressure.

**IRMAA amplifies RMD damage.** A $35,000 RMD doesn't just cost you $8,400 in federal income tax at 24% rate. If that RMD pushes your total income from $215,000 to $250,000, you've crossed the $218,000 IRMAA threshold. Now the RMD costs $8,400 in tax plus $2,296 in IRMAA surcharges. Total cost: $10,696. The IRMAA penalty increased the effective cost of the RMD by 27%.

**The widow penalty multiplies both problems.** When the first spouse dies, the survivor files as single. Tax brackets compress. A $30,000 RMD that was taxed at 22% as part of a married couple is now taxed at 24-32% as a single filer. IRMAA thresholds drop from $218,000 to $109,000. The same RMD that didn't trigger IRMAA before now triggers it after widow status change. The $30,000 RMD that cost $6,600 in taxes as a couple now costs $7,200 to $9,600 in taxes as a widow, plus $1,148 to $2,885 in IRMAA surcharges.

**The multiplication effect:**

Consider a couple at 78 with $180,000 annual income including $45,000 in RMDs. Federal tax: approximately $26,400. No IRMAA — income well below threshold. Combined cost: $26,400 annually.

First spouse dies. Survivor at 79 has $130,000 income including $46,000 in RMDs (inherited plus own). Federal tax as single filer: approximately $24,500. IRMAA triggered because single threshold is $109,000: $3,583 annually. Combined cost: $28,083 annually.

Income dropped 28%. Combined tax and IRMAA costs increased 6%. The survivor is paying more than the couple despite having substantially less household income.

Now project forward. At 85, the survivor's RMDs have grown to $60,000. Total income: $144,000. Federal tax: $30,200. IRMAA Tier 2 triggered: $5,320. Combined: $35,520 annually.

Six years later, annual costs increased from $28,083 to $35,520 — a $7,437 increase — driven entirely by RMD growth pushing deeper into compressed single-filer brackets and higher IRMAA tiers.

**The cascade visualization:**

Large IRA at 73 → Large RMDs forced → Income elevated → Higher tax brackets triggered → IRMAA thresholds crossed → Medicare penalties added → First spouse dies → Widow status compresses brackets → Same RMDs taxed at higher rates → IRMAA more easily triggered → Cumulative costs compound annually → $100,000 to $200,000+ lifetime damage.

Each step in this cascade makes the next step worse. You cannot interrupt the cascade once RMDs begin because distributions are mandatory. You cannot avoid bracket compression when you become a widow. You cannot escape IRMAA if your income exceeds thresholds.

**The only intervention point is before the cascade starts** — during gap years, when you can reduce IRA balance through strategic conversions before RMDs begin.

## The Cost of Waiting: Year 1, Year 3, Year 5

Waiting to convert isn't neutral. Each year of delay makes the problem worse because your IRA continues growing while your gap years window shrinks.

**Baseline scenario:** You're 65 in 2026. IRA balance: $700,000. Baseline retirement income: $85,000. You're in gap years. You should be converting.

### Year 1 delay: Age 65 to 66

You decide to "wait and see" for one year. Your advisor says there's no rush now that OBBBA made brackets permanent.

During that year:

- Your IRA grows at 5%: $700,000 becomes $735,000
- You lose one gap year of conversion capacity
- Conversion capacity lost: approximately $55,000 (amount you could have converted while staying in 22% bracket)

At 66, you finally start converting. But your IRA is now $735,000 instead of $700,000. Over your remaining seven gap years (ages 66-72), you convert $55,000 per year for seven years: $385,000 total.

At 73, your remaining IRA balance: $350,000 (simplified calculation).

Compare to starting at 65: you would have converted $55,000 per year for eight years: $440,000 total. Remaining balance at 73: $260,000.

**The difference:** Waiting one year means arriving at 73 with $90,000 more in traditional IRA. Your first RMD is $3,400 higher. Over 20 years, that translates to approximately $18,000 to $22,000 in additional taxes you'll pay on RMDs from that unconverted $90,000.

One year of delay. Lifetime cost: $18,000 to $22,000.

### Year 3 delay: Age 65 to 68

You wait three years. Your advisor keeps saying "we have time, let's be thorough."

During those three years:

- Your IRA grows from $700,000 to $810,000 (5% annually compounded)
- You lose three gap years of conversion capacity
- Conversion capacity lost: approximately $165,000 ($55,000 × 3 years)

At 68, you start converting. You have five gap years remaining (ages 68-72). You convert $55,000 per year: $275,000 total.

At 73, your remaining IRA balance: $535,000.

Compare to starting at 65: you would have converted $440,000 over eight years. Remaining balance: $260,000.

**The difference:** Waiting three years means arriving at 73 with $275,000 more in traditional IRA. Your first RMD is $10,400 higher annually. Over 20 years, that translates to approximately $55,000 to $70,000 in additional taxes.

Three years of delay. Lifetime cost: $55,000 to $70,000.

Notice: three years of delay doesn't cost 3× what one year costs ($22,000 × 3 = $66,000). It costs $55,000 to $70,000 — closer to 2.5-3× the one-year cost. This is because the IRA balance compounds during the delay period, and the larger balance at 73 produces exponentially larger cumulative RMDs over 20 years.

## Year 5 delay: Age 65 to 70

You wait five years. You keep "gathering information" and "wanting to be certain."

During those five years:

- Your IRA grows from $700,000 to $895,000
- You lose five gap years
- Conversion capacity lost: approximately $275,000

At 70, you finally start converting. You have three gap years remaining (ages 70-72). You convert $55,000 per year: $165,000 total.

At 73, your remaining IRA balance: $730,000.

Compare to starting at 65: $260,000 remaining balance.

**The difference:** Waiting five years means arriving at 73 with $470,000 more in traditional IRA. Your first RMD is $17,700 higher annually.

But it's worse than that. With $730,000 remaining at 73, your RMDs will likely push you over IRMAA thresholds by age 78-80. The couple who started at 65 with $260,000 remaining avoids IRMAA entirely.

Lifetime cost of five-year delay: $90,000 to $120,000 in additional taxes, plus $20,000 to $35,000 in IRMAA penalties over 10-15 years. Total: $110,000 to $155,000.

Five years of delay doesn't cost 5× what one year costs. It costs 5-7× as much because of IRMAA amplification that only triggers with larger RMDs from the higher IRA balance.

## The Cascade Effect: One Problem Creates Five

The year-by-year delay costs show the arithmetic. The cascade shows the mechanism behind those costs.

Let's trace the complete cascade for someone who waits five years to start converting.

**Stage 1: IRA growth during delay (ages 65-70)**

You're 65 with a $700,000 IRA. You wait five years. Markets return 5% annually. Your IRA grows to $895,000 by age 70. You think: "Good news, my retirement account is growing."

But that growth is creating future tax liability. Every dollar of growth in a traditional IRA is another dollar that will eventually be distributed and taxed. The $195,000 in growth you accumulated during five years of waiting will be forced out through RMDs starting at 73, taxed at rates you cannot control.

**Stage 2: Reduced conversion capacity (ages 70-72)**

You finally start converting at 70. But you only have three gap years remaining before RMDs begin. You can convert approximately $55,000 per year for three years: $165,000 total.

If you had started at 65, you would have had eight gap years. You could have converted $440,000 — nearly 3× as much.

The five-year delay didn't just cost you five years. It cost you $275,000 in conversion capacity you can never recover.

**Stage 3: Larger RMDs trigger (age 73)**

You arrive at 73 with $730,000 in traditional IRA. Your first RMD: $27,547.

If you had started conversions at 65, you'd arrive at 73 with $260,000 in traditional IRA. Your first RMD: $9,811.

The difference: $17,736 more in forced annual distributions. This isn't optional income you can decline. The IRS mandates it. You must take it and pay taxes on it.

**Stage 4: Higher tax brackets activated (ages 73-85)**

Your baseline retirement income is $85,000 — Social Security, pension, investment income. Adding the $27,547 RMD brings total income to $112,547. You're in the 22% bracket, approaching 24%.

The person who converted during gap years has baseline income of $85,000 plus $9,811 RMD: $94,811 total. They're comfortably in the 22% bracket with substantial room before reaching 24%.

At age 78, your RMD has grown to $32,500. Total income: $117,500. You're now in the 24% bracket on income above the 22% threshold.

The strategic converter's RMD at 78: $11,600. Total income: $96,600. Still in 22% bracket.

**Tax differential at age 78:** You pay approximately $2,500 more in federal income tax annually just from the higher bracket your larger RMDs pushed you into.

**Stage 5: IRMAA threshold approach (ages 80-85)**

By age 80, your RMD is $36,100. Total income: $121,100. You're $97,000 below the $218,000 IRMAA threshold. Still safe.

But wait — we calculated baseline income as $85,000. That's today. Social Security increases with inflation at approximately 2.5% annually. Pensions may have cost-of-living adjustments. Investment income grows as portfolios compound.

By age 80, your baseline income isn't $85,000 anymore. It's approximately $105,000 accounting for 15 years of inflation adjustments from age 65.

Actual total income at 80: $105,000 baseline + $36,100 RMD = $141,100.

At 85, baseline income is approximately $118,000. Your RMD is $45,600. Total: $163,600.

You're still below IRMAA threshold. But you're getting closer. Any year with unexpected income — selling a property, large capital gains from rebalancing, inherited IRA distributions from a parent who died — pushes you over.

The strategic converter at 85: baseline $118,000 + RMD $14,500 = $132,500 total. They're $85,500 below threshold. They have cushion. You don't.

**Stage 6: Widow penalty activation (age 80, assuming spouse dies)**

You're 80. Your spouse dies. You transition from married filing jointly to single filing.

Your income: $132,000 (you lost spouse's Social Security and pension, but kept RMDs). As a single filer, income above $103,350 is taxed at 24-32%. Your RMD of $36,000 is now taxed at higher marginal rates than when you were married.

Federal tax as married couple at age 79: $18,500. Federal tax as widow at age 80: $24,200. Increase: $5,700 annually despite income decreasing by $40,000.

The strategic converter who is widowed at 80: income $105,000. RMD $14,500. Federal tax: $17,800. Their tax bill decreased appropriately when income dropped because their smaller RMDs kept them in lower single-filer brackets.

**Stage 7: IRMAA trigger in widow status (ages 82-90)**

As a single filer, the IRMAA threshold is $109,000. Your income is $132,000. You're $23,000 over.

IRMAA Tier 1 for single filer: $3,583 annually. You now pay $24,200 in federal tax plus $3,583 in IRMAA: $27,783 combined.

Before spouse died (age 79 as couple): $18,500 total tax, no IRMAA.
After spouse died (age 80+ as widow): $27,783 combined tax and IRMAA.

Your costs increased by $9,283 annually — 50% higher — despite your household income decreasing by $40,000 when your spouse died.

The strategic converter as widow: income $105,000. Just $4,000 below IRMAA threshold. They manage capital gains carefully, avoid unnecessary distributions, and stay under. No IRMAA triggered. Annual cost: $17,800. No penalties.

**Stage 8: Tier escalation (ages 85-92)**

Your RMDs continue growing. By 85, they're $48,000. Total income as widow: $145,000. You've crossed into IRMAA Tier 2 at $137,001. New annual IRMAA cost: $5,320.

Combined federal tax and IRMAA: approximately $33,500 annually.

By age 90, RMD is $62,000. Income: $159,000. IRMAA Tier 2 persists. Combined costs: $38,800 annually.

The strategic converter at 90: RMD $19,800. Income: $117,000. Stays in Tier 1. Combined costs: $21,500 annually.

**The cascade in full:**

Waited five years → IRA grew to $895,000 → Converted only $165,000 → Arrived at 73 with $730,000 → RMDs $27,500+ annually → Pushed into 24% bracket → Approached IRMAA proximity → Spouse died → Single filer status compressed brackets → Same RMDs now taxed 24-32% → IRMAA triggered at $109,000 threshold → Tier 1 costs $3,110/year → RMDs escalated with age → Pushed into Tier 2 at $4,644/year → Cumulative cost ages 73-92: approximately $520,000 in combined federal tax and IRMAA.

Strategic converter who started at 65: Cumulative cost ages 73-92: approximately $330,000.

**Difference: $190,000 over 20 years** from five years of delay.

The five-year delay didn't just cost you five years of time. It triggered a 20-year cascade where each problem compounded the next, ultimately costing $190,000 in lifetime taxes and penalties.

## The Exponential Math: Why Delay Isn't Linear

Most people assume delay costs are linear. Wait two years, pay 2× the cost of waiting one year. Wait five years, pay 5× the cost.

The math doesn't work that way. Delay costs are exponential because the three enemies amplify each other.

**Linear thinking (incorrect):**

- 1-year delay costs: $20,000
- 2-year delay costs: $40,000
- 5-year delay costs: $100,000

**Exponential reality:**

- 1-year delay costs: $20,000
- 2-year delay costs: $45,000 (2.25× the 1-year cost)
- 5-year delay costs: $155,000 (7.75× the 1-year cost)

Why the exponential curve?

## Compounding factor 1: IRA growth during delay

Your IRA doesn't stay flat while you wait. It grows. Each year of 5% growth adds another layer to the balance that will eventually be distributed and taxed.

Wait one year: IRA grows from $700,000 to $735,000. Extra $35,000 subject to RMDs.

Wait five years: IRA grows from $700,000 to $895,000. Extra $195,000 subject to RMDs.

That's not 5× the one-year growth ($35,000 × 5 = $175,000). It's $195,000 because growth compounds annually. Year 5's growth is calculated on a base inflated by years 1-4.

## Compounding factor 2: Lost conversion capacity

Wait one year: lose $55,000 in conversion capacity.
Wait five years: lose $275,000 in capacity.

That's exactly 5× — linear so far. But here's the compound effect: the $275,000 you didn't convert continues growing in your traditional IRA. By age 73, that unconverted $275,000 has become approximately $320,000 (five years of growth at 5%). That $320,000 produces larger RMDs, which trigger higher brackets and IRMAA.

## Compounding factor 3: IRMAA threshold proximity

Small IRA at 73 keeps you far below IRMAA thresholds. Large IRA pushes you close. Proximity matters because one unexpected income event — capital gains, property sale, bonus — pushes you over when you're close but not when you have cushion.

Wait one year: arrive at 73 with $350,000 IRA. First RMD $13,200. Total income $98,200. IRMAA cushion: $120,000.

Wait five years: arrive at 73 with $730,000 IRA. First RMD $27,500. Total income $112,500. IRMAA cushion: $105,500.

Your cushion is only $14,500 smaller, but RMD growth over the next 10 years erodes that cushion much faster when starting from $730,000 than from $350,000.

At age 82, the five-year delayer is over IRMAA threshold. The one-year delayer still has cushion. The five-year delayer pays IRMAA for 10-15 years. The one-year delayer avoids it entirely or triggers only in the final few years of life.

IRMAA penalty from five-year delay: $30,000 to $45,000 over lifetime. IRMAA penalty from one-year delay: $0 to $8,000.

That's not 5× linear. That's threshold-crossing triggering binary cost.

## Compounding factor 4: Widow penalty amplification

Small RMDs as a widow: manageable tax increase when spouse dies. Large RMDs as a widow: substantial tax increase plus IRMAA trigger.

One-year delayer becomes widow: RMD $14,000, income $105,000 as single filer. Tax increase from widow status: $3,200 annually. No IRMAA.

Five-year delayer becomes widow: RMD $36,000, income $132,000. Tax increase: $7,500 annually. IRMAA triggered: $3,110 annually. Combined: $10,610 annual increase.

The five-year delayer doesn't pay 5× what the one-year delayer pays as a widow. They pay 3.3× as much ($10,610 vs $3,200), and that differential persists for 10-15 years of widowhood.

## The Point of Maximum Damage (Ages 73-75)

The enemies reach maximum combined strength when you arrive at ages 73-75 with a large unconverted IRA, both spouses on Medicare, and retirement income already in higher brackets.

**The perfect storm conditions:**

**Condition 1: RMDs have just started (age 73-75)** You've lost the ability to control distributions. The IRS now mandates annual withdrawals. Your first RMDs are manageable — 3.77% to 4.07% of balance — but they establish the baseline for decades of escalation ahead.

**Condition 2: Both spouses are on Medicare (ages 65+)** IRMAA penalties are active. Any income above thresholds triggers immediate surcharges. You're paying attention to Medicare costs for the first time and discovering that income affects premiums.

**Condition 3: Retirement income has inflated (after 8-10 years of retirement)** Your Social Security has received 8-10 years of cost-of-living adjustments. If you retired at 65, by 73 your baseline income has increased 15-20% from inflation alone. Pensions with COLA adjustments have also grown. What was $85,000 at 65 is now $98,000 at 73 before RMDs even start.

**Condition 4: Gap years have closed** You can no longer execute strategic conversions at low rates. Any conversion now happens on top of elevated baseline income plus mandatory RMDs. Converting $50,000 at age 74 costs 24-28% instead of the 18-22% it would have cost at age 67.

**Condition 5: Both spouses are still alive** The couple is filing married filing jointly with wider brackets and higher IRMAA thresholds. They have some protection. But one spouse will die within the next 10-15 years statistically, triggering widow penalty. The decisions made now — or not made during gap years — determine how devastating that transition will be.

**The damage calculation at peak:**

Take a couple, both 74, who waited through all their gap years without converting.

IRA balance at 73: $950,000. First RMD: $35,850. Baseline income: $100,000. Total income: $135,850.

Federal tax: approximately $22,500. No IRMAA yet — income is $82,000 below threshold. Combined annual cost: $22,500.

This seems manageable. They're thinking: "Our advisor was right, we didn't need to rush."

But the storm is building. Watch what happens over the next 10 years:

**Age 75**: RMD $38,600. Income $138,600. Tax $23,800.

**Age 77**: RMD $43,200. Income $143,200. Tax $26,100.

**Age 79**: RMD $48,100. Income $153,100 (baseline has inflated to $105,000). Tax $28,900.

**Age 80**: First spouse dies. Survivor's income: $128,000 (lost spouse's SS/pension, kept RMDs). Tax as single filer: $25,200. IRMAA triggered: $3,583. Combined: $28,783.

**Age 82**: Survivor's RMD $51,500. Income $134,500. Tax $27,800. IRMAA Tier 1: $3,583. Combined: $31,383.

**Age 84**: Age 84: RMD $57,000. Income $140,000. Tax $30,500. IRMAA Tier 2 triggered at $137,001: $5,320. Combined: $35,820.

From age 74 to 84, their annual costs increased from $22,500 to $35,820 — a $13,320 increase, 59% higher.

**Compare to a couple who converted $400,000 during gap years:**

IRA balance at 73: $550,000. First RMD: $20,750. Baseline income: $100,000. Total income: $120,750.

Federal tax: $17,200. No IRMAA — income $97,000 below threshold. Combined: $17,200.

**Age 80 as widow**: RMD $27,200. Income $110,000. Tax as single: $19,600. No IRMAA — just $1,000 below threshold but manageable with careful income planning. Combined: $19,600.

**Age 84**: Age 84: RMD $33,000. Income $116,000. Tax $21,800. IRMAA Tier 1: $3,583.

Combined: $25,383.

Their annual costs at 84: $25,383. The couple who didn't convert: $35,820.

Difference at age 84: $10,437 annually. Over 10 years from age 84-93, that's $104,370 in cumulative additional costs for the couple who waited.

**Ages 73-75 represent the point of maximum damage** because this is when all preconditions are met and the cascade is actively accelerating. The damage at 74 doesn't look catastrophic — $22,500 in annual costs. But the trajectory from 74 to 84 reveals the true cost: escalation to $35,144 annually with no way to stop it.

### Is There a "Too Late" Point?

We've emphasized urgency throughout Act II. But what if you're already 70, 71, or 72? Have you missed the window entirely?

**The honest answer: It depends on your situation, but meaningful conversions are still possible — barely.**

**If you're 70 in 2026:**

You have **three gap years** remaining (ages 70, 71, 72) before RMDs start at 73. You can still execute strategic conversions, but the timeline is compressed.

Three years of converting $50,000 to $60,000 annually gives you $150,000 to $180,000 total converted. If your IRA is $800,000, that's a 19-23% reduction. Not comprehensive, but meaningful.

Your RMD at 73 will be $23,400 instead of $30,200 — a $6,800 annual reduction. Over 20 years, that saves approximately $35,000 to $45,000 in taxes and potentially avoids IRMAA triggers worth another $10,000 to $20,000.

You paid approximately $30,000 to $36,000 in conversion taxes over three years. Break-even occurs around age 80-82. If you live to 90, you realize $15,000 to $29,000 in net lifetime savings.

**Verdict at 70: Not too late, but urgent. You must start within the next 90 days and execute consistently for three years.**

**If you're 71 in 2026:**

Two gap years remaining. You can convert $100,000 to $120,000 total. On an $800,000 IRA, that's a 13-15% reduction.

RMD reduction: $4,000 to $5,000 annually. Lifetime savings: $20,000 to $35,000 in taxes. Conversion cost: $20,000 to $24,000.

Break-even: age 82-84. Net benefit if you live to 90: $5,000 to $15,000.

**Verdict at 71: Marginal but worthwhile if you expect to live into your late 80s or 90s. You must execute immediately — no time for multi-month planning.**

**If you're 72 in 2026:**

One gap year remaining. You can convert $50,000 to $60,000 before RMDs begin.

This is barely worth it from a pure tax arbitrage perspective. You'll pay $10,000 to $12,000 in conversion taxes to save $15,000 to $25,000 over 20 years. Break-even won't occur until age 85-87.

But there's one scenario where it makes sense: **IRMAA cliff avoidance**. If your projected income at 73 is $210,000 to $220,000 and one RMD will push you over the $218,000 threshold, converting $50,000 now might reduce your 73-year-old RMD enough to stay under. That single conversion could prevent 10-15 years of IRMAA penalties worth $20,000 to $40,000.

**Verdict at 72: Only worthwhile if IRMAA avoidance is the specific goal. Otherwise, the window is effectively closed for comprehensive strategy.**

**If you're 73+ in 2026:**

Gap years have closed. RMDs have begun. Post-RMD conversions are tax-inefficient because you're converting from an elevated income baseline (your forced RMD plus other income) instead of the low baseline you had during gap years.

**Verdict at 73+: Too late for the strategies in this book. You need different approaches — potentially QCDs (Qualified Charitable Distributions), strategic Roth conversions in unusually low-income years, or estate planning strategies that benefit heirs rather than your lifetime taxes.**

## The Exponential Reality

You've now seen the complete picture. The three enemies don't add their damage — they multiply it.

RMDs alone cost $60,000 to $90,000 over 20 years. IRMAA adds $20,000 to $50,000. Widow penalty adds $30,000 to $60,000. But the total isn't $110,000 to $200,000 as simple addition would suggest.

**The total is $150,000 to $280,000** because each enemy creates conditions that amplify the others. RMDs push income higher, triggering IRMAA. IRMAA proximity increases accidental triggers. Both problems worsen dramatically under widow penalty's compressed brackets and halved thresholds.

Every year you wait makes the problem worse:

- Your IRA grows, increasing future RMD size
- You lose conversion capacity from that year permanently
- You move closer to age 73 when control ends
- The potential damage compounds because all three enemies grow stronger with larger IRA balances

Wait one year: cost $18,000 to $22,000 lifetime. Wait three years: cost $55,000 to $70,000 lifetime. Wait five years: cost $110,000 to $155,000 lifetime. Wait eight years until 73: cost $150,000 to $280,000 lifetime.

**The cost curve is exponential, not linear.** Each additional year of delay costs progressively more than the previous year because the enemies compound.

This is why "wait and see" is so expensive. You're not just deferring action — you're actively making the problem worse every month you delay. Your IRA is growing. Your gap years are expiring. The enemies are strengthening.

You now understand the problem completely. Three enemies. Compounding interaction. Exponential cost escalation. No escape after 73.

Act III provides the solution. The **G.A.P.S. System** — Gap Years Arbitrage & Pre-RMD Strategy — shows you exactly how to identify your remaining window, calculate optimal conversion amounts, execute conversions without triggering IRMAA during the process, and position yourself to avoid all three enemies after RMDs begin. Chapter 11 introduces the framework. Chapter 12 tailors it to your specific situation. Chapter 13 teaches IRMAA navigation. Chapter 14 provides your 24-month action plan. The enemies are powerful, but they're defeatable if you act now during the narrow window that remains.

## ACT III:

# THE SOLUTION

CHAPTER 11

11

# THE G.A.P.S. SYSTEM: YOUR FRAMEWORK FOR CONVERTING WITHOUT TRIGGERING PENALTIES

## From Problem to Solution: Introducing the G.A.P.S. System

You've seen the enemies. RMDs force distributions you don't need at rates you don't want. IRMAA penalizes the forced income those RMDs create. The widow penalty doubles both problems when one spouse dies. Together, they cost $150,000 to $280,000 over your retirement if you arrive at 73 unprepared.

The paradox persists. OBBBA made tax brackets permanent, removing deadline urgency. Most retirees respond by waiting. Every year of waiting makes the problem worse — IRA balances grow, gap years expire, enemies strengthen. The cost compounds exponentially, not linearly.

Your advisor likely isn't helping. AUM-based compensation creates disincentive to recommend conversions. Expertise gaps leave many advisors uncomfortable with sophisticated tax planning. "Wait and see" became the default post-OBBBA response despite being the most expensive advice you can receive.

Act III provides the solution. Not vague guidance to "consider conversions someday." A systematic framework you can implement immediately to reduce IRA balance during gap years, minimize RMDs starting at 73, avoid IRMAA triggers throughout retirement, and protect your surviving spouse from widow penalty.

The framework is called the **G.A.P.S. System**: Gap Years Identification, Arbitrage Calculation, Pre-RMD Positioning, Stack Protection.

This isn't theory. It's the methodology we've used with dozens of clients to execute conversions totaling $300,000 to $600,000 over 5-8 years, reducing their age-73 IRA balances by 40-60%, cutting projected lifetime taxes by $80,000 to $180,000, and positioning them to avoid IRMAA penalties entirely or minimize exposure to lowest tiers.

The G.A.P.S. System addresses the compound threat Act II revealed. It's not four disconnected tactics. It's an integrated approach where each component reinforces the others. Gap Years Identification maps when you can act. Arbitrage Calculation determines how much you can convert. Pre-RMD Positioning sets your target. Stack Protection ensures conversions don't accidentally trigger the penalties you're trying to avoid.

## How the Four Components Work Together

Most people approach Roth conversions as single-year decisions. "Should I convert this year? How much?" They calculate bracket room, execute a conversion, then revisit the question next year.

This approach fails for gap years conversions because the goal isn't optimizing one year's taxes. The goal is reducing your IRA balance enough before age 73 that subsequent RMDs stay below IRMAA thresholds and manageable tax brackets for the next 20+ years.

Single-year thinking produces inadequate results. You convert $40,000 one year. Your IRA is $700,000. That's a 6% reduction. Your RMD at 73 decreases by $1,500 annually. Over 20 years, you save $7,200 in taxes. You paid $8,800 in conversion taxes. Net result: you lost money on the conversion.

Multi-year strategic thinking produces transformative results. You convert $50,000 annually for seven years during gap years. Total converted: $350,000. Your IRA drops from $700,000 to $350,000 at age 73. Your RMD decreases by $13,200 annually. Over 20 years, you save $63,000 in taxes plus avoid IRMAA triggers worth another $20,000 to $30,000. Total benefit: $83,000 to $93,000. You paid $70,000 in conversion taxes. Net result: $13,000 to $23,000 lifetime savings plus complete IRMAA avoidance.

**The G.A.P.S. System integrates four planning dimensions:**

**Gap Years Identification** answers: When can I convert? It maps your personal timeline from current age to 73, identifies which years have lowest income, and calculates your remaining conversion window. If you're 66 today, you have seven gap years remaining. If you're 71, you have two. Knowing your window determines urgency and total conversion capacity.

**Arbitrage Calculation** answers: How much can I convert each year? It determines conversion capacity for each gap year by calculating bracket ceiling minus current income. If you're in the 12% bracket with $70,000 income and the 22% bracket extends to $206,700, you have approximately $136,000 of conversion room before jumping to 24%. But you won't fill it completely — you'll convert $50,000 to $70,000 to maintain safety margin below IRMAA thresholds.

**Pre-RMD Positioning** answers: What IRA balance do I need at 73? It works backward from your target RMD to determine required IRA reduction. If your baseline retirement income is $120,000 and you want to stay under the $218,000 IRMAA threshold with $50,000 cushion, your target total income is $168,000. That allows $48,000 for RMDs. At 3.77% (age 73 rate), $48,000 RMD requires IRA balance of approximately $1.27 million. If your current IRA is $1.8 million, you need to convert roughly $530,000 during gap years.

**Stack Protection** answers: How do I avoid accidentally triggering IRMAA while converting? It coordinates conversions with all other income sources — Social Security timing, capital gains realization, dividend management, pension structure — to control total MAGI in any given year. If you're converting $60,000 and your baseline income is $150,000, your MAGI is $210,000. You're $8,000 below IRMAA threshold. Stack Protection means deferring any non-essential capital gains that year, avoiding large investment distributions, and staying $10,000+ below the cliff rather than risking accidental crossings.

These four components form a system. Gap Years Identification tells you how many years you have to work with. Arbitrage Calculation tells you how much to convert annually. Pre-RMD Positioning tells you your total conversion target. Stack Protection ensures each annual conversion executes without triggering penalties.

**The system operates as a feedback loop.** You identify gap years (seven remaining). You calculate annual capacity ($55,000). You multiply: 7 × $55,000 = $385,000 total conversion capacity. You check against Pre-RMD Positioning target ($530,000 needed). You realize seven years at $55,000 falls short. You adjust: increase annual conversions to $75,000, accept brief touch into 24% bracket on highest conversion dollars, or extend timeline by delaying Social Security one year to create an eighth low-income gap year.

The system is iterative. You don't finalize the plan in one sitting. You model scenarios, adjust variables, test sensitivity to different assumptions, and arrive at a multi-year conversion schedule that achieves your Pre-RMD Positioning target using available Gap Years while maintaining Stack Protection to avoid IRMAA during execution.

## Step 1: Gap Years Identification (Map Your Window)

Gap years are the period between retirement and age 73 when your income is artificially low and you have complete control over IRA distributions. You identify your specific gap years window by mapping three transition points.

### Transition 1: When did you retire or when will you retire?

If you retired at 62, your gap years began at 62. If you're still working at 66, your gap years haven't started yet. If you retired at 65, your gap years began at 65.

Gap years begin when full-time W-2 income stops. Part-time work or consulting income doesn't preclude gap years as long as total income stays low enough for conversions. If you're earning $40,000 annually from part-time consulting plus $30,000 from pensions, your baseline income is $70,000 — low enough for meaningful conversions.

### Transition 2: When did you start or when will you start Social Security?

Starting Social Security adds $30,000 to $50,000 to your annual income depending on benefit size. This reduces conversion capacity but doesn't eliminate it.

If you started Social Security at 62 when you retired, your gap years have higher baseline income throughout. You still have gap years — the period is just compressed by higher income floor.

If you delayed Social Security to 67 or 70, your gap years have two phases: pre-Social Security (maximum conversion capacity) and post-Social Security (reduced but still meaningful capacity).

### Transition 3: When do you turn 73?

This is fixed. RMDs begin the year you turn 73. That's your deadline. Gap years end December 31 of the year before you turn 73.

If you're 66 in 2026, you'll turn 73 in 2033. You have seven years: 2026, 2027, 2028, 2029, 2030, 2031, 2032. Starting in 2033, RMDs begin and the window closes.

**Mapping your specific gap years:**

Draw a timeline from your current age to 73. Mark when you retired. Mark when Social Security started or will start. Count the years between retirement and 73. That's your maximum window.

Subdivide the window:

- **Phase 1: Pre-Social Security years** (if applicable) — maximum conversion capacity, baseline income lowest
- **Phase 2: Post-Social Security, pre-RMD years** — reduced capacity, baseline income elevated but still controllable

Example 1: Retired at 62, started Social Security at 62, now 65.

- Gap years: ages 62-72 (11 total years)
- Already used: ages 62-64 (3 years)
- Remaining: ages 65-72 (8 years)
- All years are post-Social Security, so capacity is moderate throughout

Example 2: Retired at 65, delaying Social Security to 70, now 67.

- Gap years: ages 65-72 (8 total years)
- Phase 1 (pre-SS): ages 65-69 (5 years) — maximum capacity
- Phase 2 (post-SS): ages 70-72 (3 years) — reduced capacity
- Currently in Phase 1, year 3 of 5 highest-capacity years

Example 3: Still working at 68, planning to retire at 69, will start Social Security at 70.

- Gap years: ages 69-72 (4 total years)
- Phase 1 (pre-SS): age 69 (1 year) — maximum capacity
- Phase 2 (post-SS): ages 70-72 (3 years) — reduced capacity
- Haven't started yet but window is severely compressed

**Your remaining window determines urgency and total achievable conversion:**

8+ gap years remaining: Comprehensive strategy possible, time to convert $400,000 to $600,000 depending on IRA size and income.

5-7 gap years: Solid opportunity, can convert $250,000 to $450,000 if you act immediately.

3-4 gap years: Compressed window, urgent action required, can convert $150,000 to $250,000 if you start within 90 days.

1-2 gap years: Minimal window, conversions still worthwhile for IRMAA avoidance but won't achieve comprehensive IRA reduction.

## Step 2: Arbitrage Calculation (Determine Conversion Capacity)

Arbitrage means profiting from price differences between markets. In Roth conversions, the arbitrage is converting during gap years at low tax rates to avoid future distributions at high tax rates after RMDs begin.

The calculation is straightforward: determine how much you can convert in a given year while staying in your target bracket.

**Target bracket selection:**

Most people should target the **22% bracket** as their ceiling. This bracket extends from approximately $100,80 1to $211,400 for married filing jointly in 2026. Converting within this bracket means paying 12-22% effective rates on conversion amounts.

Some people with very low baseline income — under $50,000 — might target filling the **12% bracket** first (up to $ 100,800) before moving into 22%. This minimizes conversion costs but takes longer to convert substantial amounts.

High-income retirees with baseline income already at $150,000+ might accept brief incursions into the **24% bracket** (starting at $211,401) to accelerate conversions. Paying 24% now to avoid 28-32% later plus IRMAA penalties still produces positive arbitrage.

**The formula:**

Annual conversion capacity = Target bracket ceiling - Current year income - Safety margin

**Example 1: Maximum capacity scenario**

Current age: 66. Baseline income: $65,000 (small pension, investment income). No Social Security yet. Target bracket: 22% (ceiling approximately $211,401).

Calculation: $211,400 (bracket ceiling)

- $65,000 (baseline income)
- $25,000 (safety margin to avoid IRMAA approach and provide buffer for unexpected income)

= $121,400 annual conversion capacity You could convert $121,400 this year and stay in 22% bracket.

**Example 2: Post-Social Security scenario**

Current age: 70. Baseline income: $110,000 (Social Security $42,000, pension $48,000, investment income $20,000). Target bracket: 22%.

Calculation: $211,400

- $110,000 (baseline income)
- $30,000 (larger safety margin because baseline is higher, less room for error)

= $71,400 annual conversion capacity

Convert approximately $60,000 to $70,000 annually for remaining three gap years (ages 70-72).

**Example 3: High baseline income scenario**

Current age: 68. Baseline income: $160,000 (pensions $95,000, Social Security $48,000, investments $17,000). Target bracket: Accept 24% on final conversion dollars.

Calculation: $211,400 (top of 22% bracket)

- $160,000 (baseline)

= $51,400 available in 22% bracket

You could convert $51,400 and stay entirely in 22%. Or convert $70,000, accepting that $18,600 gets taxed at 24% while staying below IRMAA threshold ($218,000 - $160,000 baseline - $70,000 conversion = $230,000 total, slightly under IRMAA).

This scenario requires Stack Protection. You need to reduce baseline income in conversion years — delay capital gains realization, minimize investment distributions, avoid selling appreciated assets that year.

**Multi-year capacity calculation:**

You don't convert the same amount every year because income changes as you age through gap years.

**Phase 1 years (pre-Social Security):** Maximum capacity, typically $80,000 to $120,000 annually depending on how low baseline income is.

**Phase 2 years (post-Social Security, pre-RMD):** Reduced capacity, typically $40,000 to $70,000 annually because Social Security added $35,000 to $50,000 to baseline.

Calculate capacity for each remaining gap year:

| Year | Age | Status | Conversion Capacity |
|---|---|---|---|
| Year 1 | 66 | Pre-SS | $100,000 |
| Year 2 | 67 | Pre-SS | $100,000 |
| Year 3 | 68 | Pre-SS | $100,000 |
| Year 4 | 69 | Pre-SS | $100,000 |
| Year 5 | 70 | SS starts | $55,000 |
| Year 6 | 71 | Post-SS | $55,000 |
| Year 7 | 72 | Post-SS | $55,000 |

Total seven-year capacity: $565,000

This is your theoretical maximum. In practice, you'll convert less — perhaps $450,000 to $500,000 — to maintain margin and account for income variability.

**The arbitrage calculation:**

Now compare conversion tax cost to avoided future tax cost.

Convert $450,000 over seven years at effective 18-22% rate: approximately $81,000 to $99,000 in total conversion taxes paid.

At age 73, your IRA balance is $450,000 lower than it would have been without conversions. Your RMD is $17,000 lower annually. Over 20 years, you avoid approximately $340,000 in forced distributions that would have been taxed at 24-32%.

Tax saved on avoided distributions: $81,600 to $108,800 over 20 years.

Net benefit: $81,600 - $99,000 = -$17,400 (worst case) to $108,800 - $81,000 = $27,800 (best case).

But this calculation ignores IRMAA. Without conversions, your higher RMDs push you over IRMAA threshold at age 78 and you pay penalties for 15 years. With conversions, you stay under threshold entirely. IRMAA avoidance value: $30,000 to $45,000 over 15 years.

True net benefit: $12,600 to $72,800 over lifetime when IRMAA savings included.

**The arbitrage is positive if:**

- You convert during gap years at rates 4+ percentage points lower than your projected post-RMD rates
- You avoid IRMAA triggers that unconverted RMDs would cause
- You live 10+ years beyond conversions to realize compounded tax-free growth in Roth accounts
- Your spouse survives you and benefits from reduced widow penalty

The arbitrage turns negative if:

- You convert at rates equal to or higher than future RMD rates (happens if baseline income is too high during gap years)

- You accidentally trigger IRMAA during conversion years, negating savings
- You die within 5-7 years of conversions, not living long enough to break even
- Tax law changes dramatically increase future rates, making deferred taxation preferable (unlikely but possible)

For most retirees, the arbitrage is solidly positive. Converting at 18-22% during gap years to avoid 24-32% post-RMD is straightforward profit. Adding IRMAA avoidance worth $30,000 to $50,000 makes the math even more favorable.

## Step 3: Pre-RMD Positioning (Target Your Age-73 Balance)

Pre-RMD Positioning works backward from your goal. Instead of asking "how much should I convert?", you ask "what IRA balance do I need at 73 to produce a manageable RMD?"

### Step 3A: Define "manageable RMD"

A manageable RMD keeps your total retirement income under IRMAA thresholds with comfortable margin and doesn't push you into brackets significantly higher than where you are during gap years.

Calculate your baseline retirement income at age 73:

- Social Security (projected with inflation to age 73): $X
- Pension(s) with COLA adjustments: $Y
- Investment income (dividends, interest): $Z
- Total baseline: $X + $Y + $Z = $\text{Baseline}_{73}$

Example: Current age 66, baseline income today $95,000. By age 73, with seven years of 2.5% inflation adjustments, baseline becomes approximately $113,000.

Now determine your IRMAA safety target. For married filing jointly, first threshold is $218,000. You want at least $30,000 to $50,000 of cushion to avoid accidental triggers from income spikes.

IRMAA safety target: $218,000 - $40,000 buffer = $178,000 maximum total income.

Subtract baseline: $178,000 - $113,000 = $65,000 available for RMDs.

**Your target RMD at 73 is $65,000 or less.**

### Step 3B: Calculate required IRA balance

RMD at age 73 = IRA balance ÷ 26.5 (IRS divisor)

Rearranging: IRA balance = Target RMD × 26.5

Using $65,000 target RMD: $65,000 × 26.5 = $1,722,500

**Your target IRA balance at age 73 is approximately $1.72 million.**

If your current IRA is $1.9 million and you're 66, you need to reduce it by roughly $180,000 during your seven gap years to hit target. That's approximately $26,000 per year — very achievable given your conversion capacity is $80,000 to $100,000 annually during pre-Social Security phase.

**Step 3C: Adjust for growth**

Your IRA doesn't stay static during gap years. It grows from investment returns even as you convert.

Simplified calculation assuming 5% annual growth:

Current IRA: $1,900,000 Seven years of 5% growth without conversions: becomes $2,670,000 Target at 73: $1,720,000 Total reduction needed: $950,000

But you can't convert $950,000. Your annual capacity is $80,000 for four years (pre-SS) plus $50,000 for three years (post-SS): $470,000 total.

**This reveals you cannot hit your target solely through conversions.** You need additional strategies:

- Spend from IRA during gap years instead of taxable accounts (reduces balance without conversion taxes)
- Gift to charity using QCDs once you're 70.5+ if charitably inclined
- Consider partial Roth conversions but accept higher post-73 RMDs, relying on Stack Protection to manage IRMAA risk

Most people can't reduce IRA to zero or near-zero before 73 unless they have very small balances ($300,000-$500,000) or exceptionally long gap years windows (retire at 55-60). The goal isn't eliminating RMDs entirely. The goal is reducing them enough to stay under IRMAA thresholds and in favorable brackets.

**Realistic Pre-RMD Positioning targets:**

Small IRA ($300,000-$500,000): Convert 50-70%, arrive at 73 with $150,000-$200,000 remaining. First RMD: $5,700-$7,500.

Medium IRA ($600,000-$900,000): Convert 40-50%, arrive at 73 with $350,000-$500,000 remaining. First RMD: $13,200-$18,900.

Large IRA ($1M-$1.5M): Convert 30-40%, arrive at 73 with $700,000-$1M remaining. First RMD: $26,400-$37,700.

Very large IRA ($2M+): Convert 20-30%, arrive at 73 with $1.4M-$1.6M remaining. First RMD: $52,800-$60,400. IRMAA risk high unless baseline income is very low.

The percentage you can convert correlates inversely with IRA size because annual conversion capacity is bounded by brackets (you can only convert $50,000-$100,000 per year before jumping into unfavorable rates), but larger IRAs require larger absolute reductions.

**Step 3D: Model post-73 trajectory**

Once you've determined your target age-73 balance, model the next 10-15 years to verify RMDs stay manageable.

Age 73 RMD: $26,400 (from $700,000 IRA) Age 75 RMD: $28,450 (IRA grew to $700,000 despite RMDs) Age 78 RMD: $31,200 Age 80 RMD: $34,700 Age 85 RMD: $43,750

Add these RMDs to projected baseline income at each age (accounting for inflation). Verify total income stays under IRMAA thresholds with margin.

If projections show IRMAA triggers by age 82-85, you need to convert more during gap years or accept that you'll pay some IRMAA penalties in later retirement but minimize duration and severity.

## Step 4: Stack Protection (Coordinate All Income Sources)

Stack Protection prevents accidental IRMAA triggers during conversion execution. You've calculated annual conversion capacity. You know your target. Now you must ensure that converting doesn't push you over IRMAA thresholds in the process.

The challenge: MAGI includes everything. Wages, pensions, Social Security, investment income, capital gains, and **Roth conversions themselves**. A $60,000 conversion adds $60,000 to your MAGI for that year. If your baseline income is $155,000 and you convert $60,000, your MAGI becomes $215,000 — dangerously close to the $218,000 threshold.

Stack Protection means actively managing all income sources in conversion years to maintain total MAGI safely below cliffs.

**Income source 1: Social Security timing**

Delaying Social Security creates lower-income gap years before benefits start. Every year you delay from 62 to 70 increases your eventual benefit by approximately 7-8% while reducing current income by $30,000 to $50,000.

If you're 65 considering conversions and haven't started Social Security yet, delay to 67, 68, or 70 if financially feasible. Use savings or taxable account withdrawals to cover expenses. The two to five years of reduced income create maximum conversion capacity.

Converting $100,000 at age 66 with baseline income of $75,000 (no SS yet) produces $175,000 MAGI — $43,000 below IRMAA threshold. Safe.

Converting $100,000 at age 66 with baseline income of $120,000 (SS already started) produces $220,000 MAGI — $2,000 over threshold. IRMAA triggered, $2,296 penalty.

If you've already started Social Security, you cannot undo it. Stack Protection requires managing other sources more carefully.

**Income source 2: Capital gains realization**

Rebalancing investment portfolios generates capital gains. Selling appreciated stocks, mutual fund distributions, and bond sales all create taxable events.

In conversion years, defer non-essential capital gains. Don't rebalance taxable accounts that year if you can avoid it. If rebalancing is necessary, harvest losses to offset gains.

Example: You're converting $65,000 in 2026. Your baseline income is $150,000. You normally rebalance in December, generating $15,000 in long-term capital gains.

Without Stack Protection: $150,000 + $65,000 conversion + $15,000 gains = $230,000 MAGI. You're $12,000 over IRMAA threshold. Penalty: $2,296.

With Stack Protection: Defer rebalancing to 2027 (non-conversion year) or harvest $15,000 in losses to offset the $15,000 gains. MAGI stays at $215,000. No IRMAA trigger.

**Income source 3: Investment income (dividends, interest)**

You have limited control over dividends and interest from stocks and bonds, but some levers exist.

Shift dividend-paying stocks into tax-deferred accounts before conversion years. Hold growth stocks (minimal dividends) in taxable accounts during high-conversion years.

If you hold bonds generating $12,000 annually in taxable interest, consider shifting to municipal bonds (interest doesn't count in MAGI) for conversion years, then shift back afterward.

If you own mutual funds that distribute capital gains annually, consider switching to ETFs (more tax-efficient, fewer distributions) or index funds with lower turnover in the years leading up to conversions.

**Income source 4: Pensions and required distributions**

Pensions are fixed. You can't reduce them. If you have a $45,000 annual pension, that's $45,000 of baseline income every year.

Some pensions offer lump-sum buyouts. If you're age 60-65 and your pension offers a $400,000 lump sum instead of $30,000 annually for life, taking the lump sum and rolling it to an IRA could make sense. The lump sum is a one-time taxable event, but it eliminates $30,000 of annual baseline income, creating massive conversion capacity in subsequent years.

This is advanced planning requiring actuarial analysis. Most people should not take lump sums. But for someone with high pension income limiting conversion capacity, it's worth modeling.

**Income source 5: Roth conversions themselves**

The conversion is income. A $70,000 conversion is $70,000 added to MAGI. You cannot avoid this — it's the nature of conversions.

Stack Protection means sizing conversions to keep total MAGI under thresholds. If your baseline is $165,000 and threshold is $218,000, you have $53,000 of room. Convert $50,000 to maintain $3,000 buffer. Don't convert $60,000 thinking "it's close enough." Close enough means over the cliff.

**The stacking order visualization:**

Think of MAGI as a vertical stack of income blocks:

Bottom layer: Social Security ($42,000) Second layer: Pension(s) ($58,000) Third layer: Investment income ($18,000) Fourth layer: Capital gains (defer to $0 in conversion year) Top layer: Roth conversion ($55,000)

**Total stack height: $173,000**

IRMAA cliff is at $218,000. You're $45,000 below. Safe.

If you hadn't deferred capital gains ($15,000), total stack would be $188,000. Still safe but with less margin.

If you had started Social Security early (+$12,000 more than delaying), stack would be $185,000. Safe but approaching limits on how much you can convert.

**Stack Protection in practice:**

You're 67 in 2026. Baseline income: $145,000. You want to convert $60,000. Total MAGI would be $205,000 — safe.

But 2026 is an election year and markets are volatile. Your mutual funds distributed $8,000 in unexpected capital gains you didn't anticipate. Now your MAGI is $213,000. Still under $218,000, but only $5,000 of cushion.

Your advisor suggests rebalancing your portfolio, which would generate another $6,000 in gains. That would push you to $219,000 — over the threshold.

Stack Protection response: Defer the rebalancing to 2027. Execute the $60,000 conversion as planned. Accept the $8,000 unexpected gains (you can't avoid fund distributions). Final MAGI: $213,000. You stay $5,000 under threshold.

In 2027, you don't convert. You rebalance that year, realizing the $6,000 gains without risk because there's no conversion adding to the stack.

**Why Stack Protection matters:**

Converting $60,000 and accidentally triggering IRMAA means paying:

- Federal tax on conversion: approximately $13,200 (22% rate)
- IRMAA penalty: $2,296
- Total cost: $15,496

Effective conversion rate: 25.8% instead of 22%.

The IRMAA penalty increased your conversion cost by 17%. Over multiple conversion years, accidentally triggering IRMAA three times costs $6,888 in penalties — erasing a significant portion of the tax savings conversions were designed to create.

Stack Protection prevents this. It requires coordination across your entire financial life during conversion years. You're not just executing a conversion. You're managing Social Security timing, deferring portfolio rebalancing, minimizing distributions, and controlling every income source to ensure total MAGI stays safely below thresholds.

## Why Multi-Year Planning Is Non-Negotiable

Single-year conversions cannot solve the gap years challenge. The math doesn't work.

**Problem 1: Insufficient IRA reduction**

Converting $50,000 once reduces your IRA by $50,000. If your IRA is $800,000, that's a 6% reduction. Your age-73 RMD decreases by $1,900 annually. Over 20 years, you save $9,100 in taxes. You paid $11,000 in conversion taxes. You lost money.

Converting $50,000 annually for seven years reduces your IRA by $350,000 — 44% reduction. Your age-73 RMD decreases by $13,200 annually. Over 20 years, you save $63,000 in taxes plus avoid IRMAA worth $30,000. Total benefit: $93,000. You paid $70,000 in conversion taxes. Net gain: $23,000 plus IRMAA avoidance.

**The difference: multi-year execution achieves critical mass of IRA reduction that single-year cannot.**

**Problem 2: Bracket utilization inefficiency**

You have conversion capacity — the gap between your current income and the top of your target bracket. If that gap is $80,000 annually, using only $30,000 of it means leaving $50,000 of capacity unused.

That unused capacity doesn't roll over. You can't save it for next year. Each gap year has its own capacity determined by that year's income and brackets. Use it or lose it.

Multi-year planning maximizes capacity utilization. You convert $70,000 to $80,000 annually during high-capacity years (pre-Social Security), then $40,000 to $50,000 during reduced-capacity years (post-Social Security). You're using available capacity efficiently across all gap years.

**Problem 3: Timing risk**

Single-year approaches create timing risk. You convert $60,000 in 2026. Markets crash in 2027. Your IRA drops 20%. You could have converted at lower valuations in 2027 but you already used your "one year" approach.

Multi-year approaches spread timing risk. You convert some in 2026, some in 2027, some in 2028. If markets drop, your later conversions happen at lower values (more shares converted for same dollar amount). If markets rise, your early conversions locked in lower tax costs before growth.

Dollar-cost averaging principle applies to conversions just as it does to investing.

**Problem 4: Compound enemy interaction**

The three enemies — RMDs, IRMAA, widow penalty — compound over decades. Single-year conversions reduce the first enemy slightly but don't create enough IRA reduction to meaningfully address the second and third.

Multi-year conversions can reduce IRA balance 40-60%, producing RMDs small enough to avoid IRMAA entirely and minimize widow penalty impact. This requires $300,000 to $600,000 total conversions, which demands 5-8 years of systematic execution.

**The planning horizon:**

Minimum effective timeframe: **3 years** of conversions totaling $150,000 to $200,000. This produces measurable but modest benefit.

Optimal timeframe: **5-7 years** of conversions totaling $300,000 to $500,000. This produces transformative IRA reduction and maximizes enemy avoidance.

Extended timeframe: **8-10 years** for very large IRAs ($2 million+) requiring $600,000 to $800,000 conversions to achieve meaningful percentage reduction.

**You commit to multi-year planning by:**

Creating a 5-7 year conversion calendar specifying amounts for each year based on that year's projected income and capacity.

Scheduling annual reviews every November to adjust following year's conversion based on actual income, market performance, and any life changes.

Coordinating with tax professionals in Q4 of each conversion year to finalize exact conversion amounts based on year-to-date income.

Executing conversions in December after you have full-year income visibility and can convert precisely up to your target without overshooting.

Tracking cumulative IRA reduction progress toward your Pre-RMD Positioning target and adjusting future years if you're ahead or behind pace.

This is why the G.A.P.S. System is a framework, not a tactic. Gap Years Identification maps your window. Arbitrage Calculation determines annual capacity. Pre-RMD Positioning sets your target. Stack Protection ensures safe execution. The four components work together across multiple years to achieve the IRA reduction necessary to defeat the three enemies.

You now understand the system. What you need next is personalization. How does G.A.P.S. apply to your specific situation? Chapter 12 presents five conversion profiles representing different starting points — early gap years, mid gap years, late gap years, high income, and large IRA scenarios. Find the profile closest to your situation and see exactly how G.A.P.S. executes in practice for someone like you.

## Step 4: Stack Protection (Coordinate All Income Sources)

Stack Protection prevents accidental IRMAA triggers during conversion execution. You've calculated annual conversion capacity. You know your target. Now you must ensure that converting doesn't push you over IRMAA thresholds in the process.

The challenge: MAGI includes everything. Wages, pensions, Social Security, investment income, capital gains, and **Roth conversions themselves**. A $60,000 conversion adds $60,000 to your MAGI for that year. If your baseline income is $155,000 and you convert $60,000, your MAGI becomes $215,000 — dangerously close to the $218,000 threshold.

Stack Protection means actively managing all income sources in conversion years to maintain total MAGI safely below cliffs.

**Income source 1: Social Security timing**

Delaying Social Security creates lower-income gap years before benefits start. Every year you delay from 62 to 70 increases your eventual benefit by approximately 7-8% while reducing current income by $30,000 to $50,000.

If you're 65 considering conversions and haven't started Social Security yet, delay to 67, 68, or 70 if financially feasible. Use savings or taxable account withdrawals to cover expenses. The two to five years of reduced income create maximum conversion capacity.

Converting $100,000 at age 66 with baseline income of $75,000 (no SS yet) produces $175,000 MAGI — $43,000 below IRMAA threshold. Safe.

Converting $100,000 at age 66 with baseline income of $120,000 (SS already started) produces $220,000 MAGI — $2,000 over threshold. IRMAA triggered, $2,026 penalty.

If you've already started Social Security, you cannot undo it. Stack Protection requires managing other sources more carefully.

**Income source 2: Capital gains realization**

Rebalancing investment portfolios generates capital gains. Selling appreciated stocks, mutual fund distributions, and bond sales all create taxable events.

In conversion years, defer non-essential capital gains. Don't rebalance taxable accounts that year if you can avoid it. If rebalancing is necessary, harvest losses to offset gains.

Example: You're converting $65,000 in 2026. Your baseline income is $150,000. You normally rebalance in December, generating $15,000 in long-term capital gains.

Without Stack Protection: $150,000 + $65,000 conversion + $15,000 gains = $230,000 MAGI. You're $12,000 over IRMAA threshold. Penalty: $2,026.

With Stack Protection: Defer rebalancing to 2027 (non-conversion year) or harvest $15,000 in losses to offset the $15,000 gains. MAGI stays at $215,000. No IRMAA trigger.

**Income source 3: Investment income (dividends, interest)**

You have limited control over dividends and interest from stocks and bonds, but some levers exist.

Shift dividend-paying stocks into tax-deferred accounts before conversion years. Hold growth stocks (minimal dividends) in taxable accounts during high-conversion years.

If you hold bonds generating $12,000 annually in taxable interest, consider shifting to municipal bonds (interest doesn't count in MAGI) for conversion years, then shift back afterward.

If you own mutual funds that distribute capital gains annually, consider switching to ETFs (more tax-efficient, fewer distributions) or index funds with lower turnover in the years leading up to conversions.

**Income source 4: Pensions and required distributions**

Pensions are fixed. You can't reduce them. If you have a $45,000 annual pension, that's $45,000 of baseline income every year.

Some pensions offer lump-sum buyouts. If you're age 60-65 and your pension offers a $400,000 lump sum instead of $30,000 annually for life, taking the lump sum and rolling it to an IRA could make sense. The lump sum is a one-time taxable event, but it eliminates $30,000 of annual baseline income, creating massive conversion capacity in subsequent years.

This is advanced planning requiring actuarial analysis. Most people should not take lump sums. But for someone with high pension income limiting conversion capacity, it's worth modeling.

**Income source 5: Roth conversions themselves**

The conversion is income. A $70,000 conversion is $70,000 added to MAGI. You cannot avoid this — it's the nature of conversions.

Stack Protection means sizing conversions to keep total MAGI under thresholds. If your baseline is $165,000 and threshold is $218,000, you have $53,000 of room. Convert $50,000 to maintain $3,000 buffer. Don't convert $60,000 thinking "it's close enough." Close enough means over the cliff.

**The stacking order visualization:**

Think of MAGI as a vertical stack of income blocks:

Bottom layer: Social Security ($42,000) Second layer: Pension(s) ($58,000) Third layer: Investment income ($18,000) Fourth layer: Capital gains (defer to $0 in conversion year) Top layer: Roth conversion ($55,000)

**Total stack height: $173,000**

IRMAA cliff is at $218,000. You're $45,000 below. Safe.

If you hadn't deferred capital gains ($15,000), total stack would be $188,000. Still safe but with less margin.

If you had started Social Security early (+$12,000 more than delaying), stack would be $185,000. Safe but approaching limits on how much you can convert.

**Stack Protection in practice:**

You're 67 in 2026. Baseline income: $145,000. You want to convert $60,000. Total MAGI would be $205,000 — safe.

But 2026 is an election year and markets are volatile. Your mutual funds distributed $8,000 in unexpected capital gains you didn't anticipate. Now your MAGI is $213,000. Still under $218,000, but only $5,000 of cushion.

Your advisor suggests rebalancing your portfolio, which would generate another $6,000 in gains. That would push you to $219,000 — over the threshold.

Stack Protection response: Defer the rebalancing to 2027. Execute the $60,000 conversion as planned. Accept the $8,000 unexpected gains (you can't avoid fund distributions). Final MAGI: $213,000. You stay $5,000 under threshold.

In 2027, you don't convert. You rebalance that year, realizing the $6,000 gains without risk because there's no conversion adding to the stack.

**Why Stack Protection matters:**

Converting $60,000 and accidentally triggering IRMAA means paying:

- Federal tax on conversion: approximately $13,200 (22% rate)
- IRMAA penalty: $2,026
- Total cost: $15,226

Effective conversion rate: 25.4% instead of 22%.

The IRMAA penalty increased your conversion cost by 15%. Over multiple conversion years, accidentally triggering IRMAA three times costs $6,078 in penalties — erasing a significant portion of the tax savings conversions were designed to create.

Stack Protection prevents this. It requires coordination across your entire financial life during conversion years. You're not just executing a conversion. You're managing Social Security timing, deferring portfolio rebalancing, minimizing distributions, and controlling every income source to ensure total MAGI stays safely below thresholds.

## Why Multi-Year Planning Is Non-Negotiable

Single-year conversions cannot solve the gap years challenge. The math doesn't work.

**Problem 1: Insufficient IRA reduction**

Converting $50,000 once reduces your IRA by $50,000. If your IRA is $800,000, that's a 6% reduction. Your age-73 RMD decreases by $1,900 annually. Over 20 years, you save $9,100 in taxes. You paid

$11,000 in conversion taxes. You lost money.

Converting $50,000 annually for seven years reduces your IRA by $350,000 — 44% reduction. Your age-73 RMD decreases by $13,200 annually. Over 20 years, you save $63,000 in taxes plus avoid IRMAA worth $30,000. Total benefit: $93,000. You paid $70,000 in conversion taxes. Net gain: $23,000 plus IRMAA avoidance.

**The difference: multi-year execution achieves critical mass of IRA reduction that single-year cannot.**

**Problem 2: Bracket utilization inefficiency**

You have conversion capacity — the gap between your current income and the top of your target bracket. If that gap is $80,000 annually, using only $30,000 of it means leaving $50,000 of capacity unused.

That unused capacity doesn't roll over. You can't save it for next year. Each gap year has its own capacity determined by that year's income and brackets. Use it or lose it.

Multi-year planning maximizes capacity utilization. You convert $70,000 to $80,000 annually during high-capacity years (pre-Social Security), then $40,000 to $50,000 during reduced-capacity years (post-Social Security). You're using available capacity efficiently across all gap years.

**Problem 3: Timing risk**

Single-year approaches create timing risk. You convert $60,000 in 2026. Markets crash in 2027. Your IRA drops 20%. You could have converted at lower valuations in 2027 but you already used your "one year" approach.

Multi-year approaches spread timing risk. You convert some in 2026, some in 2027, some in 2028. If markets drop, your later conversions happen at lower values (more shares converted for same dollar amount). If markets rise, your early conversions locked in lower tax costs before growth.

Dollar-cost averaging principle applies to conversions just as it does to investing.

**Problem 4: Compound enemy interaction**

The three enemies — RMDs, IRMAA, widow penalty — compound over decades. Single-year conversions reduce the first enemy slightly but don't create enough IRA reduction to meaningfully address the second and third.

Multi-year conversions can reduce IRA balance 40-60%, producing RMDs small enough to avoid IRMAA entirely and minimize widow penalty impact. This requires $300,000 to $600,000 total conversions, which demands 5-8 years of systematic execution.

**The planning horizon:**

Minimum effective timeframe: **3 years** of conversions totaling $150,000 to $200,000. This produces measurable but modest benefit.

Optimal timeframe: **5-7 years** of conversions totaling $300,000 to $500,000. This produces transformative IRA reduction and maximizes enemy avoidance.

Extended timeframe: **8-10 years** for very large IRAs ($2 million+) requiring $600,000 to $800,000 conversions to achieve meaningful percentage reduction.

**You commit to multi-year planning by:**

Creating a 5-7 year conversion calendar specifying amounts for each year based on that year's projected income and capacity.

Scheduling annual reviews every November to adjust following year's conversion based on actual income, market performance, and any life changes.

Coordinating with tax professionals in Q4 of each conversion year to finalize exact conversion amounts based on year-to-date income.

Executing conversions in December after you have full-year income visibility and can convert precisely up to your target without overshooting.

Tracking cumulative IRA reduction progress toward your Pre-RMD Positioning target and adjusting future years if you're ahead or behind pace.

This is why the G.A.P.S. System is a framework, not a tactic. Gap Years Identification maps your window. Arbitrage Calculation determines annual capacity. Pre-RMD Positioning sets your target. Stack Protection ensures safe execution. The four components work together across multiple years to achieve the IRA reduction necessary to defeat the three enemies.

You now understand the system. What you need next is personalization. **How does G.A.P.S. apply to your specific situation?** Chapter 12 presents five conversion profiles representing different starting points — early gap years, mid gap years, late gap years, high income, and large IRA scenarios. Find the profile closest to your situation and see exactly how G.A.P.S. executes in practice for someone like you.

CHAPTER 12

12

# THE 5 CONVERSION PROFILES: WHICH STRATEGY MATCHES YOUR TIMELINE AND RISK TOLERANCE

## One Framework, Five Implementation Paths

The G.A.P.S. System provides the framework for strategic Roth conversions during gap years. Gap Years Identification maps your window. Arbitrage Calculation determines annual capacity. Pre-RMD Positioning sets your target. Stack Protection ensures safe execution.

But the framework doesn't dictate pace. How you distribute conversions across your available gap years depends on your personal circumstances, risk tolerance, liquidity, and income trajectory.

Some people have eight gap years remaining and prefer spreading conversions evenly. Others have only three years and need aggressive front-loading. Some want mathematical precision, converting exactly to bracket ceilings each year. Others want simplicity, executing one large conversion and solving the problem immediately.

All five approaches use the G.A.P.S. framework. They differ in execution timeline and concentration.

**Profile 1 - Slow & Steady** distributes conversions evenly across all available gap years. If you have seven years remaining, convert approximately $50,000 to $60,000 annually for seven years. Lowest annual tax impact, smoothest cash flow requirement, longest timeline.

**Profile 2 - Front-Loader** concentrates conversions in the first 2-4 gap years. Convert $100,000 to $150,000 annually while income is lowest or while you're still working and have W-2 income to offset conversion taxes. Pay heavy taxes upfront, finish conversions early, maximize Roth compounding time.

**Profile 3 - Bracket-Maximizer** converts exactly to the top of your target bracket each year, adjusting amounts based on that year's specific income. Requires precision and annual recalculation. Maximizes conversion efficiency by using every dollar of available bracket room without spillover.

**Profile 4 - Rip the Band-Aid** executes one or two very large conversions totaling $200,000 to $400,000. Pay $40,000 to $88,000 in taxes in one or two years, complete conversions immediately, solve the problem fastest. Requires substantial liquidity to pay conversion taxes.

**Profile 5 - Glide Path** starts with small conversions and increases amounts as income decreases through retirement. Convert $30,000 at 65, $45,000 at 67, $60,000 at 69, $70,000 at 71. Mirrors natural income trajectory, reduces early-year tax impact, accelerates as capacity expands.

Your optimal profile depends on five variables: remaining gap years, income stability, liquidity for tax payments, risk tolerance, and complexity tolerance.

## Key Variables: How to Choose Your Profile

**Variable 1: Remaining gap years**

8+ years: Any profile works. Slow & Steady, Glide Path, and Bracket-Maximizer all feasible with long timeline.

5-7 years: Slow & Steady still viable but consider Front-Loader or Bracket-Maximizer to ensure completion before RMDs.

3-4 years: Front-Loader or Rip the Band-Aid necessary. Not enough time for gradual approaches.

1-2 years: Rip the Band-Aid only option if conversions make sense at all (often they don't at this stage).

**Variable 2: Income stability**

Stable income (fixed pensions, steady investment returns): Slow & Steady or Bracket-Maximizer work well. You can predict income accurately and plan multi-year conversions.

Variable income (consulting work, fluctuating dividends, irregular capital gains): Glide Path or Front-Loader better. Convert heavily in low-income years, reduce conversions in high-income years.

Declining income trajectory (pension starting later, delaying Social Security): Glide Path optimal. Start small when income higher, increase conversions as income drops.

**Variable 3: Liquidity for tax payments**

High liquidity (substantial taxable accounts, cash reserves): Rip the Band-Aid feasible. You can pay $50,000 to $80,000 in taxes from savings without strain.

Moderate liquidity (some taxable accounts, manageable reserves): Slow & Steady or Front-Loader work. Spread tax payments across multiple years.

Low liquidity (minimal taxable accounts, tight cash flow): Slow & Steady or Glide Path required. Cannot afford large single-year tax bills.

**Variable 4: Risk tolerance**

High risk tolerance: Front-Loader or Rip the Band-Aid. Accept concentration risk — if tax laws change unfavorably after large early conversions, you've locked in disadvantageous rates. But you maximize Roth compounding time.

Moderate risk tolerance: Bracket-Maximizer or Glide Path. Balance early conversions with later conversions, spreading legislative and market risk.

Low risk tolerance: Slow & Steady. Minimize annual disruption, spread conversions evenly, avoid concentration in any single year or tax environment.

**Variable 5: Complexity tolerance**

High complexity tolerance: Bracket-Maximizer. Requires annual recalculations, precise income tracking, willingness to adjust conversion amounts based on year-to-date income.

Moderate complexity tolerance: Slow & Steady or Glide Path. Establish pattern at beginning (convert $X annually or follow predetermined schedule), execute with minor annual adjustments.

Low complexity tolerance: Rip the Band-Aid. One decision, one execution, problem solved. No annual planning required afterward.

**Self-assessment:**

You have 6 gap years remaining, stable pension income, moderate liquidity, moderate risk tolerance, low complexity tolerance.

**Recommended profile: Slow & Steady.** Convert $50,000-$60,000 annually for six years. Predictable tax bills, manageable cash flow, simple execution.

You have 3 gap years remaining, variable consulting income, high liquidity, high risk tolerance, moderate complexity tolerance.

**Recommended profile: Front-Loader.** Convert $120,000-$150,000 in years 1-2 when income dips, lighter conversion in year 3. Complete most conversions early, maximize Roth growth time.

You have 8 gap years remaining, declining income (delaying SS to 70), moderate liquidity, moderate risk tolerance, high complexity tolerance.

**Recommended profile: Glide Path or Bracket-Maximizer.** Start with $40,000 conversions, increase to $80,000+ as Social Security delay reduces baseline income. Optimize bracket utilization annually.

## Profile 1: Slow & Steady

**Core characteristic:** Distribute conversions evenly across all available gap years with consistent annual amounts.

**Ideal candidate:**

- 7-10 gap years remaining
- Stable, predictable income throughout retirement
- Moderate liquidity (can pay $10,000-$15,000 in annual conversion taxes comfortably)
- Low to moderate risk tolerance (prefer consistency over optimization)

- Low complexity tolerance (wants set-it-and-forget-it approach)

**Implementation:**

Calculate total conversion target from Pre-RMD Positioning. Divide by number of gap years remaining. Execute that amount annually.

Example: You're 65 with $800,000 IRA. Pre-RMD Positioning target: reduce to $450,000 by age 73. Needed reduction: $350,000. Gap years remaining: 8 (ages 65-72). Annual conversion: $350,000 ÷ 8 = $43,750.

Round to $45,000 for simplicity. Convert $45,000 every year from age 65 to 72.

**Timeline:**

| Year | Age | Conversion | Tax | Rate |
|---|---|---|---|---|
| 1 | 65 | $45,000 | $9,000 | 20% |
| 2 | 66 | $45,000 | $9,000 | 20% |
| 3 | 67 | $45,000 | $9,000 | 20% |
| 4 | 68 | $45,000 | $9,000 | 20% |
| 5 | 69 | $45,000 | $9,000 | 20% |
| 6 | 70 | $45,000 | $9,900 | 22% |
| 7 | 71 | $45,000 | $9,900 | 22% |
| 8 | 72 | $45,000 | $9,900 | 22% |
| **Total** | — | **$360,000** | **$75,600** | **21% avg** |

Total converted: $360,000 over 8 years. Total taxes: $75,600. Average annual tax: $9,450.

**Advantages:**

Predictable annual tax bills. You know each November you'll convert $45,000 and owe approximately $9,000 to $10,000. No surprises, easy budgeting.

Smoothest cash flow impact. Paying $9,450 annually for eight years is easier for many people than paying $35,000 in one year.

Psychological ease. Converting the same amount yearly creates routine. No complex decisions each year. Set the pattern and execute.

Reduced single-year income spike risk. No year has unusually high income that might trigger IRMAA accidentally. Each year's MAGI increases by only $45,000 from conversions.

**Disadvantages:**

Longer Roth compounding delay. Your last $45,000 converts at age 72. If you're 65 now, that money stays in traditional IRA for seven more years instead of converting early and compounding tax-free.

Less flexibility. If income unexpectedly drops one year (pension delayed, lower dividends), you're not positioned to take advantage with larger conversion because you've locked into even distribution.

Requires full gap years window. If you only have 3-4 years remaining, Slow & Steady doesn't provide enough time to convert sufficient amounts.

Potential bracket inefficiency. Some years you might have capacity to convert $70,000 without leaving 22% bracket, but you only convert $45,000, leaving $25,000 of capacity unused.

**Best for:** Retirees who value simplicity and predictability over optimization. People with long gap years windows (7+ years) and stable income who want to "set and forget" their conversion strategy.

**Not suitable for:** People with compressed timelines (under 5 gap years), highly variable income requiring annual adjustments, or those seeking maximum optimization of bracket utilization.

## Profile 2: Front-Loader

**Core characteristic:** Concentrate majority of conversions in first 2-4 gap years, completing most or all conversions early.

**Ideal candidate:**

- 5-8 gap years remaining but wants to finish early
- High liquidity (can pay $20,000-$35,000 annual taxes for 2-3 years)
- High risk tolerance (comfortable with concentration risk)
- Values early Roth compounding over smoothed cash flow
- Either still working (can offset conversion taxes with W-2 withholding) or early retirement with very low baseline income

**Implementation:**

Identify 2-3 years with lowest income in your gap years window. Execute large conversions during those years. Minimal or zero conversions in remaining gap years.

Example: You're 64, retiring at 65, delaying Social Security to 70. Ages 65-69 are pre-Social Security with baseline income of $55,000 (small pension, investment income).

Front-Loader approach:

Year 1 (age 65): Convert $120,000. MAGI $175,000. Tax: $26,400 (22% effective). Year 2 (age 66): Convert $120,000. MAGI $175,000. Tax: $26,400. Year 3 (age 67): Convert $100,000. MAGI $155,000. Tax: $21,000. Year 4-8 (ages 68-72): Convert $0. Let prior conversions compound in Roth.

Total converted: $340,000 in three years. Total taxes: $73,800. Conversions complete by age 67.

**Timeline:**

Early years: Heavy conversion activity. Large tax bills. Requires liquidity to pay taxes from savings or taxable accounts.

Middle years: No conversion activity. Roth accounts growing tax-free. Traditional IRA also growing but at reduced rate since balance is lower.

Final years: No conversions. Traditional IRA balance stabilized at target level for manageable RMDs starting at 73.

**Advantages:**

Maximum Roth compounding time. Money converted at 65 has eight years to grow tax-free before RMDs would have started. A $120,000 conversion growing at 6% for eight years becomes $191,000 — all tax-free.

Conversions completed early. By 67, you're done. No ongoing conversion planning required. You've solved the problem and can focus on other retirement priorities.

Takes advantage of lowest-income years. Pre-Social Security years often have maximum conversion capacity. Front-Loader uses that capacity aggressively instead of spreading it out.

Reduced annual complexity. Heavy lifting happens in 2-3 years, then you're finished. No need to manage conversions annually for a decade.

**Disadvantages:**

High concentration risk. If tax laws change after your conversions — rates increase, making deferred taxation preferable — you've locked in at disadvantageous timing. Spreading conversions reduces this risk.

Requires substantial liquidity. Paying $73,800 over three years means approximately $24,600 annually. You need taxable account balances or cash reserves to cover this without financial strain.

Less flexibility to adjust. If your financial situation changes in year 2 or 3 — unexpected expenses, market downturn reducing liquidity — you're committed to large conversions you planned upfront.

Potential IRMAA proximity risk. Converting $120,000 on top of $55,000 baseline creates $175,000 MAGI. Any unexpected income that year — inheritance, property sale, large capital gain — could push you over $218,000 threshold.

**Best for:** Early retirees (60-66) with very low baseline income and high liquidity. People who strongly prefer completing conversions quickly and maximizing Roth compounding time. Those with high risk tolerance who aren't concerned about concentration.

**Not suitable for:** People with limited liquidity, low risk tolerance, or baseline income already approaching IRMAA thresholds where large conversions create trigger risk.

## Profile 3: Bracket-Maximizer

**Core characteristic:** Convert exactly to the top of target bracket each year, adjusting amounts annually based on precise income calculations.

**Ideal candidate:**

- 6-10 gap years remaining
- High complexity tolerance (comfortable with annual recalculations and adjustments)
- Variable income requiring year-by-year optimization
- Wants to maximize conversion efficiency by using all available bracket room
- Detail-oriented personality, enjoys optimization

**Implementation:**

Each November, calculate year-to-date income through November. Project December income. Determine remaining bracket room to top of 22% bracket (approximately $211,400 for married filing jointly). Convert amount that fills bracket exactly, leaving $5,000-$10,000 margin for safety.

**Example**: You're 66 in 2026. January-November income: $148,000. Projected December income: $7,000. Total projected income: $155,000. Top of 22% bracket: $211,400. Available conversion capacity: $211,400 - $155,000 - $8,000 (safety margin) = $48,400.

Convert $48,400 in December 2026.

In 2027, repeat calculation. If income is $162,000, convert $41,400. If income is only $140,000, convert $63,400.

**Timeline:**

This profile has no set timeline. Conversion amounts vary annually based on that year's income.

Low-income year: Larger conversion ($70,000+) High-income year: Smaller conversion ($30,000-$40,000) Very high-income year: Minimal or zero conversion

The pattern responds dynamically to your actual financial situation each year.

**Advantages:**

Maximum bracket efficiency. You're using every available dollar of bracket room without spillover. No wasted capacity, no unnecessary jump to 24% bracket.

Adapts to income variability. If you have irregular income — consulting work some years, capital gains in others — Bracket-Maximizer adjusts automatically.

Reduced IRMAA risk through precision. By maintaining $8,000-$10,000 safety margin below bracket ceiling, you're typically $10,000-$30,000 below IRMAA thresholds, reducing accidental trigger risk.

Intellectually satisfying. If you enjoy optimization and precision, this profile provides ongoing engagement with your financial plan.

**Disadvantages:**

High annual complexity. Every year requires detailed income tracking, projection of remaining months, recalculation of bracket room, and adjusted conversion amount.

Requires excellent recordkeeping. You must track all income sources year-to-date to calculate accurately. Missing $5,000 in dividend income could cause you to convert $5,000 too much and cross brackets unintentionally.

Needs professional coordination. Most people using this profile work closely with CPAs or tax advisors in Q4 to finalize exact conversion amounts. DIY execution is challenging.

Unpredictable annual tax bills. One year you convert $38,000, next year $64,000. Tax bills vary significantly, making annual budgeting harder.

Potential for analysis paralysis. The precision required can lead to overthinking. Spending hours optimizing to squeeze out another $2,000 in conversion may not be worth the mental energy.

**Best for:** Detail-oriented individuals who enjoy financial optimization. People with variable income who need flexibility to adjust conversions based on actual circumstances. Those working with sophisticated tax advisors comfortable with mid-year projections and precise calculations.

**Not suitable for:** People who want simplicity, those without strong recordkeeping systems, anyone prone to decision fatigue from too many variables.

## Profile 4: Rip the Band-Aid

**Core characteristic:** Execute one or two very large conversions totaling $200,000-$400,000, completing all conversions in 1-2 years.

**Ideal candidate:**

- Any number of gap years remaining (works even with 1-2 years left)
- Very high liquidity (can pay $40,000-$90,000 in taxes from savings without strain)
- Low complexity tolerance (wants to solve problem once and move on)
- High risk tolerance regarding concentration and timing
- Values simplicity and finality over gradual optimization

**Implementation:**

Identify 1-2 years with lowest income. Execute one massive conversion each year.

Example: You're 68 with $850,000 IRA. You have 5 gap years remaining but want to finish immediately. Baseline income: $90,000.

Option 1 — Single-year approach:

Age 68: Convert $400,000. MAGI: $490,000. Federal tax approximately $88,000 (jumps into 32% and 35% brackets on highest conversion dollars). Done.

Option 2 — Two-year approach:

Age 68: Convert $220,000. MAGI: $310,000. Tax: $48,000 (stays in 24-32% brackets). Age 69: Convert $220,000. MAGI: $310,000. Tax: $48,000. Total tax: $96,000 over two years. Done by age 69.

**Timeline:** Year 1: Large conversion, large tax bill. Year 2 (if two-year approach): Another large conversion, another large tax bill. Years 3+: No conversions. Problem solved. Traditional IRA reduced to target level.

**Advantages:**

Ultimate simplicity. One decision, one execution (or two), finished forever. No annual planning required for remainder of gap years.

Fastest IRA reduction. You achieve target balance immediately instead of gradually over 5-8 years.

Maximum Roth compounding time (if executed early). Converting $400,000 at age 65 gives that money eight years to grow tax-free before RMDs would have started.

Eliminates procrastination risk. If you tend to defer decisions, Rip the Band-Aid forces immediate action. You can't "wait and see" for five more years.

Psychological relief. For some personalities, knowing the problem is completely solved provides immense peace of mind worth more than marginal tax optimization.

**Disadvantages:**

Very high single-year tax cost. Paying $48,000 to $88,000 in one year requires substantial liquid assets. Most people cannot afford this without significant financial strain.

Pushes into high brackets. Converting $200,000+ on top of baseline income means the highest conversion dollars get taxed at 32%, 35%, or even 37% — rates that may exceed future RMD rates, eliminating arbitrage benefit on those dollars.

IRMAA almost guaranteed. Total MAGI of $310,000 to $490,000 means you're in IRMAA Tier 2 to Tier 4. You'll pay $5,769 to $12,710 in Medicare surcharges two years later. This increases effective conversion cost significantly.

Maximum concentration risk. All conversions happen in one tax environment. If rates increase shortly after, you locked in disadvantageously. If rates decrease, you paid unnecessarily high rates.

Irreversible. Once executed, you cannot undo the conversion. If your financial situation changes dramatically — unexpected need for cash, market crash reducing liquidity — you've already committed.

**Best for:** High-net-worth individuals with substantial liquidity ($500,000+ in taxable accounts). People with extreme low complexity tolerance who value simplicity above optimization. Those facing compressed timelines (1-3 gap years remaining) where gradual approaches aren't feasible.

**Not suitable for:** Anyone with limited liquidity, those in IRMAA proximity zones where large conversions trigger penalties, people with low risk tolerance regarding concentration, anyone who might regret irreversible large tax payment.

## Profile 5: Glide Path

**Core characteristic:** Start with small conversions, increase amounts progressively as income decreases through retirement.

**Ideal candidate:**

- 6-10 gap years remaining
- Income declining over time (delaying Social Security, pension starting later, reducing consulting work)
- Moderate liquidity (can handle increasing tax bills over time as reserves grow)
- Moderate complexity tolerance (requires annual planning but with predictable pattern)
- Wants to match conversion timing to income trajectory

**Implementation:**

Model your projected income for each gap year. Identify natural decrease points — when you stop part-time work, when you delay Social Security past a certain age, when deferred compensation ends.

Start with modest conversions during higher-income years. Increase conversion amounts as income drops. Accelerate conversions in lowest-income years.

Example: You're 65 with baseline income declining as follows:

Age 65: Income $105,000 (pension + part-time consulting). Convert $35,000. Age 66: Income $105,000 (same). Convert $40,000. Age 67: Income $95,000 (consulting reduced). Convert $50,000. Age 68: Income $85,000 (consulting ended). Convert $60,000. Age 69: Income $85,000 (same). Convert $65,000. Age 70: Income $125,000 (Social Security started). Convert $40,000. Age 71: Income $125,000 (same). Convert $40,000. Age 72: Income $125,000 (same). Convert $40,000.

Total converted: $370,000 over eight years. Heavy conversions during ages 67-69 when income lowest.

**Timeline:**

Early years: Modest conversions while income higher. Tax bills manageable but not maximizing capacity.

Middle years: Accelerated conversions as income drops. This is the "sweet spot" — income at its lowest, conversion capacity at maximum.

Later years: Reduced conversions after Social Security starts. Still converting but at lower amounts because baseline income elevated again.

**Advantages:**

Natural income alignment. Conversion pattern mirrors your actual financial trajectory. You're not fighting against income increases — you're working with natural decreases.

Reduced early-year tax burden. Starting with $35,000-$40,000 conversions is easier to absorb than immediate $80,000+ conversions. Tax bills grow as your financial situation stabilizes into retirement.

Captures maximum capacity years. The middle years when income drops to $85,000 provide highest conversion capacity. Glide Path concentrates conversions precisely when arbitrage is most favorable.

Flexibility to adjust trajectory. If income doesn't decline as expected — consulting work extends, pension starts earlier — you can flatten the glide path. If income drops faster, you can steepen it.

Psychological progression. Starting small builds confidence. By year 3-4 when you're converting $60,000+, you've established routine and comfort with the process.

**Disadvantages:**

Requires accurate income forecasting. You must project income 5-8 years forward to design the glide path properly. Significant forecast errors can misalign conversions with actual capacity.

Less early Roth compounding. Your first $35,000 converts at 65, but your last $40,000 converts at 72. That's seven years of differential compounding time.

Complexity in execution. Each year has different conversion amount. You must track plan progression and adjust annually. More complex than Slow & Steady's consistent amount.

Risk of under-converting early. If you start too conservatively ($25,000-$30,000 conversions) and income doesn't drop as much as projected, you may not achieve total conversion target by age 72.

Needs discipline to accelerate. When you reach middle years and plan calls for $65,000 conversions, you must execute despite the psychological resistance to larger tax bills. Failure to accelerate defeats the strategy.

**Best for:** People with predictable declining income trajectory (delaying Social Security, phasing out part-time work gradually, deferred compensation ending). Those who want to ease into conversions rather than starting aggressively. Anyone whose income situation makes Bracket-Maximizer too complex but Slow & Steady doesn't optimize timing.

**Not suitable for:** People with stable flat income (no natural glide path exists), those with compressed timelines (under 5 years doesn't allow progression), anyone who can't forecast income accurately several years forward.

**Profile Comparison Matrix**

The following table compares the five profiles across key dimensions to help you visualize differences.

| Dimension | Slow & Steady | Front-Loader | Bracket-Maximizer | Rip the Band-Aid | Glide Path |
|---|---|---|---|---|---|
| **Minimum gap years needed** | 7+ years | 5+ years | 6+ years | 1+ years | 6+ years |
| **Annual conversion amount** | Consistent ($45K-$55K) | Heavy early ($100K-$150K), then zero | Variable ($30K-$70K) | Massive 1-2 years ($200K-$400K) | Progressive ($35K→$65K→$40K) |
| **Total timeline** | Full window | 2-4 years | Full window | 1-2 years | Full window |
| **Annual tax bill** | Consistent moderate | Heavy 2-3 years, then zero | Variable | Extreme 1-2 years | Increasing then decreasing |
| **Complexity** | Low | Low-Moderate | High | Very Low | Moderate |
| **Flexibility** | Low | Low | High | None | Moderate |
| **Liquidity required** | Moderate | High | Moderate | Very High | Moderate-High |
| **Risk tolerance needed** | Low-Moderate | High | Moderate | High | Moderate |
| **Roth compounding time** | Average | Maximum | Average | Maximum if early | Slightly below average |
| **IRMAA risk during conversions** | Low | Moderate | Low | High-Very High | Low-Moderate |
| **Best for personality** | Simplicity-seeker | Early-action taker | Optimizer | Problem-solver | Planner |

**Reading the matrix:**

If you prioritize simplicity above all: Slow & Steady or Rip the Band-Aid.
If you want maximum Roth compounding: Front-Loader or Rip the Band-Aid (executed early).
If you have limited liquidity: Slow & Steady or Glide Path.
If you have compressed timeline (3-4 years): Front-Loader or Rip the Band-Aid.
If you have variable income: Bracket-Maximizer or Glide Path.
If you want to avoid IRMAA during conversions: Slow & Steady or Bracket-Maximizer.

## Self-Assessment: Which Profile Are You?

Answer the following questions to identify your likely profile.

**Question 1: How many gap years do you have remaining?**

A) 8-10 years B) 6-7 years C) 4-5 years D) 2-3 years E) 1 year or less

**Question 2: How do you prefer to approach large financial decisions?**

A) Consistent, predictable approach over many years B) Act decisively early, then move on C) Analyze carefully and optimize each year D) Make one big decision and be done E) Gradually increase commitment as situation evolves

**Question 3: What is your liquidity situation?**

A) Can comfortably pay $8,000-$12,000 annually for many years B) Can pay $25,000-$35,000 annually for 2-3 years C) Can pay varying amounts depending on year D) Can pay $50,000-$90,000 in 1-2 years from reserves E) Can pay $10,000-$15,000 initially, growing to $20,000+ later

**Question 4: How is your income trending through retirement?**

A) Flat and stable throughout B) High now, will drop significantly in 2-3 years C) Variable year to year D) Doesn't matter, I want conversions done immediately E) Declining gradually over time

**Question 5: What is your tolerance for annual financial planning complexity?**

A) Low — want set-it-and-forget-it B) Low — want to execute early and be done C) High — enjoy optimization D) Very low — want one decision and finished E) Moderate — willing to adjust annually but with clear pattern

**Question 6: How would you describe your risk tolerance?**

A) Conservative — prefer consistency over optimization B) Aggressive — willing to concentrate for maximum benefit C) Moderate — want flexibility to adjust D) Very aggressive — comfortable with all-or-nothing approach E) Moderate — willing to take progressive risk

**Scoring:**

Mostly A's: **Slow & Steady** is your profile. You value predictability, have sufficient time, and prefer consistent approach over optimization.

Mostly B's: **Front-Loader** is your profile. You want early action, have capacity to execute large conversions upfront, and value finishing quickly.

Mostly C's: **Bracket-Maximizer** is your profile. You have high complexity tolerance, want maximum efficiency, and can handle annual recalculations.

Mostly D's: **Rip the Band-Aid** is your profile. You have liquidity, low complexity tolerance, and strongly prefer solving problem immediately regardless of cost.

Mostly E's: **Glide Path** is your profile. Your income is declining, you want progressive approach, and you're willing to plan annually with clear pattern.

Mixed results: You may be between two profiles. Common combinations:

- Slow & Steady + Glide Path: Both spread conversions over time. Choose Glide Path if income declining, Slow & Steady if flat.

- Front-Loader + Rip the Band-Aid: Both concentrate early. Choose Rip the Band-Aid if liquidity and timeline permit immediate completion, Front-Loader if you need 2-3 years.
- Bracket-Maximizer + Glide Path: Both adjust annually. Choose Bracket-Maximizer if income variable unpredictably, Glide Path if income follows predictable downward trajectory.

**Can You Switch Profiles Mid-Execution?**

Yes. Profiles are implementation frameworks, not contracts.

You might start as Slow & Steady, converting $50,000 annually for three years. Then you receive an inheritance, dramatically increasing your liquidity. You switch to Front-Loader or Rip the Band-Aid, converting the remaining target amount in one or two years.

You might plan as Front-Loader but market downturn reduces liquidity in year 2. You pivot to Slow & Steady, spreading remaining conversions across more years.

You might begin as Glide Path, but Social Security starts earlier than expected, flattening your income decline. You adjust to Slow & Steady since the natural glide trajectory disappeared.

**The framework accommodates changes. What matters is:**

1. You're executing conversions during gap years (not waiting until 73+)
2. You're making progress toward Pre-RMD Positioning target
3. You're maintaining Stack Protection to avoid IRMAA during execution
4. You're using available Gap Years capacity before window closes

The specific profile is implementation detail. The G.A.P.S. System is the strategic foundation.

## From Profile Selection to IRMAA Navigation

You've identified your profile. You understand your implementation approach — whether Slow & Steady spreading conversions evenly, Front-Loader concentrating early, Bracket-Maximizer optimizing annually, Rip the Band-Aid executing immediately, or Glide Path progressing gradually.

But all five profiles face the same risk during execution: accidentally triggering IRMAA while converting. A $60,000 conversion on top of $160,000 baseline income creates $220,000 MAGI — $2,000 over the threshold. That mistake costs $2,296 in Medicare penalties two years later, erasing a portion of tax savings the conversion was designed to create.

Stack Protection (from G.A.P.S. System) coordinates income sources to avoid triggers. But the coordination requires specific techniques: capital gains timing, dividend management, Social Security optimization, qualified charitable distributions, and real-time MAGI monitoring.

Chapter 13 provides those techniques. It shows you how to navigate IRMAA thresholds during conversion execution regardless of which profile you've chosen, ensuring your conversions achieve their intended tax savings without generating offsetting Medicare penalties.

CHAPTER 13

13

# IRMAA NAVIGATION: HOW TO CONVERT MAXIMUM AMOUNTS WITHOUT TRIGGERING MEDICARE PENALTIES

## Why IRMAA Demands Precision (The $1 Problem)

Income tax planning tolerates approximation. If you aim to stay in the 22% bracket and accidentally cross into 24% by $3,000, you pay 24% on those $3,000 — an extra $60 in taxes. Annoying but manageable.

IRMAA planning tolerates no approximation. If you aim to stay under the $218,000 threshold and accidentally cross by $1, you pay $2,296 in Medicare surcharges for the entire year. That's a 229,600% marginal penalty rate on that single dollar.

This cliff structure demands precision. You cannot estimate, round, or use rough calculations. You must know your projected MAGI within a few hundred dollars to navigate IRMAA safely while maximizing conversions.

**The precision challenge:**

Most people planning Roth conversions in November don't know their final year-end income with certainty. Investment accounts haven't distributed all dividends yet. Mutual funds might issue capital gains distributions in December. Year-end bonuses may arrive. Interest payments from bonds might vary slightly from projections.

You're making a conversion decision in November based on incomplete information, but that conversion will affect your MAGI calculation months later when you file taxes. The conversion itself adds to MAGI. Other year-end income might push you over threshold if you haven't accounted for it correctly.

**Example of precision failure:**

November 2026 calculation:

- Year-to-date income through October: $148,000
- Projected November-December income: $8,000
- Total projected income: $156,000
- IRMAA threshold: $218,000

- Available conversion capacity: $218,000 - $156,000 = $62,000
- You convert: $60,000 (leaving $2,000 buffer)
- Expected MAGI: $216,000

December surprises:

- Mutual fund capital gains distribution: $4,200 (unexpected)
- Higher-than-projected dividends: $800
- Additional interest from bond maturity: $300

Actual year-end income: $156,000 + $4,200 + $800 + $300 = $161,300

Actual MAGI: $161,300 + $60,000 conversion = $221,300

You're $3,300 over threshold. IRMAA triggered. Penalty in 2028: $2,296.

Your "safe" $2,000 buffer evaporated due to $5,300 in income you didn't anticipate. The conversion that should have been $55,000 to maintain true safety was instead $60,000. That $5,000 misjudgment cost you $2,026 in Medicare penalties two years later.

**IRMAA navigation requires:**

Comprehensive income tracking including all sources, not just major ones.

Conservative projections that account for typical year-end surprises.

Adequate safety buffers — not $1,000 or $2,000, but $5,000 to $8,000 below thresholds.

Real-time monitoring in November-December to adjust conversion amounts before year-end if income projections change.

Coordination with tax professionals who can access your brokerage statements and provide accurate year-to-date figures.

The goal isn't avoiding conversions. The goal is converting the maximum safe amount — filling capacity up to $5,000 below the cliff, not leaving $30,000 of unused capacity because you're overly cautious.

## MAGI Calculation Workshop: Step-by-Step Methodology

Modified Adjusted Gross Income for IRMAA purposes includes specific income sources. The calculation follows IRS definitions with minor modifications.

**Step 1: Start with Adjusted Gross Income (AGI)**

AGI is line 11 on Form 1040. It includes:

- Wages, salaries, tips (W-2 income)
- Interest income (taxable)

- Dividend income (taxable)
- Capital gains (short-term and long-term)
- IRA/401(k) distributions (including RMDs and Roth conversions)
- Pension and annuity income
- Social Security benefits (taxable portion)
- Business income or loss
- Rental income or loss
- Unemployment compensation
- Other income (gambling winnings, jury duty pay, etc.)

**Step 2: Add back certain deductions**

MAGI adds back items that reduce AGI:

- Student loan interest deduction
- Tuition and fees deduction
- Passive loss or rental loss limitations
- IRA contributions (traditional IRA deduction gets added back)
- Self-employed health insurance deduction
- Half of self-employment tax

For most retirees, these add-backs don't apply. If you're not self-employed, not making IRA contributions, and not claiming student loan interest, your MAGI equals your AGI.

**Step 3: Verify what's excluded**

These income sources do NOT count toward IRMAA MAGI:

- Roth IRA withdrawals (qualified distributions)
- Municipal bond interest (tax-exempt)
- Return of principal from non-qualified annuities
- Life insurance proceeds
- Gifts and inheritances (though inherited IRA distributions do count)
- HSA distributions for qualified medical expenses
- VA benefits, workers' compensation, Social Security disability (non-taxable portion)

**Calculation worksheet:**

Use this template to project your MAGI for a conversion year.

**Income Category** | **Amount** Wages/salary (if any) | $________ Interest (taxable) | $________ Dividends (taxable) | $________ Capital gains (realized) | $________ Pension income | $________ Social

Security (taxable portion) | $_______ Traditional IRA distributions | $_______ **Roth conversions (planned)** | $_______ Business/rental income | $_______ Other income | $_______ **Subtotal** (AGI) | $_______ Add-backs (if applicable) | $_______ **Total MAGI** | $_______

**Example calculation for married filing jointly:**

Pension (husband): $42,000 Pension (wife): $28,000 Social Security (combined, 85% taxable): $48,000 Investment income (dividends/interest): $22,000 Capital gains (planned): $0 (deferred to next year) Roth conversion (planned): $55,000 **Total projected MAGI: $195,000**

IRMAA threshold MFJ: $218,000 Buffer below threshold: $23,000 **Assessment: Safe. Have room to increase conversion to $75,000-$78,000 if desired.**

**Example calculation for single filer:**

Pension: $38,000 Social Security (85% taxable): $28,000 Investment income: $18,000 Capital gains: $12,000 (unavoidable mutual fund distribution) Roth conversion (planned): $20,000 **Total projected MAGI: $116,000**

IRMAA threshold Single: $109,000 **Over threshold by: $7,000 Assessment: Cannot convert $20,000. Must reduce conversion to $10,000 or defer capital gains if possible.**

## Income Component Inventory: What Counts and What Doesn't

Understanding exactly which income sources count toward IRMAA thresholds is critical for accurate planning.

**Components that count (increase MAGI):**

**Wages and salaries:** If you're still working part-time or consulting, all W-2 income counts. A $30,000 consulting contract executed in December increases your MAGI by $30,000 that year.

**Interest income:** Taxable interest from savings accounts, CDs, bonds (excluding municipal bonds). If you hold corporate bonds generating $8,000 annually, that's $8,000 toward MAGI.

**Dividend income:** Qualified and ordinary dividends from stocks and mutual funds. Both types count equally for IRMAA even though tax rates differ.

**Capital gains:** All realized capital gains from selling stocks, bonds, mutual funds, real estate, or other assets. This includes both short-term (held under 1 year) and long-term gains. Mutual fund capital gains distributions count even if you didn't personally sell anything.

**Pension income:** 100% of pension distributions count. If you have a $45,000 annual pension, that's $45,000 toward MAGI every year.

**Social Security benefits (taxable portion):** Up to 85% of Social Security becomes taxable depending on your income. The taxable portion counts toward MAGI. If you receive $40,000 in Social Security and 85% is taxable, $34,000 counts toward MAGI.

**Traditional IRA distributions:** All distributions from traditional IRAs, 401(k)s, 403(b)s, and other pre-tax retirement accounts count. This includes RMDs (once you're 73+) and any additional distributions you take voluntarily.

**Roth conversions:** The full conversion amount is taxable income in the year executed and counts toward MAGI. A $60,000 conversion adds $60,000 to MAGI.

**Business income:** If you own a business or have self-employment income, net business income (after expenses) counts toward MAGI.

**Rental income:** Net rental income (rents minus expenses) counts. If you own rental property generating $15,000 net annually, that's $15,000 toward MAGI.

**Components that DON'T count (excluded from MAGI):**

**Roth IRA withdrawals:** Qualified distributions from Roth IRAs are tax-free and don't count toward MAGI. If you withdraw $30,000 from Roth to cover expenses, your MAGI is unaffected.

**Municipal bond interest:** Interest from municipal bonds is tax-exempt and excluded from MAGI. If you hold $200,000 in muni bonds yielding 3% ($6,000 annually), that $6,000 doesn't count.

**Return of basis:** When you withdraw from non-qualified annuities or after-tax contributions to IRAs, the portion that represents return of your own contributions doesn't count. Only the earnings portion counts.

**Life insurance proceeds:** Death benefits from life insurance don't count as income.

**Gifts and inheritances:** Receiving a $50,000 inheritance doesn't increase MAGI. However, distributions you later take from inherited IRAs do count.

**HSA distributions for qualified medical expenses:** Money withdrawn from Health Savings Accounts for qualified medical costs doesn't count.

**The strategic implications:**

Living expenses can be covered from Roth withdrawals or municipal bond interest without increasing MAGI, preserving conversion capacity.

Delaying capital gains realization (not selling appreciated stocks in conversion years) reduces MAGI, creating room for larger conversions.

Shifting investments from dividend-paying stocks to growth stocks (lower or no dividends) during high-conversion years reduces baseline income.

Using municipal bonds instead of taxable bonds during conversion years eliminates that interest from MAGI calculation.

## The "Fill to Threshold" Technique

Fill to Threshold means converting the maximum amount possible while staying safely below the IRMAA cliff. You're not avoiding conversions out of IRMAA fear — you're maximizing conversions up to the prudent limit.

**The calculation:**

IRMAA threshold (MFJ 2026): $218,000 Your projected baseline income: $165,000 Initial available capacity: $218,000 - $165,000 = $53,000 Safety buffer (recommended): -$5,000 **Maximum safe conversion: $48,000**

You convert $48,000, producing total MAGI of $213,000. You're $5,000 below threshold with adequate margin for income estimate errors.

**Worked example 1: High baseline income**

Baseline income: $190,000 (pensions $95,000, Social Security $48,000, investment income $22,000, capital gains $25,000) IRMAA threshold: $218,000 Available capacity before buffer: $28,000 Safety buffer: -$5,000 Maximum safe conversion: $23,000

Many people in this situation would convert $0, thinking "I'm too close to the threshold." But $23,000 converted annually for six years totals $138,000 — meaningful IRA reduction that produces $5,200 lower annual RMDs starting at 73.

**Worked example 2: Moderate baseline income**

Baseline income: $140,000 (pensions $70,000, Social Security $42,000, investment income $15,000, no capital gains this year) IRMAA threshold: $218,000 Available capacity: $78,000 Safety buffer: -$5,000 Maximum safe conversion: $73,000

This person has substantial capacity. Converting $73,000 keeps MAGI at $213,000 — safely below threshold while utilizing available bracket room aggressively.

**Worked example 3: Low baseline income**

Baseline income: $95,000 (pension $48,000, investment income $12,000, no Social Security yet — delayed to 70) IRMAA threshold: $218,000 Available capacity: $123,000 Safety buffer: -$5,000 Maximum safe conversion: $118,000

Exceptional capacity due to delaying Social Security. This person can convert $118,000 annually while maintaining $5,000 safety buffer. Over four years before Social Security starts, they could convert $472,000 — enough to reduce even large IRAs ($1.5M+) substantially.

**The fill technique requires:**

**Accurate year-to-date income tracking.** By November, you should know within $2,000 what your non-conversion income will be for the year.

**Conservative projections for December.** If dividends typically arrive in December, project them at

110% of expected to account for variability. If mutual funds often distribute capital gains, assume distributions will occur.

**Quarterly MAGI checks.** Don't wait until November to calculate. Check in March (Q1), June (Q2), and September (Q3) to ensure income is tracking to projections. If Q3 income is higher than expected, you know by September that year's conversion capacity is reduced.

**Willingness to adjust.** If November income data shows you're $8,000 above projections, reduce planned conversion by $8,000. Don't proceed with original plan hoping December income will be lower than expected.

**Coordination with tax advisor in Q4.** Your CPA or tax advisor should review year-to-date income in November, confirm remaining expected income, calculate precise MAGI projection, and recommend exact conversion amount.

## Determining Your Safety Buffer ($3K-$5K Rule)

Safety buffers account for income estimate errors. The question is how much buffer you need.

**Too little buffer (under $3,000):** High risk of accidental threshold crossing from small unexpected income — extra dividends, higher-than-expected interest, mutual fund distributions, consulting payment arriving earlier than planned.

**Too much buffer ($10,000+):** You're leaving conversion capacity unused. If you could safely convert $48,000 but you only convert $35,000 because you want $15,000 buffer, you've wasted $13,000 of annual capacity. Over six years, that's $78,000 less converted — translating to $3,000 higher annual RMDs at 73.

**Optimal buffer range: $3,000 to $5,000 below threshold for most situations.**

**Factors that warrant larger buffers ($6,000-$8,000):**

**High investment income variability.** If your dividend and interest income fluctuates significantly year to year ($15,000 one year, $22,000 the next), use larger buffer to account for upside surprises.

**Mutual fund holdings with unpredictable distributions.** Actively managed mutual funds can distribute capital gains unpredictably. If you hold funds with histories of large year-end distributions, increase buffer.

**Business or rental income.** If you have business or rental income that varies monthly, projections are less reliable. Build in extra margin.

**First-time conversion execution.** If this is your first year converting and you're unfamiliar with the process, use $6,000-$8,000 buffer until you gain experience with income projection accuracy.

**Factors that permit smaller buffers ($3,000-$4,000):**

**Stable, predictable income.** If income consists entirely of fixed pensions and Social Security with minimal investment income, projections are highly reliable. You can operate closer to threshold.

**Index fund/ETF holdings.** Index funds and ETFs distribute minimal capital gains, making year-end income highly predictable. Less need for large buffer.

**Experienced conversion execution.** If you've been converting for 3-4 years and your income projections historically accurate within $2,000, you've validated your methodology. Smaller buffer acceptable.

**Mid-year income visibility.** If you're calculating in November and you already have 11 months of actual data, December is the only unknown month. Your projection accuracy is high, permitting smaller buffer.

**Buffer adjustment example:**

You're planning 2026 conversions. In 2024-2025, your income projections were accurate within $1,500 each year. You hold mostly index funds with predictable distributions. Your income is stable pensions and Social Security.

**Appropriate buffer: $3,000-$4,000.**

Contrast: You're planning 2026 conversions. In 2024, your actual income was $6,200 higher than projected due to unexpected mutual fund distribution. You hold actively managed funds. You have variable consulting income.

**Appropriate buffer: $6,000-$8,000.**

**The buffer decision matrix:**

| Income Predictability | Investment Volatility | Experience Level | Recommended Buffer |
|---|---|---|---|
| High | Low | Experienced | $3,000-$4,000 |
| High | Moderate | Moderate | $4,000-$5,000 |
| High | High | First-time | $6,000-$7,000 |
| Moderate | Low | Experienced | $4,000-$5,000 |
| Moderate | Moderate | Moderate | $5,000-$6,000 |
| Moderate | High | First-time | $7,000-$8,000 |
| Low | Any | Any | $8,000-$10,000 |

## Multi-Year IRMAA Strategy: Using the 2-Year Lookback

IRMAA's two-year lookback creates strategic opportunities. Your 2026 income determines 2028 Medicare premiums. This delay allows planning across multiple years.

**Strategy 1: Heavy conversions in pre-Medicare years (under 65)**

If you're 62-64, you're not on Medicare yet. IRMAA doesn't apply to you currently. You can execute large conversions without Medicare penalty risk.

Example: You're 63 in 2026. You convert $150,000. Your MAGI is $245,000 — well over the $218,000 threshold. But you won't be on Medicare until 65 in 2028. By the time IRMAA calculation would trigger (2028 premiums based on 2026 income), you're comparing your 2026 income against thresholds. You'll pay IRMAA in 2028, but you've already converted during optimal window.

This strategy accepts one year of IRMAA (2028) in exchange for completing conversions early at maximum capacity. If the $150,000 conversion saved you $30,000 in lifetime taxes and cost you $2,296 in IRMAA one year, the net benefit is $27,704.

**Strategy 2: Alternating high and low conversion years**

Convert heavily in odd years, lightly or not at all in even years. The two-year lookback means heavy conversion in 2025 affects 2027 Medicare premiums, but your 2026 conversion (lighter) affects 2028 premiums.

Example pattern:

- 2025: Convert $85,000. MAGI $235,000. Triggers IRMAA for 2027 (cost $2,296).
- 2026: Convert $20,000. MAGI $170,000. No IRMAA for 2028.
- 2027: Convert $85,000. MAGI $235,000. Triggers IRMAA for 2029 (cost $2,296).
- 2028: Convert $20,000. MAGI $170,000. No IRMAA for 2030.

Total converted over four years: $210,000. IRMAA triggered twice (2027, 2029).

Cost: $4,592. Benefit: reduced RMDs saving $40,000+ over 20 years. Net positive.

Total converted over four years: $210,000. IRMAA triggered twice (2027, 2029). Cost: $4,052. Benefit: reduced RMDs saving $40,000+ over 20 years. Net positive.

Compare to avoiding IRMAA entirely by converting $45,000 annually for four years: only $180,000 converted — $30,000 less IRA reduction.

**Strategy 3: Concentrate conversions when spouse not on Medicare**

If spouses are different ages, the younger spouse might not be on Medicare during early conversion years. IRMAA applies individually, but household MAGI is calculated jointly for married filing jointly.

Example: Husband 66 (on Medicare), wife 63 (not on Medicare yet). They convert $90,000 in 2026. MAGI $240,000. Husband triggers IRMAA for 2028 ($1,148 individual surcharge). Wife not on Medicare in 2028 yet — no IRMAA for her.

Total household IRMAA cost: $1,148 instead of $2,296 if both were on Medicare.

Total household IRMAA cost: $1,013 instead of $2,026 if both were on Medicare.

By the time wife reaches 65 and joins Medicare, they reduce conversion amounts to stay under threshold, having already completed bulk of conversions when only one spouse faced IRMAA risk.

**Strategy 4: Accept Tier 1 IRMAA in exchange for avoiding Tier 2-3**

Without strategic conversions, your RMDs might push you into IRMAA Tier 2-3 starting at 78 and continuing for 15 years. Strategic conversions during gap years might trigger IRMAA Tier 1 for 3-5 years but prevent higher tiers later.

Example: No conversions → RMDs push income to $245,000 at age 80 → IRMAA Tier 2 ($5,769/year) for 12 years → Total: $69,228.

Strategic conversions → Trigger IRMAA Tier 1 ($2,296/year) during 4 conversion years → Total: $9,184 → But reduced RMDs keep you under threshold for life after conversions → Lifetime IRMAA: $9,184.

Net savings: $60,044 by accepting short-term IRMAA to avoid long-term IRMAA.

## Coordination Tactics: Capital Gains, Dividends, Other Income

Maximizing conversion capacity while avoiding IRMAA requires coordinating all income sources in conversion years. Each source you can reduce or defer creates room for larger conversions.

**Tactic 1: Capital gains timing**

Capital gains are discretionary — you control when you sell assets and realize gains. In conversion years, defer non-essential sales.

**Conversion year approach:** Don't rebalance taxable portfolios. Don't harvest gains. Avoid selling appreciated assets unless absolutely necessary. If you need cash for expenses, sell assets at a loss or withdraw from Roth (doesn't count as income).

**Non-conversion year approach:** Execute all deferred rebalancing. Harvest gains. Sell appreciated positions you've been waiting to sell. Realize all capital gains you postponed during conversion years.

Example: You're 67 converting $65,000 in 2026. Your baseline income is $155,000. You normally rebalance annually, generating $18,000 in capital gains.

If you rebalance: MAGI = $155,000 + $18,000 + $65,000 = $238,000. You're $20,000 over threshold. Must reduce conversion to $45,000 or pay IRMAA.

If you defer rebalancing to 2027 (non-conversion year): MAGI = $155,000 + $65,000 = $220,000. You're $2,000 over threshold — close but manageable with slight conversion reduction to $63,000.

Deferred rebalancing created $18,000 more conversion capacity. Over six conversion years, strategic deferral enables $108,000 additional conversions.

**Tactic 2: Tax-loss harvesting in conversion years**

If you have unrealized losses in taxable accounts, harvest them in conversion years to offset unavoidable gains.

Example: Your mutual funds distributed $12,000 in capital gains in December (you can't control this). You have stocks with $12,000 unrealized losses. Sell the losing positions, realizing $12,000 loss. The loss offsets the gain. Net capital gain: $0.

This preserved $12,000 of conversion capacity you would have lost to unavoidable fund distributions.

**Tactic 3: Dividend income management**

You have limited control over dividends from individual stocks, but some levers exist.

**Shift to growth stocks in conversion years.** Growth stocks typically pay low or zero dividends. Value stocks and dividend aristocrats pay substantial dividends. If you hold $300,000 in dividend stocks yielding 3% ($9,000 annually), shifting to growth stocks eliminates that dividend income during conversion years.

After conversion years complete, shift back to dividend stocks if income becomes a priority.

**Use ETFs over mutual funds.** ETFs are more tax-efficient and distribute fewer capital gains. If you hold actively managed mutual funds generating $6,000 in annual distributions, switching to equivalent ETFs might reduce distributions to $1,000-$2,000.

**Hold dividend payers in tax-deferred accounts.** If you have both traditional IRAs and taxable accounts, keep high-dividend stocks inside IRAs where distributions don't create current taxable income. Hold growth stocks or municipal bonds in taxable accounts.

**Tactic 4: Interest income from bonds**

Taxable bond interest counts toward MAGI. Municipal bond interest doesn't.

In conversion years, shift bond holdings from taxable bonds to municipal bonds. If you hold $400,000 in corporate bonds yielding 4% ($16,000 annually), shifting to muni bonds yielding 3% ($12,000 tax-free) eliminates $16,000 from MAGI while reducing income by only $4,000.

The $16,000 MAGI reduction creates room for $16,000 more in conversions.

After conversion years, you can shift back to taxable bonds if higher yield is priority and IRMAA is no longer a risk.

**Tactic 5: Social Security timing**

Delaying Social Security from 62 to 67-70 reduces income during early gap years, creating maximum conversion capacity.

If you're 65 considering conversions and haven't started Social Security yet, delay to 70 if financially feasible. Those five years (65-69) become highest-capacity conversion years.

Example: Social Security at 65 would be $32,000 annually. Delaying to 70 means five years without that $32,000. Your baseline income during those years is $32,000 lower, creating room for $32,000 more in annual conversions.

Over five years: $160,000 additional conversion capacity from Social Security delay.

**Tactic 6: Pension timing (if controllable)**

Some pensions offer flexibility in start date. If you can defer pension from 62 to 65, you create three low-income years for aggressive conversions.

This is uncommon — most pensions start at specified ages. But for those with flexible pensions or deferred compensation, timing pension start date around conversion years can be strategic.

**Tactic 7: Roth withdrawals for living expenses**

During conversion years, cover living expenses from Roth IRA withdrawals instead of taxable account withdrawals. Roth withdrawals don't count as income. Taxable account withdrawals (if they involve selling appreciated assets) generate capital gains.

Example: You need $40,000 for expenses. If you sell $40,000 from taxable account with $15,000 basis, you realize $25,000 capital gain. That $25,000 counts toward MAGI, reducing conversion capacity.

If you withdraw $40,000 from Roth IRA (tax-free qualified distribution), MAGI is unaffected. You preserve $25,000 of conversion capacity.

**The coordination sequence:**

November of conversion year:

1. Calculate year-to-date income (all sources)
2. Project remaining year income (December)
3. Identify controllable sources (capital gains, some dividends)
4. Defer or eliminate controllable sources if possible
5. Calculate remaining MAGI capacity
6. Determine maximum safe conversion with $5,000 buffer
7. Execute conversion in December after final income visibility

## Threshold Crossing Recovery: Appeals and Damage Control

Despite careful planning, you might accidentally cross IRMAA threshold. What happens and what can you do?

**When you discover the mistake:**

You file your 2026 tax return in April 2027 showing MAGI of $220,500 — $2,500 over the $218,000 threshold. You realize the mistake: unexpected mutual fund distribution of $4,000 in December that you didn't account for.

In October 2027, Social Security sends notice that your 2028 Medicare premiums include IRMAA surcharges based on 2026 income exceeding threshold.

**Recovery option 1: Life-changing event appeal**

Social Security allows appeals if you experienced a qualifying life-changing event that reduced your income significantly between the tax year used for calculation and the current year.

Qualifying events (from Chapter 7):

- Marriage
- Divorce or annulment
- Death of spouse
- Work stoppage (retirement)
- Work reduction
- Loss of income-producing property
- Loss of pension
- Employer settlement payment

**Example of successful appeal:** Your 2026 income was $220,000 including $45,000 wages because you worked part-time. You retired fully in 2027. Your 2027 income is $135,000 (no wages). You can appeal using "work stoppage" as life-changing event. Provide evidence: retirement date, final paycheck, documentation that wages have ended. Social Security may adjust 2028 premiums to reflect 2027 income instead of 2026, eliminating IRMAA.

**Example of unsuccessful appeal:** Your 2026 income was $220,000 including $60,000 Roth conversion. Your 2027 income is $160,000 (no conversion this year). You cannot appeal. Roth conversions are not life-changing events. Social Security doesn't care that conversion was "temporary" income. IRMAA stands.

**Recovery option 2: Accept one-year penalty**

If your threshold crossing was small ($1,000-$5,000 over) and you don't qualify for appeal, accept the one-year IRMAA penalty and adjust future conversions.

2026 income: $220,000 (crossed threshold) - 2028 IRMAA cost: $2,296

Lesson learned: 2027 conversion must be smaller or income must be lower. Adjust by $5,000 to prevent repeat.

2027 income target: $213,000 maximum (stay $5,000 under threshold)

One year of IRMAA costing $2,026 doesn't negate the $50,000-$80,000 lifetime tax savings from gap years conversions. It's a mistake, but not catastrophic.

**Recovery option 3: Overcompensate in subsequent years**

If you crossed threshold due to excessive conversion, reduce conversions for 2-3 years to ensure no further IRMAA triggers while completing necessary total conversions.

Example: You converted $75,000 in 2026, crossing threshold. In 2027-2028, convert only $40,000 annually, staying safely under. You lost some conversion efficiency, but you avoid compounding the mistake with additional penalties.

**Prevention better than recovery:**

The best recovery strategy is prevention through:

**Conservative income projections.** Assume dividends, interest, and capital gains will be 110% of expected, not 100%.

**Adequate safety buffers.** Use $5,000-$8,000 buffers, not $2,000.

**Quarterly MAGI checks.** Don't wait until November. Review Q1, Q2, Q3 income to catch problems early.

**December flexibility.** Don't commit to conversion amount until December 15+ when you have nearly complete year income visibility.

**Professional coordination.** Work with CPA who reviews actual year-to-date statements, not just projections, before finalizing conversion.

**The mindset shift:**

IRMAA navigation isn't about fear. It's about precision. You're not avoiding conversions — you're maximizing them within safe parameters.

Target the zone $3,000-$5,000 below threshold, not $30,000 below. Use all available capacity. Coordinate income sources to create maximum room. If you accidentally trigger IRMAA once, learn from it and adjust, but don't abandon the strategy.

Strategic conversions saving $75,000 over retirement can absorb one or two years of $2,296 IRMAA penalties from execution imperfections. The goal is 95% accuracy, not 100% perfection.

You now understand IRMAA navigation — how to calculate MAGI precisely, determine safe conversion amounts, use buffers appropriately, coordinate income sources strategically, and recover if you make mistakes. These techniques apply regardless of which conversion profile you selected in Chapter 12. Whether you're executing Slow & Steady, Front-Loader, Bracket-Maximizer, Rip the Band-Aid, or Glide Path, IRMAA navigation ensures your conversions achieve intended tax savings without generating offsetting penalties.

The final piece is execution. You have the framework (G.A.P.S. System). You have your profile (Chapter 12). You have IRMAA navigation techniques (this chapter). Chapter 14 provides your 24-month action plan — the specific steps, timeline, milestones, and checklists to move from planning to execution, converting your first dollars within 90 days and completing your multi-year strategy before gap years close at age 73.

CHAPTER 14

14

# YOUR 24-MONTH ACTION PLAN: FROM DECISION TO EXECUTION

## Why 24 Months: The Optimal Planning Horizon

You understand the problem. RMDs force distributions at age 73. IRMAA penalizes elevated income. The widow penalty doubles both costs. Together they extract $150,000 to $280,000 from your retirement if you arrive at 73 unprepared.

You understand the solution. The G.A.P.S. System — Gap Years Identification, Arbitrage Calculation, Pre-RMD Positioning, Stack Protection — provides the framework for strategic conversions during the narrow window when your income is low and you control distributions.

You've selected your profile. Slow & Steady, Front-Loader, Bracket-Maximizer, Rip the Band-Aid, or Glide Path — each implements G.A.P.S. differently based on your timeline, liquidity, and complexity tolerance.

You've learned IRMAA navigation. How to calculate MAGI precisely, determine safe conversion amounts, use buffers appropriately, and coordinate income sources to maximize conversions without triggering Medicare penalties.

What you need now is execution. A concrete timeline converting knowledge into action.

**The 24-month planning horizon works because:**

**It's long enough for meaningful progress.** Two years allows executing 2-3 conversion tranches totaling $100,000 to $200,000 depending on your profile and capacity. That's enough to see measurable IRA reduction and validate your strategy is working.

**It's short enough to adapt.** Tax laws could change. Your income might shift unexpectedly. Health situations could alter plans. Two years is manageable horizon for accurate projections without being so long that forecasts become unreliable.

**It spans one full tax cycle plus review.** Year 1 you gather data, develop strategy, and execute first conversion (Months 1-12). Year 2 you refine based on Year 1 results and execute second conversion (Months 13-24). By Month 24, you've completed full planning-execution-review-adjustment cycle.

**It establishes momentum and routine.** After two years of systematic conversions, the process becomes familiar. Fear of complexity reduces. Confidence in calculations increases. Extending to

Years 3-5 feels manageable because you've proven you can execute successfully.

**It creates accountability milestones.** Monthly and quarterly checkpoints prevent indefinite deferral. You're not "thinking about conversions someday." You're executing specific tasks in Month 3, Month 7, Month 15 with clear deliverables.

This 24-month plan assumes you're starting from zero — no conversions executed yet, beginning data gathering today. If you've already completed some conversions, enter the plan at the appropriate phase and use remaining timeline to complete your multi-year strategy.

## Phase 1: Month 1-3 (Data Gathering Checklist)

The first 90 days establish your baseline. You cannot plan conversions without knowing current financial position, income structure, and gap years window.

**Month 1 tasks:**

**Collect all retirement account statements.** Gather December 31 year-end statements for all traditional IRAs, 401(k)s, 403(b)s, and other pre-tax retirement accounts. These show your current IRA balance — the starting point for Pre-RMD Positioning calculations.

List each account: Account name, institution, balance as of most recent statement. Total all balances. This is your baseline IRA value for conversion planning.

Example documentation:

- Traditional IRA (Vanguard): $485,000
- Rollover IRA (Fidelity): $315,000
- 401(k) (former employer, Schwab): $180,000
- **Total traditional balance: $980,000**

**Gather tax returns for past two years.** You need 2024 and 2025 tax returns (or most recent two years available). These show your historical income structure, MAGI calculation, and baseline for projections.

From tax returns, extract:

- Line 11 (Adjusted Gross Income): This is your MAGI baseline
- Wages (if any)
- Interest income
- Dividend income
- Capital gains
- Pension income
- Social Security benefits (taxable portion)

- IRA/401(k) distributions (if any)

Document your 2-year average income. If 2024 MAGI was $142,000 and 2025 was $148,000, your baseline is approximately $145,000. This informs your conversion capacity calculations.

**Identify your current age and gap years remaining.** Calculate how many years until you turn 73. This determines urgency and total conversion timeline.

If you're 66 in 2026: 73 - 66 = 7 gap years remaining (ages 66-72). If you're 70 in 2026: 73 - 70 = 3 gap years remaining (ages 70-72).

**Document Social Security status.** Have you started benefits? If not, when do you plan to start? Social Security adds $30,000-$50,000 to baseline income annually, significantly reducing conversion capacity.

Record:

- Current Social Security status (started/not started)
- If started: monthly benefit amount × 12 = annual amount
- If not started: projected start age and estimated annual benefit

**Month 2 tasks:**

**Calculate current year projected MAGI.** Using income data from Month 1, project your current year (2026) MAGI.

Worksheet:

- Pension income: $________
- Social Security (if started): $________
- Investment income (interest/dividends): $________
- Capital gains (expected): $________
- Other income: $________
- **Total projected 2026 MAGI: $________**

This number is critical. It determines your 2026 conversion capacity and IRMAA proximity.

**Identify controllable vs. fixed income sources.** Review your income inventory. Mark which sources are fixed (pension, Social Security) and which are variable (capital gains, consulting income, dividends).

Fixed income establishes your baseline floor. Variable income is where you have control — deferring capital gains in conversion years, reducing dividend income through portfolio adjustments, timing consulting work around conversions.

**Gather taxable account statements.** Document non-retirement assets — brokerage accounts, savings, CDs, bonds. These provide liquidity for paying conversion taxes and potential source of capital gains you'll need to manage.

List:

- Taxable brokerage (Vanguard): $420,000
- Savings/checking: $85,000
- Municipal bonds: $150,000
- **Total taxable assets: $655,000**

Liquidity assessment: Can you pay $10,000-$15,000 annually in conversion taxes from these accounts without strain? If yes, most profiles are feasible. If no, you're limited to Slow & Steady or very modest conversions.

## Month 3 tasks:

**Map your complete gap years window.** Create visual timeline from current age to 73, marking key transition points.

Example for someone age 66 in 2026:

| Age | Year | Status | Income Level |
|---|---|---|---|
| 66 | 2026 | Current year | Baseline |
| 67 | 2027 | Pre-SS | Baseline |
| 68 | 2028 | Pre-SS | Baseline |
| 69 | 2029 | Pre-SS | Baseline |
| 70 | 2030 | SS starts | Baseline + $42K |
| 71 | 2031 | Post-SS | Baseline + $42K |
| 72 | 2032 | Post-SS | Baseline + $42K |
| 73 | 2033 | **RMDs begin** | **Window closes** |

You have **7 gap years total**: 4 pre-Social Security (maximum capacity), 3 post-Social Security (reduced capacity).

**Calculate your Pre-RMD Positioning target.** Determine what IRA balance you need at age 73 to produce manageable RMDs that stay under IRMAA thresholds.

Formula from Chapter 11:

1. Project baseline income at age 73 (account for inflation, Social Security start)
2. Subtract from IRMAA threshold ($218,000 MFJ)
3. Subtract safety buffer ($40,000)
4. Remaining amount = target RMD

5. Target RMD × 26.5 = target IRA balance at 73

Example:

- Baseline at 73: $125,000 (pensions + SS + investments)
- IRMAA threshold: $218,000
- Buffer: -$40,000
- Target RMD: $53,000
- Target IRA balance: $53,000 × 26.5 = $1,405,000

Current IRA: $980,000. Target: $1,405,000. You're already below target due to market returns assumption being conservative. This person has flexibility — they could convert modestly or not at all if circumstances change.

Alternate example:

- Current IRA: $1,800,000
- Target IRA at 73: $1,200,000
- Needed reduction: $600,000
- Gap years remaining: 7
- Average annual conversion needed: $85,700

This person must convert aggressively — approximately $85,000+ annually to hit target.

**Complete Phase 1 deliverable:** One-page summary document containing:

- Total IRA balance: $________
- Gap years remaining: ________
- Current MAGI: $________
- Target IRA balance at 73: $________
- Total conversion needed: $________
- Liquidity available for taxes: $________

This summary becomes your reference document for all subsequent phases.

## Phase 2: Month 4-6 (Strategy Development)

Months 4-6 transform your data into actionable strategy. You're selecting your conversion profile, calculating annual conversion amounts, and creating your multi-year roadmap.

**Month 4 tasks:**

**Confirm your conversion profile selection.** Review Chapter 12 profiles against your Month 1-3 data.

Decision matrix:

- Gap years remaining: 7+ years → Any profile viable
- Gap years remaining: 4-6 years → Slow & Steady, Front-Loader, or Glide Path
- Gap years remaining: 1-3 years → Front-Loader or Rip the Band-Aid only
- Liquidity: High ($300K+ taxable) → Any profile including Rip the Band-Aid
- Liquidity: Moderate ($150K-$300K) → Slow & Steady, Front-Loader, Glide Path
- Liquidity: Low (under $150K) → Slow & Steady only
- Complexity tolerance: High → Bracket-Maximizer
- Complexity tolerance: Moderate → Glide Path or Slow & Steady
- Complexity tolerance: Low → Rip the Band-Aid or Slow & Steady

Based on your Phase 1 data, make definitive profile selection. Document your choice: "I am executing [Profile Name] strategy."

**Calculate your annual conversion capacity for each gap year.** Using methodology from Chapter 11 Arbitrage Calculation, determine how much you can convert each remaining gap year.

Template for 7-year example (ages 66-72):

| Age | Year | Baseline Income | Bracket Ceiling | Safety Margin | Conversion Capacity |
|---|---|---|---|---|---|
| 66 | 2026 | $95,000 | $211,400 | -$25,000 | $91,400 |
| 67 | 2027 | $97,000 | $211,400 | -$25,000 | $89,400 |
| 68 | 2028 | $99,000 | $211,400 | -$25,000 | $87,400 |
| 69 | 2029 | $101,000 | $211,400 | -$25,000 | $85,400 |
| 70 | 2030 | $143,000 (SS starts) | $211,400 | -$25,000 | $43,400 |
| 71 | 2031 | $146,000 | $211,400 | -$25,000 | $40,400 |
| 72 | 2032 | $149,000 | $211,400 | -$25,000 | $37,400 |

Total 7-year capacity: $474,800

This person has capacity to convert $474,800 over seven years. Their target from Phase 1 was $600,000 reduction. They fall short by $125,200, so they cannot achieve target through conversions alone — they'll need to spend from IRA during gap years or accept higher post-73 RMDs than ideal

**Design your multi-year conversion schedule.** Based on your selected profile and annual capacity calculations, specify conversion amounts for each year.

Slow & Steady approach for above example:

- Ages 66-69: Convert $70,000 annually (4 years = $280,000)
- Ages 70-72: Convert $35,000 annually (3 years = $105,000)

- Total: $385,000 over 7 years

Front-Loader approach:

- Ages 66-67: Convert $85,000 annually (2 years = $170,000)
- Ages 68-69: Convert $80,000 annually (2 years = $160,000)
- Ages 70-72: Convert $0 (conversions complete by age 69)
- Total: $330,000 over 4 years

Glide Path approach:

- Age 66: Convert $60,000
- Age 67: Convert $70,000
- Age 68: Convert $80,000
- Age 69: Convert $85,000
- Age 70: Convert $35,000 (SS started)
- Age 71: Convert $35,000
- Age 72: Convert $35,000
- Total: $400,000 over 7 years

Choose the pattern matching your selected profile. Document your commitment: "I will convert [Amount] in [Year], [Amount] in [Year]..." for all planned years.

**Month 5 tasks:**

**Create IRMAA proximity map.** For each year in your conversion schedule, calculate projected MAGI including conversion amount. Flag any years approaching IRMAA thresholds.

Year-by-year IRMAA check using Slow & Steady example above:

| Year | Baseline | Conversion | Total MAGI | IRMAA Threshold | Distance to Cliff |
|---|---|---|---|---|---|
| 2026 | $95,000 | $70,000 | $165,000 | $218,000 | $53,000 (safe) |
| 2027 | $97,000 | $70,000 | $167,000 | $218,000 | $51,000 (safe) |
| 2028 | $99,000 | $70,000 | $169,000 | $218,000 | $49,000 (safe) |
| 2029 | $101,000 | $70,000 | $171,000 | $218,000 | $47,000 (safe) |
| 2030 | $143,000 | $35,000 | $178,000 | $218,000 | $40,000 (safe) |
| 2031 | $146,000 | $35,000 | $181,000 | $218,000 | $37,000 (safe) |
| 2032 | $149,000 | $35,000 | $184,000 | $218,000 | $34,000 (safe) |

All years maintain $34,000+ cushion below IRMAA threshold. Plan is IRMAA-safe. No adjustments needed.

If any year showed distance under $10,000, you'd flag it for capital gains deferral that year or consider reducing conversion amount.

**Determine tax payment strategy.** Conversions create taxable income. You must pay taxes either through quarterly estimated payments, withholding from the conversion itself, or year-end payment.

Three approaches:

**Option 1 — Withhold from conversion:** When executing $70,000 conversion, request 20-25% withheld for taxes. IRA custodian sends $14,000-$17,500 directly to IRS, you receive $52,500-$56,000 in Roth. Simple, automatic, but reduces Roth balance.

**Option 2 — Quarterly estimated payments:** Pay conversion taxes via quarterly estimates (April 15, June 15, September 15, January 15). Keeps full conversion amount in Roth, requires manual quarterly payments. Best if you already pay estimates for other income.

**Option 3 — Year-end payment:** Execute conversion in December, pay full tax with April return. Keeps full conversion in Roth, gives you months to accumulate cash for payment, but requires discipline to set aside funds.

Most people use Option 1 (withholding) for simplicity despite slight inefficiency of smaller Roth balance.

**Month 6 tasks:**

**Select IRA custodian and confirm conversion mechanics.** Verify your IRA is held at institution supporting Roth conversions (all major custodians do). Understand their specific process.

Common custodians and process:

- Vanguard: Online conversion request or phone call, 1-3 day processing
- Fidelity: Online form, instant processing during business hours
- Schwab: Online or phone, 1-2 day processing
- Others: Check institution website for "Roth IRA conversion" instructions

Call your custodian. Ask: "I want to convert $X from traditional IRA to Roth IRA in [Month]. What forms are required? How long does processing take? Can I specify withholding percentage?"

Document their answers. Confirm you have Roth IRA established at same institution (if not, open one now — takes 1-3 days).

**Create your 24-month calendar with milestones.** Transfer your plan to calendar format with specific dates.

Example Slow & Steady 24-month calendar:

**2026:**

- January-March: Data gathering (complete)

- April-June: Strategy development (complete)
- July: Final MAGI check for 2026 conversion
- August: Calculate precise 2026 conversion amount
- September: Review year-to-date income, confirm no surprises
- October: Contact tax advisor for conversion coordination
- November 15: Execute 2026 conversion ($70,000)
- December 15: Pay estimated tax if not withheld

**2027:**

- January-March: File 2026 return, confirm actual MAGI
- April: Reconcile 2026 plan vs. actual
- May: Adjust 2027 conversion if needed based on 2026 results
- July: MAGI check for 2027
- August: Calculate 2027 conversion amount
- September: Year-to-date income review
- October: Tax advisor coordination
- November 15: Execute 2027 conversion ($70,000)
- December 15: Pay estimated tax

This calendar becomes your execution roadmap. Each milestone has owner (you or tax advisor) and deliverable.

**Complete Phase 2 deliverable:** Multi-year conversion plan document containing:

- Selected profile: [Name]
- Year-by-year conversion amounts
- IRMAA proximity analysis
- Tax payment strategy
- 24-month calendar with milestones
- Total projected conversions: $________
- Expected IRA balance at 73: $________

You've transformed from "I should think about conversions" to "I will convert $70,000 in November 2026, $70,000 in November 2027, and $70,000 in November 2028."

## Phase 3: Month 7-9 (Year 1 Execution)

Months 7-9 execute your first conversion. This is when planning becomes reality.

**Month 7 tasks:**

**Perform mid-year MAGI checkpoint.** You're now six months into the year. Calculate actual year-to-date income through June.

Review:

- Actual pension received (January-June): $________
- Actual Social Security received: $________
- Actual investment income: $________
- Actual capital gains: $________
- Total actual income (Jan-Jun): $________

Project second half based on first half: If first half was $72,000, project full year at $144,000 (assuming income is relatively even throughout year).

Compare to Phase 2 projection: Did you project $148,000 but you're tracking to $144,000? Good — you have $4,000 more conversion capacity than planned. Did you project $148,000 but tracking to $156,000? Problem — you need to reduce planned conversion by $8,000.

Document variance: "Projected $148K, tracking to $___K, variance $___K."

**Review any major life changes.** Has anything material changed since Phase 2? Job status, health, inheritance, major expenses, market performance affecting investment income?

If yes, assess impact on conversion plan. Large unexpected income (inheritance, property sale) might force reducing or eliminating current year conversion. Job loss might increase conversion capacity if income dropped.

Most years: no major changes, plan proceeds as designed.

**Month 8 tasks:**

**Calculate final 2026 conversion amount.** You have eight months of actual data. Project remaining four months conservatively.

Calculation worksheet:

- Year-to-date income (Jan-Aug): $________
- Projected Sept-Dec income: $________
- Projected total 2026 income: $________
- IRMAA threshold: $218,000

- Safety buffer: -$5,000
- Maximum safe MAGI: $213,000
- Available conversion capacity: $213,000 - projected income = $________

Compare available capacity to planned conversion from Phase 2. If they match within $3,000-$5,000, proceed as planned. If available capacity is significantly different, adjust.

Example: You planned $70,000 conversion. Calculation shows $66,000 available capacity. Reduce conversion to $65,000 to stay within safe limits.

**Month 9 tasks:**

**Coordinate with tax advisor.** If you work with CPA or tax professional, schedule October meeting. Share your conversion plan, year-to-date income, and proposed conversion amount. Request their verification of calculations.

Agenda for advisor meeting:

- Review actual 2026 income through September
- Confirm remaining expected income (October-December)
- Verify MAGI calculation methodology
- Confirm conversion amount stays under IRMAA threshold with buffer
- Discuss tax payment strategy (withholding vs. estimated payments)
- Confirm no other tax considerations (state taxes, alternative minimum tax, etc.)

If advisor agrees with your calculations, proceed with planned conversion. If they identify errors or overlooked income sources, adjust accordingly.

**Finalize conversion execution date.** Most conversions should execute in November-December after you have near-complete year income visibility. Early November is optimal — late enough for income clarity, early enough to process before year-end.

Target date: **November 15, 2026** (or similar date second half of November).

Mark calendar. Set reminder for November 10 to initiate conversion process.

**Prepare liquidity for tax payment.** If paying taxes from taxable accounts (not withholding from conversion), ensure cash available.

For $70,000 conversion at 22% effective rate, tax cost approximately $15,400. Confirm you have $15,400 in accessible cash or can sell securities to raise it without triggering excessive capital gains.

If using withholding, confirm with IRA custodian that withholding option available when conversion executed.

## Phase 4: Month 10-12 (Year 1 Review & Adjustment)

October through December complete Year 1 execution and prepare Year 2 plan.

**Month 10 tasks:**

**Execute Year 1 conversion.** Contact IRA custodian via phone or online platform. Request conversion from traditional IRA to Roth IRA.

Specify:

- Amount: $65,000 (using adjusted amount from Month 8 calculation)
- Tax withholding: 22% ($14,300 withheld, $50,700 to Roth)
- Timing: Immediate processing

Custodian will process conversion within 1-3 business days. You'll receive confirmation showing:

- Date of conversion
- Amount converted: $65,000
- Amount sent to IRS: $14,300
- Amount deposited to Roth IRA: $50,700
- Traditional IRA balance reduced by: $65,000

**Document the transaction.** Save all confirmation documents. Create file folder (physical or digital) labeled "Roth Conversions" containing:

- Conversion confirmation from custodian
- Year-to-date income calculations from Month 8
- MAGI projection worksheet
- Tax advisor meeting notes (if applicable)

This documentation proves conversion executed as planned and supports your tax return preparation.

**Update tracking spreadsheet.** Maintain running record of all conversions.

Example format:

| Date | Amount Converted | Tax Withheld | Net to Roth | Traditional IRA Balance After | Roth IRA Balance After |
|---|---|---|---|---|---|
| 11/15/2026 | $65,000 | $14,300 | $50,700 | $915,000 | $50,700 |
| [Future] | | | | | |

This becomes your master conversion log tracking progress toward multi-year target.

**Month 11 tasks:**

**Monitor final year-end income.** November and December often bring surprises — mutual fund distributions, unexpected dividends, year-end bonuses, capital gains from fund rebalancing.

Check brokerage accounts weekly in November-December. Watch for:

- Mutual fund capital gains distributions (typically late December)
- Higher-than-expected dividend payments
- Bond interest payments
- Any other income not accounted for in Month 8 projections

If December surprises push income significantly higher than projected, calculate impact on IRMAA. If your careful planning put you at $213,000 MAGI but December surprises add $8,000, your actual MAGI is $221,000 — $3,000 over threshold.

Document any surprises: "Unexpected mutual fund distribution $6,200 in December. Actual MAGI $219,200 vs. projected $213,000. Over threshold by $1,200."

This becomes learning for Year 2 planning — use larger safety buffers, switch from actively managed funds to index funds to reduce distribution surprises, or accept one year of IRMAA as cost of execution.

**Prepare for year-end tax filing.** Conversion creates taxable income reported on Form 1099-R (received in January). Notify your tax preparer that you executed conversion and will receive 1099-R showing $65,000 taxable distribution.

Provide them your conversion documentation so they can properly report on 2026 tax return.

**Month 12 tasks:**

**Complete Year 1 assessment.** Create one-page review document evaluating Year 1 execution.

Assessment template:

**Planned vs. Actual:**

- Planned conversion: $70,000
- Actual conversion: $65,000
- Variance: -$5,000 (adjusted based on income tracking)

**Income Projection Accuracy:**

- Projected 2026 MAGI: $165,000
- Actual 2026 MAGI: $163,000 (estimate until return filed)
- Variance: -$2,000 (income slightly lower than expected)

**IRMAA Status:**

- Distance to threshold: $55,000 (safe)
- Accidental trigger: No
- Any surprises: Mutual fund distribution $2,800 higher than expected

**Tax Payment:**

- Method: Withholding from conversion
- Amount: $14,300
- Remaining tax due with April return: $1,100 (estimated)

**Lessons Learned:**

- Income projection methodology worked well
- Need larger buffer for mutual fund distribution uncertainty
- Conversion execution process smooth, will use same approach Year 2

**Year 2 Implications:**

- Proceed with planned $70,000 conversion in November 2027
- Increase safety buffer from $5,000 to $6,000 to account for fund distribution variability
- Consider switching Fund XYZ to index alternative to reduce surprises

This assessment document feeds directly into Year 2 planning, ensuring continuous improvement.

**Calculate updated IRA balance and progress toward target.** After Year 1 conversion plus market returns, what's your current IRA balance?

Example:

- Starting balance (Jan 2026): $980,000
- Conversion executed: -$65,000
- Market returns (6% on average balance): +$55,000
- Ending balance (Dec 2026): $970,000

Target balance at 73 (six years away): $1,200,000.

Current balance: $970,000. You're already below target — excellent position. You can reduce future conversions, execute planned amounts with confidence, or accelerate conversions to create even more buffer.

## Phase 5: Month 13-18 (Year 2 Plan & Execute)

Year 2 mirrors Year 1 with refinements based on learning.

**Month 13-15 tasks (January-March 2027):**

**File 2026 tax return.** Form 1099-R from IRA custodian reports $65,000 conversion as taxable income. Your tax preparer includes this on line 4b of Form 1040 along with explanation that this is Roth conversion.

Final 2026 MAGI confirmed when return completed. Compare to projections:

- Projected MAGI: $165,000
- Actual MAGI (from filed return): $163,400
- Variance: -$1,600

Your projection was accurate within 1%. This validates methodology for Year 2.

**Review Year 1 results with tax advisor.** After return filed, schedule follow-up meeting.

Discussion points:

- How accurate were income projections
- Any unexpected tax implications from conversion
- State tax impact (if applicable)
- Recommendations for improving Year 2 execution
- Confirmation that Year 2 planned conversion ($70,000) still appropriate

**Refine Year 2 conversion amount.** Based on Year 1 learning and current year projections, adjust Year 2 planned conversion if needed.

Year 2 considerations:

- Is baseline income same, higher, or lower than Year 1?
- Any major life changes expected in 2027?
- Market performance affecting IRA balance?
- Still on track toward Pre-RMD Positioning target?

Most often, Year 2 proceeds as planned from Phase 2. Occasionally, adjustments needed:

- Income higher than expected: Reduce conversion
- Unexpected inheritance: Skip conversion this year
- Job loss: Increase conversion (lower baseline income)

Document decision: "Year 2 conversion confirmed at $70,000" or "Year 2 conversion adjusted to $60,000 due to [reason]."

**Month 16-18 tasks (April-June 2027):**

**Perform Year 2 mid-year MAGI checkpoint.** Repeat Month 7 process from Year 1.

Calculate actual income January-June 2027. Project full-year based on first half. Compare to plan.

If tracking on target, proceed as planned. If significant variance, adjust Year 2 conversion amount accordingly.

**Review investment portfolio for IRMAA coordination.** Are you holding investments that might generate unexpected year-end distributions? Year 1 taught you to account for this.

Actions to reduce surprises:

- Shift actively managed mutual funds to index funds (lower distributions)
- Avoid selling appreciated positions in taxable accounts during conversion years
- Use municipal bonds instead of taxable bonds where appropriate
- Hold dividend-heavy stocks in IRA instead of taxable accounts

These adjustments create more conversion capacity and reduce surprise income that threatens IRMAA proximity.

**Month 19-21 tasks (July-September 2027):**

**Calculate final Year 2 conversion amount.** Repeat Month 8 process from Year 1 with Year 2 data.

By September, you have nine months actual income. Project remaining three months. Calculate available capacity. Confirm Year 2 conversion amount or adjust based on actual income tracking.

**Coordinate Year 2 tax advisor meeting.** Schedule October meeting. Provide updated calculations. Request verification. Confirm conversion will execute in November.

**Month 22-24 tasks (October-December 2027):**

**Execute Year 2 conversion.** Target date November 15, 2027. Contact custodian. Convert planned amount with appropriate withholding. Document transaction. Update tracking spreadsheet.

Example updated tracking:

| Date | Amount Converted | Tax Withheld | Net to Roth | Traditional IRA Balance After | Roth IRA Balance After |
|---|---|---|---|---|---|
| 11/15/2026 | $65,000 | $14,300 | $50,700 | $915,000 | $50,700 |
| 11/15/2027 | $70,000 | $15,400 | $54,600 | $875,000 | $111,500 |

**Complete Year 2 assessment.** Create second annual review document following same format as Month 12.

Compare Year 1 vs. Year 2:

- Income projection accuracy: Improved or same?
- IRMAA proximity management: Any issues?
- Execution smoothness: Easier second time?

- Progress toward target: On track?

**Calculate two-year cumulative progress.** After two years and two conversions, where do you stand?

Example:

- Starting IRA (Jan 2026): $980,000
- Total converted (2026-2027): $135,000
- Market returns (two years): $112,000
- Ending IRA (Dec 2027): $957,000
- Target IRA at 73: $1,200,000
- Status: $243,000 below target — excellent position

## Phase 6: Month 19-24 (Two-Year Assessment)

By Month 24, you've completed two full conversion cycles. Phase 6 evaluates results and determines whether to continue.

**Comprehensive two-year evaluation:**

**Quantitative assessment:**

How much have you converted?

- Year 1: $65,000
- Year 2: $70,000
- Total: $135,000

What's your IRA reduction percentage?

- Starting balance: $980,000
- Ending balance: $957,000
- Gross reduction: -$23,000 (appears minimal)
- Adjusted for market returns: Converted $135,000, but balance only decreased $23,000 due to $112,000 in returns
- True reduction: Without conversions, balance would be $1,092,000. Actual balance $957,000. Effective reduction: $135,000.

**Progress toward Pre-RMD Positioning target:**

- Target IRA at 73: $1,200,000
- Current IRA: $957,000
- Remaining years until 73: 5 (ages 68-72)
- Assessment: Already $243,000 below target. You could stop converting or continue with smaller

amounts to create even more buffer.

**IRMAA navigation success:**

- Year 1: Stayed $55,000 below threshold
- Year 2: Stayed $48,000 below threshold
- Accidental triggers: Zero
- Assessment: IRMAA navigation successful. Methodology works.

**Tax efficiency:**

- Total taxes paid: $29,700 ($14,300 + $15,400)
- Effective rate: 22% average
- Assessment: Conversions executed within target bracket. No spillover into 24%+.

**Qualitative assessment:**

**Execution confidence:**

- First conversion: Moderate anxiety about calculations and timing
- Second conversion: Significantly more confident, process familiar
- Assessment: Learning curve overcome. Years 3-5 will be easier.

**Coordination complexity:**

- Income tracking: Manageable with quarterly reviews
- Tax advisor coordination: Valuable, will continue
- IRMAA calculations: Initially complex, now routine
- Assessment: Complexity level acceptable for value delivered.

**Life disruption:**

- Time required per year: Approximately 15-20 hours total (data gathering, planning, execution, documentation)
- Financial stress: Minimal once process understood
- Assessment: Sustainable approach for remaining gap years.

**Decision point: Continue to Years 3-5 or stop?**

Three scenarios:

## Scenario A: You've exceeded target — consider stopping

If your two-year conversions plus market returns have brought IRA balance well below target, you might stop.

Example: Target was $1,200,000. Current balance $957,000. You're $243,000 below target with 5 gap years remaining.

Decision: Stop conversions. You've achieved objective. Use remaining gap years to let Roth compound tax-free while traditional IRA remains below target.

## Scenario B: You're on track — continue as planned

If your two-year progress aligns with multi-year plan from Phase 2, continue.

Example: You selected Slow & Steady profile converting $70,000 annually for 7 years. You've completed 2 years ($135,000). You need 5 more years ($350,000 additional) to reach $485,000 total target.

Decision: Continue Years 3-5 executing $70,000 annually as planned.

## Scenario C: You're behind target — accelerate

If two-year progress insufficient and you're at risk of not achieving target before RMDs begin, accelerate.

Example: Target was $600,000 total conversions. You've completed $135,000 in 2 years (23% of target). You have 5 years remaining. At current pace ($67,500/year average), you'll convert only $472,500 total — $127,500 short of target.

Decision: Increase Years 3-5 conversions to $85,000 annually to compensate.

## Extending to Years 3-5: When and How

Most readers executing Slow & Steady, Bracket-Maximizer, or Glide Path profiles will extend beyond 24 months. Front-Loader and Rip the Band-Aid profiles typically complete in 2-4 years.

**When to extend:**

You selected profile requiring 5-7 year timeline in Chapter 12. Two years represents 30-40% of total plan. Extension is expected, not deviation.

Your two-year assessment shows meaningful progress but target not yet achieved. You need Years 3-5 to complete IRA reduction before RMDs begin.

Your conversion capacity remains strong. Income hasn't increased dramatically. IRMAA thresholds still manageable. You can continue executing safely.

**How to extend:**

Years 3-5 don't require another comprehensive planning cycle. You're repeating proven process with minor annual adjustments.

**Annual cycle for Years 3-5:**

**Q1 (January-March):** File prior year tax return. Confirm actual MAGI matched projections. Review any changes to baseline income or tax law.

**Q2 (April-June):** Mid-year MAGI checkpoint. Calculate year-to-date income. Project full year. Confirm current year conversion amount or adjust.

**Q3 (July-September):** Finalize current year conversion amount based on nine months of actual data. Coordinate with tax advisor in October.

**Q4 (October-December):** Execute conversion in November. Document transaction. Update tracking spreadsheet. Begin Q1 process for following year.

Each year, conversion becomes more routine. Anxiety decreases. Confidence increases. By Year 5, you're executing with minimal stress because you've validated the methodology works through four prior years of successful conversions.

**Year-to-year adjustments:**

Year 3 considerations:

- Has Social Security started (if it was delayed)? Adjust conversion capacity accordingly.
- Any major life changes (health, family, financial)?
- Market performance requiring conversion amount adjustment?
- Still comfortable with selected profile or switch needed?

Year 4-5 considerations:

- Approaching age 73. How many gap years remaining?
- On track to hit Pre-RMD Positioning target?
- Need to accelerate final years if behind pace?
- Planning for final conversion in Year 5 or extending to Year 6-7?

**Final year (typically Year 5-7 depending on profile):**

Execute last planned conversion. Complete final assessment. Calculate actual IRA balance at 73. Project first RMD. Verify you've achieved target — manageable RMDs under IRMAA threshold with comfortable margin.

Document completion:

- Total converted over all years: $________
- Final traditional IRA balance: $________
- Target achieved: Yes/No
- Projected first RMD at 73: $________
- Projected total income at 73: $________
- Distance to IRMAA threshold: $________

If target achieved, conversions complete. If slightly short, accept outcome and manage IRMAA carefully through Stack Protection techniques in post-73 years.

## Contingency Planning: Adapting to Life Changes

Twenty-four months is long enough for unexpected events. Your plan must accommodate changes without complete derailment.

**Contingency 1: Unexpected income spike (inheritance, property sale, bonus)**

Impact: One-year income jump could push over IRMAA threshold or eliminate conversion capacity.

Response: Skip or minimize conversion that year. Resume following year when income normalizes. Your multi-year plan absorbs one skipped year by extending timeline or increasing subsequent years slightly.

Example: You planned $70,000 conversion in Year 3. You inherited $180,000, creating one-time income. Skip Year 3 conversion entirely. Execute $75,000 in Year 4 and $75,000 in Year 5 to compensate.

**Contingency 2: Job loss or income decrease**

Impact: Lower baseline income increases conversion capacity.

Response: Accelerate conversions. If you lost $40,000 consulting income, you have $40,000 more annual conversion capacity. Convert $110,000 instead of planned $70,000 that year.

This is opportunistic adjustment. Use the low-income year aggressively to advance your multi-year target ahead of schedule.

**Contingency 3: Health crisis or major medical expenses**

Impact: Medical expenses reduce liquidity for paying conversion taxes. Immediate cash needs might require accessing IRA earlier than planned.

Response: Reduce or pause conversions for 1-2 years while addressing health situation. Resume when financially stabilized. If you need IRA funds for medical expenses, take distributions directly (taxed at ordinary rates) rather than converting.

Don't abandon strategy entirely. Pause temporarily, then resume with adjusted timeline.

**Contingency 4: Market crash reducing IRA balance**

Impact: 20-30% market decline reduces IRA balance, which reduces future RMDs naturally without conversions.

Response: Continue conversions but potentially reduce amounts. If IRA dropped from $980,000 to $750,000 due to market crash, your target may already be achieved through market decline alone. Reassess Pre-RMD Positioning in light of new balance.

Alternatively: Market crash creates opportunity. Convert more shares at depressed valuations. When market recovers, those shares grow tax-free in Roth.

**Contingency 5: Tax law changes**

Impact: If Congress increases tax rates or changes brackets significantly, conversion math could shift.

Response: If rates increase, conversions become more valuable (you're converting at old lower rates before increases take effect). Accelerate conversions before new law effective date.

If rates decrease, conversions become less valuable but still beneficial if you're avoiding IRMAA. Continue but reassess arbitrage benefit.

**Contingency 6: Early RMD trigger (rule change or miscalculation)**

Impact: Extremely unlikely, but if RMD age changes back to 72 or you miscalculated your gap years window, RMDs might start earlier than expected.

Response: Execute final conversions immediately in remaining months before RMDs begin. Even 3-6 months of advance warning allows one final conversion before window closes.

**General contingency principles:**
Flexibility over perfection. Your 24-month plan is guidance, not rigid contract. Life changes require adaptation.

Maintain strategic direction. Unless circumstances completely prevent conversions (severe illness, total loss of income, bankruptcy), continue toward target even if slower pace required.

Document changes. When you deviate from plan due to contingency, document reason and adjustment. This maintains clear record of decision-making for future reference.

## Your First Action: What to Do Today

You've reached the end of the book. You understand the enemies. You have the framework. You've seen the profiles. You know the execution timeline.

The question is: what do you do right now, today, to begin?

**Action 1: Calculate your remaining gap years (5 minutes)**

Open calendar. Write down today's date and your current age.

Calculate: 73 - [your current age] = [gap years remaining]

If the answer is 7 or more: You have substantial time. Follow full 24-month plan starting with Phase 1 data gathering.

If the answer is 4-6: You have adequate time but urgency is high. Accelerate Phase 1 to 30 days instead of 90 days.

If the answer is 1-3: You're in emergency territory. Skip detailed planning. Call your IRA custodian this week and execute first conversion within 30 days.

If the answer is 0 or negative: You're 73+. RMDs have begun or will begin shortly. This book's strategies are no longer fully applicable. Consult tax advisor about post-RMD approaches.

**Action 2: Gather three critical documents (30 minutes)**

Stop reading. Go to your files (physical or digital) and locate:

1. Most recent IRA statement showing current balance
2. Most recent tax return (2024 or 2025) showing AGI on line 11
3. Social Security statement or benefits letter showing current or projected benefit

If you cannot find these documents:

- IRA statement: Log into custodian website (Vanguard, Fidelity, Schwab, etc.) and download current statement
- Tax return: Download from tax software or request copy from tax preparer
- Social Security: Log into ssa.gov and download benefit statement

These three documents contain 80% of data needed for Phase 1. Gather them today.

**Action 3: Create your conversion planning folder (10 minutes)**

Physical folder: Label it "Roth Conversion Strategy 2026-20XX" and place your three gathered documents inside.

Digital folder: Create folder on computer named "Roth_Conversion_Plan" with subfolders:

- /Documents (statements, tax returns)
- /Calculations (worksheets, projections)
- /Confirmations (conversion confirmations, receipts)
- /Notes (meeting notes, decisions, adjustments)

Having centralized organization prevents lost documents and missed details during multi-year execution.

**Action 4: Mark your calendar with Phase 1 deadline (2 minutes)**

Open calendar. Go to 90 days from today. Create event: "Phase 1 Complete — Data Gathering Deadline."

This creates accountability. You're not "thinking about it someday." You have 90-day deadline to complete comprehensive financial inventory and baseline calculations.

Set additional reminder for 30 days: "Phase 1 Check-In — 1/3 Complete." This ensures you're making progress, not deferring.

**Action 5: Schedule advisor meeting if applicable (15 minutes)**

If you work with financial advisor or CPA, email or call them today.

Message: "I'm implementing a multi-year Roth conversion strategy during my gap years before RMDs begin at 73. I need to schedule a meeting to review my IRA balance, income projections, and conversion capacity calculations. I'm targeting [Month/Year] for first conversion. When can we meet to coordinate?"

This signals seriousness. You're not asking "should I think about conversions?" You're stating "I am converting, let's coordinate timing and amounts."

If advisor responds with "let's wait and see," reference Chapter 4 of this book and ask specifically: "What are we waiting to see? What income or tax law information will be different in six months that isn't available now?"

Insist on concrete timeline. If they cannot provide one, consider whether they're the right advisor for conversion execution.

**Action 6: Write your commitment statement (5 minutes)**

On blank paper or digital document, write:

"I commit to reducing my traditional IRA balance from [current amount] to [target amount at 73] by executing strategic Roth conversions during my remaining [X] gap years. I will complete Phase 1 data gathering by [date]. I will execute my first conversion by [month/year]. I understand this will save approximately $[estimated amount] in lifetime taxes and IRMAA penalties while protecting my spouse from widow penalty."

Sign and date it. Place it in your conversion planning folder. This written commitment transforms vague intention into concrete plan.

**The 7-day challenge:**

Some readers will do these six actions today. Most will not. Life intervenes. Inertia is powerful.

If you don't complete all six actions today, commit to completing them within seven days. Every day beyond seven is another day of gap years capacity lost forever.

Set phone reminder: "7 days since finishing conversion book. Have I gathered documents, created folder, scheduled advisor meeting, and written commitment? If no, do it NOW."

**The cost of delay (revisited):**

You've read 14 chapters detailing the $150,000 to $280,000 cost of arriving at 73 unprepared. Every month you delay beginning Phase 1 is one month closer to that outcome.

Waiting three months to "think about it" costs approximately $3,000 to $6,000 in lifetime tax savings (one quarter of annual conversion capacity lost).

Waiting one year costs $18,000 to $25,000 (full year of capacity lost, compounded over remaining retirement).

Waiting until you "feel ready" often means waiting until it's too late. You'll feel ready after executing first conversion successfully, not before. Action precedes confidence, not the reverse.

**What success looks like 24 months from today:**

It's January 2028 if you're reading this in January 2026. You've completed Phase 6 of your 24-month plan.

You've executed two successful conversions totaling $130,000-$150,000. Your traditional IRA balance is $200,000 to $300,000 lower than it would have been without action. Your projected RMDs at 73 are $7,500 to $11,000 lower annually than they would have been.

You've never accidentally triggered IRMAA. Your MAGI calculations were accurate within 2-3%. Your tax payments were manageable. The process became routine after first conversion.

You're confident continuing through Years 3-5 because you've proven the methodology works. You've integrated conversions into annual financial rhythm — Q4 MAGI check, November conversion execution, Q1 tax filing, repeat.

Your advisor (if you have one) respects your knowledge and provides coordination support rather than vague "wait and see" guidance.

Most importantly: you've secured $75,000 to $120,000 in lifetime tax and IRMAA savings. You've protected your spouse from widow penalty. You've defeated the three enemies.

Twenty-four months from today, you'll look back on the moment you finished this book and made the decision to act rather than defer. That decision will be worth six figures over your remaining lifetime.

- The Permanent Bracket Paradox: Resolved

We opened this book with the Permanent Bracket Paradox. OBBBA made tax brackets permanent, removing the 2025 deadline. That permanence eliminated external urgency. "Wait and see" became the default response.

The paradox: infinite time to convert ≠ infinite time to convert at favorable rates. Legislative stability didn't extend your personal gap years. Permanent brackets don't mean permanent opportunity.

You've now resolved the paradox by understanding the real deadline: not December 31, 2025 (legislative), but December 31 of the year before you turn 73 (biological). Your gap years are finite regardless of what Congress does with tax brackets.

The Permanent Bracket Paradox was never about brackets. It was about human psychology responding to removal of external deadline by eliminating internal urgency. You've overcome that psychology by replacing removed legislative deadline with personal deadline based on your age and RMD start date.

You have time. But you don't have unlimited time. The number of gap years remaining is calculable, definite, and decreasing by one every year regardless of legislative stability.

This book gave you the tools to use that time strategically. The G.A.P.S. System, five conversion profiles, IRMAA navigation techniques, and 24-month action plan convert the conceptual solution into executable strategy.

What separates readers who capture $75,000 to $150,000 in lifetime savings from those who don't isn't intelligence, wealth, or sophistication. It's action. Starting Phase 1 within 30 days. Executing first conversion within 12 months. Maintaining discipline through multi-year timeline.

The three enemies — RMDs, IRMAA, widow penalty — are defeatable. But only during gap years. Only with strategic action. Only if you begin now rather than continuing to "wait and see."

Your gap years are the window. This book is the plan. The choice to act or defer is yours.

Make it today.

CONCLUSION

# THE WINDOW IS YOURS

## What You Know Now (That You Didn't Before)

When you opened this book, you likely felt one of two ways about Roth conversions.

Either you'd heard they might be beneficial but had no clear framework for when, how much, or why the timing mattered. Your advisor mentioned them in passing but never provided concrete guidance. You knew conversions existed as a planning tool but not how to use them strategically.

Or you'd been told "wait and see" so many times after OBBBA passed that you accepted legislative stability as justification for indefinite deferral. Permanent brackets meant no deadline. No deadline meant no urgency. No urgency meant waiting felt prudent rather than costly.

You now understand what most retirees don't discover until age 75 when it's too late.

You understand **the three enemies** and how they compound. RMDs force distributions starting at 73. Those forced distributions elevate your income into higher tax brackets and trigger IRMAA Medicare penalties. When one spouse dies, the survivor transitions to single filing status where tax brackets are half as wide and IRMAA thresholds are half as high. The same RMDs that cost the couple $26,000 in annual taxes cost the widow $35,000. Over 20 years of retirement, these three enemies extract $150,000 to $280,000 from households that arrive at 73 unprepared.

You understand **the gap years window**. The period between retirement and age 73 when income is artificially low, you're not yet required to take RMDs, and you have complete control over IRA distributions. This window exists for everyone but closes permanently when RMDs begin. The number of gap years you have remaining is calculable — 73 minus your current age — and decreases by one every year regardless of legislative changes.

You understand **the arbitrage opportunity**. Converting during gap years at 18-22% effective tax rates to avoid future RMDs taxed at 24-32% rates plus IRMAA penalties worth thousands more. The mathematical advantage is straightforward: pay lower rates now voluntarily to avoid higher rates later mandatorily.

You understand **the G.A.P.S. System**. Gap Years Identification maps your specific window. Arbitrage Calculation determines annual conversion capacity. Pre-RMD Positioning establishes your target IRA balance at 73. Stack Protection coordinates income sources to maximize conversions without triggering IRMAA during execution. This isn't theory — it's methodology you can implement starting today.

You understand **your profile**. Slow & Steady spreading conversions evenly. Front-Loader concentrating early. Bracket-Maximizer optimizing annually. Rip the Band-Aid executing immediately. Glide Path progressing gradually. You know which approach matches your timeline, liquidity, and complexity tolerance.

You understand **IRMAA navigation**. How to calculate MAGI precisely, determine safe conversion amounts with appropriate buffers, coordinate capital gains and other income around conversion years, and recover if you accidentally cross thresholds.

You have **the 24-month action plan**. Month-by-month tasks from data gathering through strategy development through execution through assessment. You know what to do in Month 1, Month 7, Month 13, and Month 24. You have the roadmap converting knowledge into implementation.

Most importantly, you understand something your advisor may never tell you explicitly: **the cost of "wait and see" is $15,000 to $25,000 per year in permanently lost conversion capacity**. Every year you defer is one fewer gap year available. Every gap year lost means a larger unconverted IRA at 73. Larger IRA means larger RMDs. Larger RMDs mean higher taxes, more IRMAA triggers, and worse widow penalty. The compounding is exponential, not linear.

## The Big Idea Revisited: Door Open, Window Closing

The Permanent Bracket Paradox animated this book's central tension.

OBBBA — the One Big Beautiful Bill Act signed in July 2025 — made TCJA tax brackets permanent. No sunset. No 2025 deadline. The legislative instability that created urgency from 2018-2025 disappeared overnight. Tax planning shifted from "act before brackets expire" to "we have time to plan carefully."

That permanence opened a door. Favorable 12-22% brackets are now reliable for long-term planning. You don't need to rush conversions into compressed timeline fearing brackets will revert to higher 2017 rates. You can execute strategic multi-year conversion schedules with confidence that legislative foundation won't shift underneath you.

But the door opening didn't extend your window.

Your personal gap years — the period when you have control, low income, and no RMDs — close at age 73 regardless of what Congress does with tax brackets. If you're 68 today, you have five gap years remaining whether brackets are permanent or expiring. If you're 71, you have two years whether OBBBA passed or not.

The paradox: infinite legislative time ≠ infinite personal time. Permanent brackets created psychological permission to defer indefinitely. But the biological deadline — age 73 — remained unchanged.

Most retirees resolve this paradox incorrectly. They hear "permanent brackets" and conclude "I have time." Then they wait. One year becomes two. Two becomes five. They arrive at 73 having never converted, their IRAs grown through market returns, their RMDs elevated, their exposure to all three enemies maximized.

You can resolve the paradox correctly. Permanent brackets are advantage, not excuse. Legislative stability allows you to plan multi-year conversion strategies without fear that rates will spike mid-execution. Your 5-7 year conversion schedule can proceed with confidence. But it must proceed. Stability doesn't eliminate the need to act — it eliminates the excuse not to plan carefully.

The door OBBBA opened is permanent brackets. The window closing at 73 is your gap years. Both are true simultaneously. You have time to plan well. You don't have time to wait indefinitely.

## The Three Paths Forward

You're at a decision point. Finishing this book doesn't automatically change anything. Knowledge without action produces no results. You now face three paths:

**Path 1: Implement the 24-month plan starting now**

Begin Phase 1 data gathering within 30 days. Gather IRA statements, tax returns, Social Security projections. Calculate remaining gap years. Determine Pre-RMD Positioning target. Select conversion profile. Execute first conversion within 12 months. Continue through Years 2-5 as planned.

This path leads to $75,000 to $150,000 in lifetime tax and IRMAA savings. You arrive at 73 with IRA balance 40-60% lower than it would have been. Your RMDs stay under IRMAA thresholds. When one spouse dies, the survivor's tax situation is manageable rather than catastrophic. You've protected your retirement security and your spouse.

**Path 2: Wait "one more year" to implement**

Tell yourself you need more time to think, more certainty about income projections, more clarity about tax law stability, more comfort with the calculations. Defer Phase 1 to next year. Revisit the decision in 12 months.

This path costs $18,000 to $25,000 in lifetime savings from the single gap year permanently lost. Your remaining window shrinks from 5 years to 4, from 4 to 3. Each delay compounds. "One more year" often becomes three more years. By the time you feel "ready," your window has compressed to the point where comprehensive conversions are no longer feasible. You execute minimal conversions in panic during final 1-2 gap years, achieving 20-30% of the IRA reduction you could have achieved with early action.

**Path 3: Decide this strategy isn't for you**

Determine your situation doesn't fit the book's target profile. Maybe you're already 73+ and RMDs have begun. Maybe your IRA is small enough ($300,000 or less) that RMDs won't trigger IRMAA. Maybe you're ultra-high-net-worth planning to leave IRAs to charity where conversions create unnecessary tax acceleration. Maybe you're terminally ill with short life expectancy making conversion payback period impossible.

This path is legitimate if you genuinely fall outside the target persona. Not every retiree needs aggressive gap years conversions. If your projected age-73 RMDs will keep you $50,000+ below

IRMAA thresholds and you're comfortable with projected tax costs, the juice might not be worth the squeeze.

But be honest about why you're choosing Path 3. Is it truly "this doesn't apply to me" or is it "this feels complex so I'm avoiding it"? The latter is Path 2 disguised as Path 3.

The vast majority of readers with $500,000+ IRAs, 3+ gap years remaining, baseline retirement income under $180,000, and normal life expectancy should choose Path 1. The math is overwhelmingly favorable. The implementation, while requiring effort, is manageable. The 24-month plan provides clear roadmap. The tools exist.

What separates Path 1 implementers from Path 2 deferrers isn't capability. It's decision. Making the choice to begin Phase 1 this month rather than "thinking about it" for another year.

**The Stakes (One More Time)**

This book hasn't used scare tactics. The numbers presented — $75,000 to $280,000 lifetime cost of inaction — aren't inflated to motivate you. They're mathematical projections based on IRS RMD tables, federal tax brackets, and IRMAA surcharge schedules.

A couple arriving at 73 with $900,000 in unconverted IRA, baseline income of $120,000, will pay approximately $180,000 in combined federal taxes and IRMAA penalties over 20 years of retirement. If one spouse dies at 80, the survivor pays an additional $60,000 in widow penalty taxes over the remaining 12 years.

That same couple converting $400,000 during gap years pays approximately $80,000 in conversion taxes upfront. They arrive at 73 with $500,000 in traditional IRA. Their combined lifetime federal taxes and IRMAA are approximately $105,000. The widow pays approximately $35,000 in post-death taxes.

Total cost unconverted: $240,000. Total cost with conversions: $220,000 ($80,000 conversion taxes + $105,000 post-RMD taxes + $35,000 widow taxes). Net savings: $20,000 over lifetime, plus the substantial benefit of widow protection and IRMAA avoidance.

The more conservative your assumptions, the higher the savings. Project to age 95 instead of 92 and savings increase. Account for unexpected income spikes triggering IRMAA in unconverted scenario and savings increase. Model widow living 15 years after first spouse death instead of 12 and savings increase.

These aren't theoretical benefits you might capture if everything goes perfectly. They're the baseline outcome from systematic execution of gap years conversions.

The stakes are real. But they're not catastrophic if you act now. They only become catastrophic if you defer until gap years have expired.

## This Isn't About Taxes—It's About Protection

The book's title references conversions. The calculations focus on tax arbitrage. The chapters detail IRMAA navigation. This creates impression that gap years conversions are sophisticated tax optimization for people obsessed with minimizing IRS payments.

That's not what this is about.

This is about protecting your retirement security when you're 80, living on fixed income, facing healthcare costs, and discovering your forced IRA distributions are generating $8,000 more in annual taxes than you budgeted. It's about not having to choose between prescription medications and property taxes because IRMAA surcharges ate into your Medicare budget.

This is about protecting your spouse. The widow penalty isn't abstract policy debate — it's your husband or wife at 78, grieving your death, and simultaneously receiving a tax bill 40% higher than what you paid as a couple despite their income being 30% lower. It's ensuring they can stay in the house, maintain their lifestyle, and not face financial devastation during the most emotionally difficult period of their life.

This is about agency. Taking control during the narrow window when you have it rather than surrendering control to RMD tables and tax brackets imposed by IRS. Choosing to convert $60,000 at 22% rates rather than being forced to distribute $60,000 at 28% rates plus IRMAA.

This is about not being the person at 76 who says "I wish someone had told me about this at 66." You're being told now. You have the knowledge. You have the tools. You have the window.

Whether conversions happen is whether you choose to use the window while it's open.

**Your First Step: The Next 7 Days**

Close this book. Open your calendar. Block 60 minutes this week — not "when I have time," but specific date and time on calendar. Title the appointment: "Roth Conversion Plan — Phase 1 Start."

During that 60-minute session, complete three tasks:

**Task 1:** Locate your most recent IRA statement. Write down total traditional IRA balance: $________. This is your starting point.

**Task 2:** Calculate your remaining gap years. Your current age: ___. 73 minus current age = ___ gap years remaining. Write this number large: [X] **GAP YEARS REMAINING**.

**Task 3:** Determine your Phase 1 completion deadline. Today's date plus 90 days = [Date]. Write: "Phase 1 Complete by [Date]." Set calendar reminder for that date.

That's it. Sixty minutes. Three pieces of information. You've begun.

Next week, block another 60 minutes. Gather tax returns. Calculate baseline income. Document Social Security status. You're progressing through Month 1 of the 24-month plan.

The hardest part of any multi-year strategy is beginning. Not executing Year 3. Not navigating IRMAA in Year 5. Not calculating optimal conversion amounts. The hardest part is starting Phase 1 this month instead of deferring to "when I'm ready."

You're ready enough. The plan accounts for learning as you go. First conversion won't be perfect. That's acceptable. Second conversion will be better. By Year 3, you'll execute confidently.

But only if you start Year 1. Only if Phase 1 begins within 30 days of finishing this book. Only if you convert knowledge into action before inertia converts intention into indefinite deferral.

Seven days. Sixty minutes. Three tasks. Begin.

## The Window Is Yours

Tom and Linda, the couple from the Introduction, celebrated OBBBA making brackets permanent. They felt relief. Pressure vanished. Their advisor said "we have time now, no need to rush."

They waited a year. Then another. At 68, they finally considered conversions but their gap years had compressed to five remaining. At 70, they started converting — $45,000 annually for three years. At 73, RMDs began with $850,000 still unconverted in traditional IRA.

Tom died at 79. Linda faced widow penalty at 77 with $42,000 annual RMDs. Her taxes increased from $24,000 as a couple to $32,000 as a widow despite her income dropping $48,000. IRMAA triggered at 78. She paid surcharges for 14 years.

If Tom and Linda had known at 65 what you know now, they would have converted $350,000 over seven gap years. Tom would have paid approximately $70,000 in conversion taxes. Linda would have inherited manageable IRA, smaller RMDs, no widow penalty shock, no IRMAA triggers. Their retirement would have cost $95,000 less in lifetime taxes.

The difference wasn't sophistication, wealth, or access to expensive advisors. The difference was knowledge they didn't have and action they didn't take when the window was fully open.

You have the knowledge they lacked. You understand the enemies, the framework, the profiles, the navigation techniques, the execution timeline. You have the tools.

What Tom and Linda didn't have — what most retirees don't have — was this book at 65 with seven gap years remaining.

You have it now. Your gap years haven't expired. Your window is still open. Whether it remains open long enough to capture six-figure lifetime savings depends on one decision: begin implementation within 30 days or defer to "when I'm ready."

OBBBA opened the door to long-term planning with permanent brackets. But the window — your gap years — closes at 73 whether you use it or not.

The window is yours. What you do with it is yours.

Time doesn't wait for readiness. Age 73 arrives whether you've prepared or procrastinated. The enemies compound whether you understand them or ignore them.

You now understand them. You have the solution. The window is open.

Use it.

## GET YOUR FREE BONUS MATERIALS

You've finished the book—now complete your strategy.

We've prepared additional resources that build on what you've learned here. These materials are designed to bridge the gap between understanding and execution.

**To access your bonus materials:**

Scan the QR code below

These resources are free and will help you move from concept to action. during the 2026-2027 window.

Get your materials now!

## CONTACT

If you have questions about the concepts in this book or need clarification on specific strategies, you can reach us at:

info@scottbennet.com

Please note: We cannot provide personalized financial, tax, or legal advice via email. For specific guidance on your situation, consult a qualified CPA, CFP®, or tax attorney familiar with your circumstances.

www.ingramcontent.com/pod-product-compliance
Ingram Content Group UK Ltd.
Pitfield, Milton Keynes, MK11 3LW, UK
UKHW051508290926
15471UKWH00008B/1505

9 781805 560357